Urbanization, Displacement and Rehabilitation

A Study of People Affected by Land Acquisition

Mohan Advani

RAWAT PUBLICATIONS

Jaipur • New Delhi • Bangalore • Guwahati • Kolkata

ISBN 978-81-316-0253-9

Reprinted, 2016

Published by
Prem Rawat for **Rawat Publications**
Satyam Apts, Sector 3, Jawahar Nagar, Jaipur 302 004 (India)
Phone: 0141 265 1748 / 7006 Fax: 0141 265 1748
E-mail: info@rawatbooks.com
Website: www.rawatbooks.com

New Delhi Office
4858/24, Ansari Road, Daryaganj, New Delhi 110 002
Phone: 011 2326 3290

Also at Bangalore, Guwahati and Kolkata

Typeset by Rawat Computers, Jaipur
Printed and bound in India

Contents

Preface

Industries, trade, commerce, factories, offices, institutions and employment opportunities attract the people for settlement in urban areas. Increasing population pressure paves a way for expansion of cities. Larger cities have relatively high population growth. Population flows from rural to urban and from less developed to more developed. The population in urban centres could be checked by providing developmental and urban facilities in rural areas.

Urban and rural areas depend on each other. Living in these places should be seen as complementary rather than contradictory. With the global approach of interlinkages and modern methods of communication and transport, the growth of urban and rural areas could be optimally balanced to scatter the population flows. This probably will minimize the displacement of people whose lands are acquired for urban development.

The problem of displacement has mainly been studied as dam-centric. The movements for the people dislocated by the construction of dams have attracted worldwide attention on the problems of the displaced. The first approach of the NGOs was to stop or delay the construction of dams because thousands of the people would be displaced. The second approach focussed on providing better compensation packages along with resettlement and rehabilitation measures to minimize the sufferings of the displaced. Adopting the second approach, the development could continue while rehabilitating the displaced people.

It is now realized that the problems of displacement are affecting the people in other sectors also. Prominent among them is the displacement caused by land acquisition in urban areas. The people in villages surrounding the cities are the target for urban development. The present law provides for only monetary compensation and the price of the land determined on prevailing market price. The compensation is not welfare-oriented and people have to suffer for the sake of development. The share of development does not reach to the people affected by land acquisition in urban areas.

This study focuses on the problems of the displaced people because of the loss of land or by limiting occupational alternatives. The present approach and laws of land acquisition are seen as detrimental as the efforts in resettlement and rehabilitation are lacking. There are social conflicts and movements and the attitude of officials is not welfare-oriented. Several social and occupational dimensions of change have been analyzed. A sociological perspective on urban dynamics and displacement has been presented for a dialogue on the approaches towards urban development.

I sincerely hope that the study will be valuable for the scholars interested in the study of the problems of displacement. There is a need to orient the officials dealing with acquisition of land about the social and cultural deprivation faced by the people who are residentially or occupationally displaced. There is need to formulate policies and laws for resettlement and rehabilitation of people affected by land acquisition in urban areas. The redressal mechanism, if followed, would be helpful for the displaced people and the affected population.

Mohan Advani

Acknowledgement

I sincerely thank and acknowledge the support, help and assistance provided by the following organizations, institutions, scholars and researchers in completion of this study.

- University Grants Commission for financial support and administrative cooperation.
- Rawat Publications for constant professionalism—the labour of their editors and staff has assumed that this important topic will reach a wide audience.
- Mohanlal Sukhadia University for academic, administrative and financial accounting through the Registrar and Comptroller office of the University.
- College of Social Sciences and Humanities, the Dean, Prof R.N. Vyas and former Dean, Prof Arun Chaturvedi, Director of Women Studies, Dr (Mrs) V.L. Chouhan and office staff for academic and administrative support.
- Department of Sociology; Dr Balveer Singh, Head and Dr Monika Nagori, former Head for providing necessary facilities and cooperation. Shri S.R. Menaria, Shri Bharat Singh Chauhan and Shri Babu Lal for providing assistance from time to time.
- My friends, Prof C.L. Sharma, Prof N.K. Bhargava, Prof B.S. Nagi and Dr R.C. Swarankar for sociological discourse and Prof G.M.K. Madnani for suggestions on economic aspects. Dr G.M. Mehta, Professor of English for help in reading the manuscript.
- Dr Ajay Kumar Chaudhary for data analysis, Dr B.L. Nagda, Dr R.K. Sharma and Dr Chakrapani Upadhyay for academic interaction.

- Shri Raju Singh and Shri Tulsi Ram for data collection and analysis, especially to Shri Raju Singh (Research Scholar) for all time assistance.
- Shri Sanjay Chaudhary and Shri P.K. Paliwal for data entry and stenographic assistance; Shri B.L. Joshi and Shri M.L. Sadhwani in financial and office assistance.
- Office bearers of UIT, PWD, RIICO, Housing Board; Property Dealers, and people affected by land acquisition for cooperating in providing necessary information.
- My wife, Smt Ritu Advani and my son Shri Ashoo Advani for motivation and patience. Dear Deeya, Madhur and Mahesh Wadhwani for love, affection and inspiration.

Mohan Advani

One

Urbanization, Displacement and Rehabilitation

Urbanization: Various Dimensions

Urbanization is seen as a key indicator of development leading to transformation in the economic, social, and cultural lives of people. The United Nations Center for Human Settlements (UNCHS) estimates that by the year 2020, 60 per cent of the world's population would reside in urban centres compared to 48 per cent in 2000. The degree of urbanization in the developed and developing countries has emerged as one of the most important economic indicators in recent times. India is predominantly rural in landscape and majority of its people are living in the villages. Of the 1068.6 million population in India, only 28 per cent lives in urban areas and the rest 72 per cent reside in rural areas. India is one of the least urbanized countries in the world when we consider the levels of urbanization (Gupta, 2005).

Urbanization may be defined as a stage in social evolution at which societies are passing through their 'typical and conventional' stage to the next stage of social evolution, i.e., 'individualistic'. In other words, it is a way of living which evolves when typical societies (rural) have sufficiently stabilized in a region, nation or on a still larger area (Prasad, 2003). Urbanization is a product of various kinds of changes taking place in a society, especially in its economic sphere. However, it is essentially a process of population redistribution from the rural to the urban communities, and from one region to another; and of a continual differentiation of the society, both in its rural and urban components (D'Souza, 2003). These aspects of population redistribution inherent in the process of urbanization are revealed in the forms of population differentiation, social stratification, resettlement and rehabilitation.

Urbanization

One way to explain urbanization is through population change. It is an increase in the proportion of the urban population to the total population over a period of time. The increase in the urban population is at a rate higher than that of the increase in the rural population. The proportion of urban population increases with the rate of natural increase in population. In some phases, the death rates in the urban sector are found lower than in the rural sector because of availability of better health facilities. The birth rates are also comparatively lower due to the higher educational level and the spread of family planning ideas. The average age at marriage is also higher in urban areas. Thus, urbanization is a change in population distribution and indicator of relative increases in the urban population and urban settlements and concentration of the population in such places. In the demographic sense, urbanization refers to the proportion of a nation's population living in urban areas. This is also seen in the ratio of rural population.

The term 'urbanization' implies the movement of people to urban areas. "It is characterized by movements of people from small communities concerned chiefly or solely with agriculture to other communities generally larger, whose activities are primarily centred in Government, trade, manufacture or allied interest" (Thompson, 1935). Charles Tilly (1964) describes urbanization as a set of changes, which generally occur with the appearance and expansion of large-scale coordinated activities in a society.

Most Indian experts have analyzed urbanization in demographic terms. Only recently have spatial and functional aspects been included into defining dichotomies of urbanization. There is also growing awareness awareness that the historical growth of towns goes through successive stages with each stage having its own characteristics. Change or its absence from colonial to post-colonial stages cannot be ignored (Prasad, 2003).

Urbanization is more than a shifting of people from country to city and from land bound work to urban types of work (Anderson, 1960). Urbanization involves basic changes in the thinking and behaviour of people and changes in their social values. Jacobson and Ved Prakash (1971) define urbanization as describing a process of change in the status of populations due to changing conditions in the society at large.

Urbanization involves the total change that is brought about in a population due to the concentration of persons in areas that are designated as urban. The development in the social and economic set-up of the urban areas and the consequent impact on the cultural and behavioural aspects bring about a change in their way of life. This is observed not only in the cities but also in the country as a whole (Gopal, 1976).

In India, the following definitions of urban area prevailed from 1901 to 1960 (National Institute of Urban Research, 1978):

1. Every municipality, cantonment and all civil lines not included in a municipality; and
2. Every other continuous collection of houses permanently inhabited by not less than 5,000 persons, which the provincial superintendent of census may decide to treat as a town.

In 1951, it was considered that the definition must reflect urban characteristics and not be based solely on population size and administrative considerations. The smaller places could be treated as towns, provided they possessed some urban characteristics, and this led to a sharp increase in the number of towns designated as urban. In 1961, a new definition of urban was introduced, with the following characteristics:

1. All municipalities, corporations, cantonments or notified town areas; and
2. All places which satisfied the following criteria:
   (i) a minimum population of 5,000 persons;
   (ii) at least 75 per cent of the male working population employed in non-agricultural occupations; and
   (iii) a population density of 1,000 persons per square mile.

The above definition has remained unchanged since 1961. This definition allowed smaller places possessing urban characteristics to be identified as urban than did the former definition. A simple dichotomy of urban and rural is less useful in the study of urban development in the Third World than in developed countries, because the growth and decline of towns of different sizes and characteristics have different consequences for the processes of urbanization in developing countries. Most countries provide some crude distinctions between urban places, but in the case of India, they are quite elaborate (Prasad, 2003).

In India, the definition of urban is more rigorous. Both civic status as well as demographic criteria is taken for declaring a settlement urban (Bhagat, 2004). The directors of census operations in states/union territories were allowed to include in consultation with the concerned state governments, union territory administration and the Census Commissioner of India, some places having distinct urban characteristics. As urban, even if such places did not strictly satisfy all the criteria mentioned under the category 2 (ii) above (Jain et al., 1992). The definition adopted in India assumes that urbanization is the consequence of industrialization and therefore urban areas must have preponderance of non-agricultural activities. It considers only male workforce in the non-agricultural sectors, as quality of census data on women workforce is doubtful (Bhagat, 2002).

Process of Urbanization

Gerald (1969) characterizes urbanization as a process of becoming urban, moving to cities, changing from agriculture to other pursuits, common to cities and corresponding changing of behavioural patterns. The term 'urbanization' refers to the process by which the density of population in existing urban places is increased and rural places are changed into urban areas.

Historically, the process of urbanization has come to symbolize social and economic development reflected by the emergence of particular types of human settlements, societal institutions, social and cultural forms. Although there is not a perfect relationship between urbanization and economic growth it is difficult to demonstrate that industrial and commercial sectors have flourished in a society that remained predominantly rural. However, when masses congregate in cities due to political upheavals and economic instability, yet remain outside of the urban mainstreams, the historical linkages between urbanization and economic development need not hold up. Also, other factors such as migration policy and communication networks may affect the urbanization process irrespective of individual and social factors. Therefore, countries with comparable economic structures may show different patterns of urbanization. The differences in the urbanization experienced by different societies in this respect should not, however, lead us to conclude that urbanization, economic growth, and social and political development are autonomous processes (Prasad, 2003).

The urbanization process relates to concentration of people engaged in non-agricultural occupation and concentration of non-agricultural land-use in a specialized area, a place, as a consequence of population, occupational and land use shifts (Prakasha Rao, 1983).

The study of urban processes, particularly in a developing (or underdeveloped) economy, cannot be merely assessed on demographic situation. It has to be based on the objective conditions of social progress. Prasad (2003) has listed such conditions in following order:

The study of urban systems must involve understanding of the entire hierarchy of settlements from the highest order 'primate' cities to the smallest hamlets. The expansion and development of towns and cities are intricately linked with the processes of economic and social development in the hinterland areas of these cities. In underdeveloped economies like India, the poverty and stagnation in the villages impede generation of surplus and, therefore, the development of these towns and cities.

The second most important criterion of studying underdeveloped and dependent urban systems is the pattern and character of linkages between urban places of different order. The dependent urban system with the few metropolitan primaries and their overwhelming exploitative character determines the nature and character of development in the urban places down the order (Kidwai, 1979).

The third important aspect of the dependent urban system will be the pattern of 'linkage development' between urban places of different order. Such linkages can be of transportation, market, communication, administrative, financial and cultural functions whose character determines the degree and direction of social and economic progress.

The fourth aspect of the study of urban system would be the pattern of migrations of three streams, i.e., between rural to urban migration (R-U), urban to urban migration (U-U), and urban to rural migration (U-R). Not only these three streams are different between each other, but also they are cardinally different between different orders of urban places. Moreover, the natures of such migration streams are axiomatically different between the developed and the dependent urban systems.

The fifth important characterization of urban system would be in terms of their location in different ecological settings, like location along major transportation nodes, port location, on high altitudes and hilly location, in large mining and industrial complexes and so on. Not only the ecological conditions are changed by specific urban location but the ecology in turn sets limits and standards to the direction of urban development. When such limits and standards are greatly digressed, the viability of those urban centres gets jeopardized.

The last but not the least important characterization of urban system would be the nature and character of territorial formation and the interlink of such urban-economic regions. The formation of economic regions and its territorial organization takes place around the hinterland of major urban sub-systems within a national economy. The nature and character of urban development in these regions ultimately direct the process and the rate of urbanization. Moreover, the interlink of these economic regions are manifest through linkages between such urban sub-systems through which regional transfers of value take place. The process of regional disparities and development takes place through such transfers of value between the urban sub-systems. When one or two of such urban economic regions grow at a higher rate compared to the stagnation or even decline of the others, the system of transfers may deprive one region and boost the development of another urban economic region. The consequences of such unequal development are well known. Therefore, in the studies of regional development, the systems of value exchanges between different urban sub-systems within the national economies are of vital interest (Prasad, 2003). Thus, the process of urbanization is a culmination of various facets of modernization and development besides the change in population dynamics and socio-economic structure.

During the course of development, urbanization is considered as an inevitable process. It is a finite process experienced by all nations in the transition from an agrarian to an industrial society. The different urbanization levels reflect different degrees of economic development. In fact, higher urbanization is regarded as one of the indicators of development. The metamorphosis which occurred in European countries during the last century, a transition from preponderantly rural to preponderantly urban has been occurring in the Third World countries in this century (Yadav and Sharma, 2004). Further, it is a dynamic process both spatially and temporally. Kanstebouskaya (1976) noted that urbanization, "being a complex socio-economic process closely connected with the scientific technological revolution, exercises a growing influence on all aspects of society's life affecting the nature of economic development, the demographic, ethnic and many social processes".

Urbanization is associated with several negative tendencies, paramount amongst these being deforestation, creation of urban slums and other environmental problems. Maintenance of the urban environment poses a challenge to policy makers, administrators, all those concerned with urban development. Urban green belt is one of the ways to resolve some of the problems of environment. Trees could be made an integral part of urban environment. With varying application environmental aspects have to be associated with the growth process of the cities.

Urbanization is a process which has taken place at a rapid scale in recent years in different countries due to the influence of a variety of causes, of which industrialization is the key factor. Urban area is an outgrowth of the existing rural populace. Hence, migration plays a key role in the growth of cities in any country. It is the chief factor, which has helped urban growth in all countries in modern time. In fact, the cities could grow only because of the flocking of a large quantity of unskilled labourers to their centres from the villages. Usually, migration is from rural to urban centres and centres of lower culture to centres of higher culture. It takes place due to various reasons such as rural unemployment and attractions of the glamour of city life (Sharma, 2004).

Issues in Urbanization

It is important to highlight some issues in the context of urbanization. How urbanization is related to economic, industrial and service growth? Whether the rate of population growth could be distinguished from the rate of urbanization?

Urbanization should be looked at as a reaction to industrial and service growth. Undoubtedly, the growth of cities also stimulates economic growth. In general, urbanization is a basic precondition for development, but it does not guarantee it. Thus, to invest in improved physical infrastructure and vocational training, make land available for building and attract skilled labour as well as cheap migrant workers make sense in order to increase the speed of technological change, to innovate in industry. It is an important saying that "infrastructure should always be a little ahead of industrial activities". Thus, to stimulate economic growth, public investments ought to have an urban bias. Literature on urban bias is, however, full of misconceptions (Hesselberg, 2002).

It is important to distinguish between the rate of urban population growth and the rate of urbanization. The former implies only the growth of urban places, areas or regions. For the rate of urbanization to increase, there must be a shift of population from rural to urban areas. This does not necessarily have to imply that people move, only that the dominant economic activities change from primary to either secondary or tertiary in the places they already live in. Empirically, both the processes of reclassifying places as urban and urban migrations are important to explain urbanization. However, migration is no longer the main reason for the rapid growth of cities. The larger part of the growth now stems from natural population increase in the cities themselves (Hessedlberg, 2002).

Studies on Urbanization

Historical studies of towns and cities discussed by Sharma (2004) provide an insight into the process of urbanization in a historical perspective. Several such urban studies, taken up in the 1970s and the earlier decades, have evoked interest in the historical and comparative perspective. Ghurye's (1964) work was pioneering in explaining urban growth in the colonial settings and developments since independence. Such studies have analyzed the colonial situation under the British rule as it prevailed on the west coast. The British succeeded in minimizing the influence of many of the age-old customs and traditions of the city which had been the traditional stronghold of the trading community. The variability with which different local communities became receptive to the new ideas introduced by the British. They took advantage of the new opportunities. This was done by identifying the merging of elites in Bombay in the mid-nineteenth century. The emergence of the urban elite gave the much-needed leadership to the nascent nationalist sentiments. Their members were instrumental in shaping the early policies of the Congress Party.

Sinha (1978) traced the growth of the metropolitan city of Calcutta from a cluster of villages during the times of Job Charnock to the period when it assumed the status of the capital city of India. In this study, Sinha highlighted the emergence of the urban middle class and also the class of Western-oriented wealthy residents who had the benefit of Western education. Such studies took account of the colonial situation under the British rule. They highlight how the trading communities flourished under the alien rule, leading to its establishment as a prosperous commercial town.

Redfield and Singer (1954) have analyzed the cultural role of cities into orthogenetic and the hetrogenetic, the former transforming the little tradition into the great tradition. They observed the modern culture in the form of emergence of a new culture. They pointed out that the demands of the modern professions pursued in urban areas are of such a nature that even the most orthodox among the urban residents are not completely free from such influences. Among the other works, Rao (1974) analyzes theoretical issues, historical aspects, and the impact of urban influences on rural life.

Contemporary Studies

Hoselitz (1952) compared level of development of India with eight developed nations when their levels of urbanization were similar at various points of time to that of India's in 1951. It revealed that the composition of workforce engaged in agriculture, manufacturing and services were distinctly different compared with India in spite of its level of urbanization.

D'Souza (1968) analyzed the social organization of a modern urban community and encompassed the major areas of urban structure such as kinship, class, caste, religion, occupational structure, educational opportunity, spatial structure, housing, migration and slums etc. He concludes that city planning in India has been greatly influenced by the western tradition because of the cultural void created by the British rule. This has been a fact in the case of Chandigarh also.

Breese (1969) explained, differences in urbanization might arise because the urbanization has taken place in the periods of colonization or exploitation by foreign countries. There may also be urbanization of considerable magnitude even prior to colonial period. The urbanization of certain countries also revealed evidence of the conflicts which led to floods of refugees moving towards the large cities, and of the relationship of military staging and supply centres to the development of city themselves. Sarikwal (1972) examined the nature and process of urbanization in the growing town of Ghaziabad and also determined the pace of urbanization.

Mohan (1985) described the inter-state differences in urbanization over the last three decades in terms of variations in economic development in different states of the country. The larger towns have not grown faster than the smaller ones. He has projected urban population using the method recommended by the United Nations.

Majumdar (1986) observed that the impact of urbanization has yet to touch the societies and cultures as whole, and only gradually slight changes are taking place among the small fraction of the communities living in the town.

Sahai (1986) has analyzed the positive and negative aspects of urbanization in Madhya Pradesh. She revealed that infrastructural development in the state was very poor and highly concentrated in a few districts.

Papola (1987) observed that the explosive growth of the low-income informal sector without a corresponding growth of industries has led to the development of a dichotomous economic structure in most Indian cities. He suggested that the strategy of economic development should be to establish strong links between the formal and informal sectors so that the wage and income differences are minimized.

Dasgupta (1987) compared the existing urbanization pattern of West Bengal with Punjab, Haryana and Kerala. These were due to differing land tenure system, colonial economic policies and economic development policies pursued in post-independence period. Ghosh (1988) compared the urban growth patterns of two Indian states—West Bengal and Punjab and revealed that West Bengal and Punjab were at barely the same level of urbanization although they have shown radically opposite spatial distribution of urban population.

Uyanga (1989) suggested that urban planning should be framed more in terms of doing the best to co-ordinate organizational and spatial relationship among urban dwellers. They are space users within the city and there is an absence of continuous evaluation and monitoring of planned projects with the aim of having feedback and meaningful directions of change.

Harris (1990) gives an account of the economic significance of urbanization and of cities in the process of economic development in order to understand the demographic transition to predominately urban societies, which will occur in the developing countries over the next three decades.

Kamra (1991) assessed the impact of urban growth on social change and pointed out that urbanization is an important force of social change and modem society is gradually transforming into an urbanized society. The study further revealed that although there is a clear-cut relationship between urbanization and social change, the relationship is mediated by the traditional value patterns particularly in communities which have trade as the dominant economic activity.

In the context of the 1991 Census, Bhagat (1992) studied the components of urban growth in India with reference to Haryana based on recent censuses and revealed that India has experienced a significant decline in urban growth during 1981–91. A comparison with Haryana shows that growth rate has also slowed down in the state during 1981–91. However, the growth rate was much higher than India in both the last decades. In fact, it was very rapid during 1971–81 compared to India. Incidentally, it was also the period when Haryana experienced the green revolution and rose fast upon the ladder of economic progress in the country.

Sharma, Jha and Gupta (1992) analyzed the status of institutional preparedness for financing the future development tasks in the wake of the revised Master Plan for Delhi during 1982–2001. They revealed that given the relatively high income levels enjoyed by Delhi's citizens and the favourable disposition of the central government towards development efforts in the notional capital, the attainment of financial investment targets set out in the Development Plan 1981–2001 may not pose serious problems.

The emerging field of urban studies presents several paradoxes to anyone in understanding its scope and context because much of its subject matter is problem-oriented. It is concerned with the phenomena known as urban troubles, urban problems or urban crises. However, the label of problem-orientedness is an over-simplification since the various elements of urbanism are interwoven. The intellectual roots of urban studies lie in both traditional academic disciplines and less orthodox fields. Urban studies have evolved from aspects of city planning, sociology, economics and also from black and ethnic studies, social welfare and interdisciplinary social services (Sharma, 2004). These studies are generally focused on rural-urban differences. Most of the demographic studies compare the population structures, whereas sociologists have taken up the issues of class, caste, race relations, problems of slums. Planners analyze the growth patterns and use them in urban studies. This will provide an understanding of the dimensions of urban society.

Various studies on urbanization reveal the consequences of economic changes that are taking place in the country. It helps to contribute to the growth process at large. The positive aspect of urbanization is sometimes misrepresented by the evident deterioration in the physical environment and quality of life in the urban areas. There has been an increasing population pressure on urban centres, which are ill-equipped and lag behind in development of equitable infrastructural facilities. The analyses of urban phenomenon should cover composition of workforce, social organization, influence of colonization, variation in economic development, social change, industrial growth, organizational and spatial relationship, demographic transition and development planning. The indicators of development should cover such aspects and relate it to consequences of urbanization.

The report of the National Commission on Urbanization (NCU) presented in August 1988 is quite exhaustive and intensive in its analysis of trends and problems of urbanization in India. Yet, it has paid more attention on the pattern of rural-urban migration and little attention to growing rural-urban dichotomies, urban disparities and economic profile of various types of cities and towns.

Urban Growth and Urbanism

The terms urban growth and urbanism should be distinguished from urbanization. Urban growth indicates increase in total urban population, whereas urbanization shows an increase in the percentage of urban population to total population. That is why, urban growth may sometimes take place without urbanization.

The most important contribution of human ecology to urban sociology is the study of the processes of urban growth, which is an application of the laws of plant and animal ecology. These processes are:

1. *Concentration:* This refers to the flocking up or converging of people and functions around a main centre of attraction. Thus, all shops and traders flock around the central business districts.
2. *Centralization*: It is a further process of concentration wherein all the functions pertaining to a specific interest will be situated in a

specific area. Thus, all shops and warehouses are in the centre while factories develop along the outskirts of city.

3. *Decentralization:* It is a further negative process of centralization which results from over or excessive centralization and congestion. It results in overpopulation and consequent spillover of extra units to other suitable places. Thus, excessive congestion of shops in a place leads to cut-throat competition and small traders who fear extinction move away to suburban residential areas. This results in the creation of suburban shopping centres, which provide for the immediate need of suburban dwellers.
4. *Invasion of neighbouring areas:* Decentralization in one area or overcentralization leads to the invasion of the neighbouring area by extra units. Thus, shops of the central loop spread over and push away the neighbouring housing areas. Invasion leads to partial dislocation of the existing interests.
5. *Succession:* It is the final process in which the interest settles down in the newly invaded area. The zone of deterioration in several cities explains this process.

All these processes explain the nature of city growth, spatial pattern and mobility, changes in city pattern etc. Another important area of human ecology is urban immigration and population mobility between areas and occupations.

Urbanism refers to the way of life generally associated with identifying the phenomenon of city residence. Urbanism represents a particular way or style of life, as contrasted with the rural, agriculturally-dominated communities, while urbanization refers to the process whereby a traditionally rural-bound community, either the whole or a section, moves to adopt a different pattern of living. Wirth (1938) defines urbanism as that complex of traits, which makes up the characteristic mode of life in cities. Urbanization, which denotes the development and extension of these traits; these are not exclusively found in settlements that are cities in the physical and demographic sense. They do nevertheless find their most pronounced expression in such area especially in metropolitan cities.

Urbanism refers to those elements and factors which are internal to the urban or city setting only whereas, urbanization is a process of development and extension of these urban factors. Urbanism is a special concept which inherits within itself all the characters connected with urbanization as the urban way of life. Louis Wirth gave the concept of urbanism. It is a category of relevant elements and terms. It is a developing concept as the urban life pattern itself as it appears as a developing and constantly changing phenomenon. As such, there is no well-defined theory of urbanism, presenting in a systematic fashion all the available knowledge concerning the city as a social entity. However, we have a wealth of literature presenting insights of sociological relevance and also empirical studies offering detailed information on a variety of particular aspects of urban life. Thus, we may assume that the larger, the more densely populated and the more heterogeneous the community, the more accentuated and the more present are the characters of urbanism. Among the sociological factors that have been focused are: (i) the size of population, (ii) its density, and (iii) heterogeneity. These are the important factors for determining the urban way of life.

In the Indian context, however, the situation is typical of any other developing society. Here the cities with a population of one lakh or so do not show the typical urban characteristics as mentioned above. These, no doubt, exist in the pronounced form in big cities, super-cities, metropolises, etc. Indian cities thus, do not show the expression of these elements (Yadav and Sharma, 2004). In this context, Mckim Marriott observers that in spite of numbers, density and heterogeneity, Indian cities are free from its consequences. Even in the modern cities with big industries there need not be the phenomena of isolation, impersonalization and secularism.

Dynamics of Urbanization

The degree of urbanization cannot be merely judged by the percentage of total population living in an urban community, or number of urban places in any political or administrative territory but also by the influence which an urban place or community exerts on cultural, political and economic life of its own hinterland and abroad (Yadav and Sharma, 2004). Assessment of urbanization includes the development of urban locales and urban traits. Lynch (1969) has observed that, "urbanization and urban are process and fact respectively".

The dynamics of urbanization should reveal the factors that influence the increase in density of population on particular earth surfaces. Lampard (1965) delineates aspects of urbanization as behavioural, structural and demographic. The first is concerned with the experiences of individuals overtime and with patterns of behaviour. The second is related to the activities of the whole population and is primarily related to changes in economic structure. The third is the demographic concept where the process is seen primarily as one of population concentration.

The behavioural aspect of urbanization is usually associated with Louis Wirth's conception of urbanism as a way of life, in which he explains urban centre as a relatively large, dense and permanent settlement of socially heterogeneous individuals. He formulated a theory of urbanism based on existing knowledge of social groups. The size of aggregate population will affect relations between members, increasing the process of differentiation, which ultimately leads to segregation. Density also adds to diversification and gives rise to urban contrasts of wealth and poverty. Redfield (1941) in his 'Theory of Contrast' describes the rural-urban dichotomy and introduced the rural urban contrasts as 'Folk Urban Continuum'. The behavioural concept of urban process has generated a large literature with various hypotheses and ideas. Berg (1966), in his theory of social change, presents a progressive and historical development from rural to urban, medicated by industrialization, division of labour and role differentiation.

The second aspect of urban dynamics process is economic and relates to the movement of people out of agricultural communities into other non-agricultural communities. This approach directly correlates the economic development with urbanization. Urbanization is seen, therefore, as a product of increasing economic specialization and advancing technology. Accumulation of specialized activities and the linkage of specialism necessitates the accumulation of people and this is seen in the process of urbanization (Childe, 1950). Berry (1962), Lampard (1955), Rostow (1937) and Reissman (1964) proceeded from the assumption that associations exist between the level of economic development of country and the degree to which the country is urbanized and they found a high positive correlation between these two variables.

The third interpretation of urban dynamics is demographic. Lampard (1955) has postulated that urbanization is a process of population concentration. It is a way to ordering a population to attain a certain level of subsistence and security in a given environment. In this context, it is necessary to develop an urban system with a proper spatial distribution.

Several empirical studies of the Third World countries have shown that the linkages between urban centres and the countryside including movement of people, goods, capital and other social transactions play an important role in processes of social, economic and cultural changes in both rural and urban areas.

Global Perspective

Urbanization is a global phenomenon. The present era is sometimes referred to as 'Age of Urbanization'. There might be difference of opinion whether the present age may be considered as an age of urbanization or not, yet figures do confirm the fast growth of urbanization all over the world. For example, the proportion of world population living in urban areas is expected to increase from 50 to 60 per cent by 2000 AD from mere 8 per cent in 1900 AD. It means that by the turn of present century, nearly three billion of the total population of the world will concentrate in the urban areas (Yadav and Sharma, 2004). Industrialization and urbanization, which are related to each other, could be considered as main tenets of social change. These processes are of considerable interest and importance to the social scientists and policy makers.

The global processes of industrialization, economic development and urbanization move together in cohesion. Urbanization is one of the key motive forces behind industrial development. It provides basic requirements such as banking, insurance, brokerage, fire services, police protection and better educational facilities etc. necessary for further accelerated pace of economic development and industrialization in these areas. Concentrated urbanization in these areas strongly supports industrial development through the realization of scale and agglomerate economies (Yadav and Sharma, 2004). In global perspective, urbanization has been termed as an inevitable consequence of development and essential condition of social and economic development.

Postmodern Urbanism

Sociologists have given us incisive insights into some of the essential socio-cultural characteristics, which are considered to be typical to urbanism. Urban areas are characterized by large aggregation, fairly high density of population, predominance of manufacturing and servicing functions, monetization, large-scale segmental and diversified living, increasing dominance of formal regulation, atomization of the individual. This shows a shift from primary to secondary relations, intense mobility as a result of economic growth, growth of transport and communications as well as the emergence of numerous servicing agencies, relatively greater sophistication (Desai, 2003). These features have been considered typical for urban life.

Theories of postmodernism have inculcated a fresh approach to the understanding of urban phenomena. Postmodern urbanism operates with a conception of a radical break with the past. The new globalized postmodern city is seen as a homogeneous intervention that somehow flattens history and culture. The local/social is seen to dissolve under the influence of the global/economic (Gupta, 2004). Taylor, Evans and Fraser (1996), in their study of two 'non-postmodern' cities (Manchester and Sheffield), argue against this interpretation, that the current regeneration of old industrial cities (at least in the north of England) actually reworks and represents the facts of local identity and difference. Therefore, importantly, preserves and symbolizes these identities, albeit in a modified fashion by comparison with the custom and practice of modernist period.

Sridhar (2004) focuses on two approaches of urbanization:

1. How to decongest urban areas; and
2. How to manage urbanization through better delivery of urban infrastructure services.

While it is common knowledge that slums are caused by the migration of rural population to urban areas, it is only because non-agricultural employment in India has not grown rapidly enough to absorb the labour force, that the tide of rural-urban migration has kept increasing. To reduce disparities in backwardness among areas, and disperse industrial activity in the remote areas of the country, the Government of India introduced the 'growth centres' programme in June 1988. According to this programme, 71 growth centres were set up throughout the country that were allotted to the various states on the basis of a combined criteria of area, population and the extent of industrial backwardness. These growth centres provide basic industrial infrastructure like power, water, telecom, and banking to enable rural areas to attract industries (Sridhar, 2004).

The cities in India, therefore, face many and increasing problems as they grow—those of resources, organization, social and technological difficulties. However, there has been significant cultural efflorescence brought about in the urban settlements due to the very factors of wealth, contiguity and education. On the other hand, the malaise of an impoverished urban environment has brought about an awareness of cultural gaps, lack of contact with nature and unhappy disparities. The economics of the crisis also has grown. The cities live increasingly on the doles from the government, which accentuates the rural and urban conflicts. The deepening crisis has not yet fully overtaken us, as perhaps in the way it has overtaken New York. The federal and state governments are now refusing to fund New York for the solution of its problems. On the other hand, the city's resources have diminished because the people and the industries capable of paying more taxes have tended to move out of New York beyond the urban units. This crisis has recently been temporarily met by a large loan made by the Government of New York. Even the repayment of die loan is somewhat in doubt (Prasad, 2003).

Nature and Types of Cities

Cities are the products of higher reaches of civilization and represent the peak of the socio-cultural aspects of any society. Sharma (2004) describes following four prerequisites of any city:

- A favourable ecological basis, since cities have to support a large population.
- An advanced technology, in the agricultural and non-agricultural spheres.
- A complex social organization since cities have to harmonize patterns of a divergent population.
- A well-developed power structure.

On the basis of broad common features of the cities, we can classify them in following types:

1. Production centres
2. Centres of trade and commerce
3. Capitals
4. Health and recreation centres
5. Cultural centres
6. Diversified cities

The theory of urbanization refers to the positive aspects of urbanization as a process of development. Starting with the assumption that a city comes into being to fulfil the needs of its region, the theory of organization propounds a symbiotic relationship between the rural and the urban areas (Alexander, 1954). The urban centre utilizes the surplus produce of its countryside, while the latter consumes the services and finished products supplied by the former. Being more developed than its surrounding region, the city acts as a nucleus radiating its influence on the region (Ellefson, 1962; D'Souza and Kamra, 1981). There is, thus, an intimate interdependence between the city and its region, the latter giving sustenance to the former and the former triggering the growth of the latter, resulting in an integrated rural-urban development (D'Souza, 1976).

According to Sharma (2004), there can be no absolute classification of cities, all classifications are relative. Many cities fit in more than one category mentioned above. For example, Delhi fits in with the first three categories; it is an important production centre, an equally important centre of trade and commerce and is, of course, a capital city. Mumbai, on the other hand, satisfies the necessary conditions of first five categories listed above. It is an important production centre, an important centre of trade and commerce, capital of Maharashtra, a centre of health and recreation and also a cultural centre. Besides these, Mumbai also has many other specialties. Being on the seacoast, its climate is temperate and it is also the most important film-making centre. It is also the world's renowned centre of entertainment and amusement. Mumbai's importance lies not only in the fact that it is the capital of Maharashtra but issues from the fact that it is a famous city. Not without reason it is called Gateway of India. Again, the importance of Mumbai does not lie in its being a big centre of culture and entertainment but issues from the fact that it is a port through which import and export worth millions of rupees is made. Though Mumbai is a centre of cloth production, it is more important as a centre of trade and commerce. Therefore, after taking into consideration everything, we find that Mumbai fits in with the second category most, that is it is a centre of trade and commerce. Thus, while classifying a city we have to see as to which of its features is most prominent. Therefore, though Delhi is an important production centre as well as the centre of trade and commerce, its most important feature is that–it is a capital city.

The distribution of urban population takes place among settlements of differing sizes along a continuum from small towns to giant cities with population of tens of million (Pacione, 2001). Cities grow initially, benefiting from the increasing agglomeration economy, but after a certain stage due to congestion and crowding, diseconomies set in resulting the urban sprawl into the adjoining area. The mono-centric urban structure becomes multi-centred and dominates the rest of the urban system. In the evolving urban structure, the small and intermediate towns are expected to grow slowly compared to large cities in the early phases of urbanization. It is in the latter phases, the smaller towns are expected to grow as a result of congestion and crowding in the large and intermediate towns. This cycle of urbanization postulated by Geyer and Kontuly (1993) in terms of primate city, intermediate city and small city phase keeps on repeating not necessarily with same group of towns.

Million cities are very distinct in terms of their relatively high population growth compared to non-million categories, and some of them are fastest growing in recent years. On the other hand, the differences in growth rates between cities and different categories of towns (large, medium and small) are not very much significant. It means that the cities within themselves show very large variations. The statistical analysis shows that the size of town and city is negatively related to urban growth rates. It is quite natural that as a city grows, it expands its economic base and activities of the cities lead to increased advantage to the trade and commerce as well as to industries from the agglomeration economy. But it cannot be sustained very long. The decline in growth rate will certainly set in with increase in the size of city in the long run. Hence, an effort to restrict city size is not always necessary and it could even be detrimental to the economic growth in the early stages of economic development in a country (Mills and Becker, 1986). Therefore, cities should be allowed to grow naturally in order to reap the benefits of its growth momentum. In fact, the optimality of city size is elusive and each city could find its own in due course of time.

Urbanization in India

The urban population in India at the beginning of 20th century was only 25.85 million constituting 10.84 per cent of India's population in 1901, which increased to 285.35 million comprising 27.78 per cent of total population in 2001. The growth rate was highest observed during 1971–81 (46.14%) and there was subsequent slowing down of urbanization.

Rural and urban areas are not independent of each other. Urban areas provide several services such as marketing of agricultural products and inputs, repair of agricultural implements and also educational and health services to the rural areas. Because of the importance of urban centres in providing services to rural population, the number of urban centres per 10 lakh rural population is shown in Table 1.1. It is interesting to note that the total number of towns/UA per 10 lakh rural populations has declined from 8.6 in 1901 to 6.0 in 2001. This shows that in a relative sense the lesser number of urban centres have to serve more and more rural populations. Table 1.1 indicates the level of urbanization in India.

Table 1.1

India: The Level of Urbanization in India Since 1901

Census Year	*Urban Population (in million)*	*% Urban Population*	*Number of Towns/UA per 10 Lakh Rural Population*	*Decennial Growth Rate of Population (%)*
1901	25.85	10.84	8.6	—
1911	25.94	10.29	8.0	0.35
1921	28.08	11.18	8.7	8.27
1931	33.45	11.99	8.4	19.12
1941	44.15	13.86	8.2	31.97
1951	62.44	17.29	9.5	41.42
1961	78.93	17.97	6.6	26.41
1971	109.11	19.91	5.9	38.29
1981	159.46	23.34	6.4	46.14
1991	217.17	25.72	6.0	36.00
2001	285.35	27.78	6.0	31.30

Notes: 1. As 1981 Census was not conducted in Assam, the 1981 population figures for India include interpolated figures for Assam.

2. The 1991 Census was not held in Jammu & Kashmir. The 1991 population figures for India include projected figures for Jammu & Kashmir as projected by the Standing Committee of Experts on Population Projection (October 1989).

Source: Census of India, 1991.

http.\\www.censusindia.net (2001 Census).

In earlier decade, cities have grown faster than the small and medium towns, and the large towns and cities have identical growth rates. But the last decade shows that both small towns and cities are growing at the same rate, whereas medium and large towns have lower growth rates. This pattern of growth during the 1990s indicates that people from large and medium towns are likely to be migrating to cities for better opportunities (Table 1.2).

Table 1.2
Adjusted Decadal Urban Growth Rates by Size Class of Towns/Cities, India 1981–2001

Size Class	*1981–91*	*1991–2001*
Cities (>1,00,000)	30.2	28.4
Large Towns (50,000–100,000)	30.0	26.1
Medium Towns (20,000–50,000)	28.8	24.5
Small Towns (<20,000)	28.8	28.3
Total	29.8	27.5

Note: Adjusted rates excluded the new towns as well as classified towns based on common towns during the decade.

This is consistent with forces of privatization and liberalization of the economy, which have more benefited the cities compared with towns. The growth of small towns might be due to higher natural increase among them as they are not very different from villages. In India, cities existed throughout recorded history as capitals of the

Table 1.3
Increase in Urban Population in India

Class of Town	*1901*	*1951*	*1961*	*1971*	*1981*	*1991*	*2001*
I 1,00,000 and above	6,661 (26.0)	27,507 (44.63)	39,883 (51.42)	61,226 (57.24)	94,504 (60.42)	138,802 (65.20)	178,224 (62.31)
II 50,000–99,999	2,892 (11.29)	6,137 (9.96)	8,713 (11.23)	11,680 (10.92)	18,190 (11.63)	23,309 (10.95)	34,452 (12.04)
III 20,000–49,999	4,007 (15.64)	9,688 (15.72)	13,139 (16.94)	17,126 (16.01)	22,409 (14.33)	28,079 (13.19)	42,119 (14.72)
IV 10,000–19,999	5,335 (20.83)	8,399 (13.63)	9,902 (12.77)	11,706 (10.94)	14,930 (9.54)	16,531 (7.77)	22,593 (7.89)
V 5,000–9,999	5,159 (20.14)	7,993 (12.97)	5,329 (6.87)	4,756 (4.45)	5,603 (3.58)	5,532 (2.60)	7,890 (2.75)
VI less than 5000	1,562 (6.10)	1,906 (3.09)	0,597 (0.77)	473 (0.44)	784 (0.50)	614 (0.29)	842 (0.29)
All Class	25,616 (100.00)	61,630 (100.00)	77,562 (100.00)	106,967 (100.00)	156,420 (100.00)	212,86 (100.00)	286,120 (100.00)
Percentage of Urban in Total Population	10.84	17.24	17.97	19.91	23.34	25.72	27.82

Note: Figures in parentheses show percentage.
Source: Census of India.

various empires. These were usually centres, which enjoyed a flourishing trade. In twentieth century, several towns have taken the shape of cities. The increase in urbanization is shown in Table 1.3.

Problems of Urbanization in India

Urban problems in India vary according to their scale and intensity. The severity of the problems is reflected by the overall population growth and shortage of infrastructural resources with which to manage the additions to the urban populations. There are some problems, which are peculiar to large cities:

There are problems related to availability of basic amenities in urban areas. Banerjee's (1995) study of Guwahati city reveals the problems that arise from rapid urbanization. Guwahati city with decadal (1981–91) population growth rate of 188.25 per cent presently lacks the basic amenities of the modern city. The prime cause of this population boom in the cities is migration. Due to the population pressure, the water supply, sewerage and drainage system of the city has failed. The city roads are totally unfit for supporting the huge volume of traffic flows. Moreover, the city is experiencing a variation of temperature between the heart of the city and the outer ring of the city, which is a very disturbing trend. The problems are aggravated due to a number of development agencies and lack of scientific planning which could regulate the enormous growth of the city due to population pressure.

The rapid growth of population resulting from the introduction of the motor vehicle and improvements in the transmission of electric power, telephone, radio, television etc. expand the radical scope of the central cities. Hawley (1955) has focussed attention on the rapid development of cities, which lead to population redistribution and change the shape of the cities. He has also taken into account the distance involved in the de-concentration of metropolitan population, which impinges upon the economies of metropolitan development.

Due to population growth and immigration, cities need many new dwellings. Agricultural land has to be transformed into residential land, present areas have to be expanded, and modified over the years to play their part in the development process. Strassmann (1982) has examined the transformation of urban housing in Cartagena city,

Colombia, in his study. The growth of population and employment generates more demand and hence increases density. Households in a prospering but rapidly proliferating city may, therefore, have to change their concept of what is a minimal acceptable density, because as the city expands, neighbourhoods change in quality and access to the rest of the city.

These are several cases of unauthorized construction in urban areas. Public land is wrongfully acquired for private purpose. There is wide range encroachment on public roads. The local municipal bodies and government agencies have a tough job of clearing unauthorized construction and encroachment on public lands.

All cities in India are facing the problem of slums. Construction of unauthorized houses and unplanned development of residential colonies have resulted in creation of slum areas. This is also attributed to population pressure, flow of rural to urban migration and loopholes in government machinery. Sometimes, slum dwellings are allowed to develop because of vested interests and authorizing during the election times.

Nowadays, the problems of displacement are being discussed in various forums. Land acquisition results in displacement of agriculturists, poor people and tribals who had been residing in the fringe areas of the city. With the development of cities there is always a need to acquire more and more land for residential colonies, industries, educational institutions, offices, roads, tourist resorts and infrastructural facilities. Large areas of land are acquired for the sake of development, whereas there are problems of payment of compensation, resettlement and rehabilitation.

As a process of growth, the cities in India reveal multidimensional problems of urbanization and development. The process may degenerate into an alienated form of urban development. Many of the problems could be attributed to rural-urban development. These problems should be adjudged in the context of those who suffer because of land acquisition. We shall now analyze it as a problem of displacement of people, their resettlement and rehabilitation.

Urban Population Change in Rajasthan

The situation of urban population of Rajasthan along with decadal change is shown in Table 1.4.

Table 1.4
Urban Population Change in Rajasthan

Year	*Urban Population*	*Decadal Change*	*Urban % to total population*
1901	15,50,656	—	15.06
1911	1,47,829	- 4.83	14.34
1921	14,75,335	- 0.03	14.33
1931	17,29,205	17.21	14.71
1941	21,17,101	22.43	15.27
1951	29,55,275	39.59	18.50
1961	32,81,478	11.04	16.28
1971	45,43,761	38.47	17.63
1981	72,10,508	58.24	21.05
1991	1,00,40,118	39.34	22.88
2001	1,32,14,375	31.26	23.38

Source: Census of India, Series 18, Rajasthan 1991.Census of India, Rajasthan 2001 floppy records.

Urban population in Rajasthan has increased from 15,50,656 in 1901 to 1,32,14,375 in 2001. The decadal change shows a decline (–4.83) in 1911 and a little less (0.03) in 1921. A major decadal change has been observed (39.59) during 1941–51. This was mainly due to influx of refugees from Pakistan to the urban areas of Rajasthan. The change in urban population picked up during 1961–71 and it was maximum (58.24) during 1971–81. This appears to be due to immigration from other states and also because of rural to urban immigration. The decade change again shows after 1981 and during 1991–2001 it was restricted to 31.26. However, the percentage of urban to total has shown a gradually increasing trend.

Displacement: Various Dimensions

Displacement is a multidimensional phenomenon, affecting people's lives in their entirety, encompassing economic social and cultural spheres. In recent years, it has caused intense debate among academics, social activists and planners. The displacement of people in urban areas detaches them from their agricultural land and ancestral homes. Though the process of acquisition of land for setting up mining, irrigation, transportation and mega industrial projects (mostly in the public sector) is not new, the intensity of adverse effects was never comprehended in the past as it is today. The liberalization of the economy, growing needs of infrastructure in fast-growing cities and new partnerships in industrial and economic sectors have threatened traditional sources of sustenance of people. More and more agricultural lands are being depleted for setting up infrastructure projects. The situation is aggravated due to major conversion of agricultural lands voluntarily or involuntarily into urbanisable lands (Sharma, 2003). There is no authentic data to ascertain the extent of displacement and quantum of agricultural lands acquired for urbanization in the country.

The intensity of urbanization-induced displacement is much larger than the involuntary displacement caused by setting up of industrial/infrastructure projects It is in this context that involuntary displacement is seen as an offshoot of the model of development and people have started questioning its legitimacy. The debate has been alive for long. It has drawn wide attention in the context of the Sardar Sarovar project. The Narmada Bachao Andolan mobilized thousands of the affected families and like-minded people against the anti-people stance of such large industrial/irrigation projects. The non-government organizations not only focused on the inadequacy of resettlement and rehabilitation programmes but also questioned the very basis of such projects executed by the government in the name of public interest (Sharma, 2003). The issue is now being debated in the context of development versus displacement.

Displaced persons are those persons or groups of persons who have been forced or obliged to flee or to leave their homes or places of habitual residence, in particular, as a result of natural or man-made disasters, or social conflicts and who have been ousted by the development projects and urbanization. Development-induced displacement is considered to be included within the definition, as made clear by later provisions on arbitrary displacement, addressed below.

The displaced persons (DPs) are those who are forced to move out of their land when the development projects require acquisition of their homesteads.

The project-affected persons (PAPs), are those who lose their livelihood fully or partially without being displaced. In some cases, their individual land is acquired and in others, the common property resources (CPRs) like forests, fishing ground. Their livelihoods are acquired.

In other cases, disposal of waste affects land fertility, health etc. Some of the most common examples include the ash ponds of thermal plants, red mud ponds to store contaminated water produced by aluminum plants, waste from cement plants etc. which render the land around them waste. This often deprives the dependants on such land of their livelihood and forces them to move out. These people are indirect DPs (Ganguly Thukral, 1999).

Earlier, displacement was defined as physical transfer of the project affected population. It did not consider the associated social and economic factors which disrupted the lives of the people. Because of the changes in land use and ownership patterns, loss of livelihood and reduced accessibility to common property resources, the affected population suffers from psychological and cultural shocks. Displacement needs to be redefined in view of the emerging concerns about resettlement and rehabilitation. The definition should focus on change in norms for compensation and calculation of non-monetary items. It is equally important to recognize the customary rights and use of common property and natural resources. Compensating to the displaced should consider reconstruction of the livelihood that has to be the main objective along with the ultimate goal of the rehabilitation.

Displacement as a Problem

The problem of displacement is not merely economic, it is also a socio-cultural problem because it disturbs a network of social relationships supporting an ethos and a way of life. It affects the entire gamut of traditional activity and an established social order. It forces people to adopt new ways of occupational activities and an unknown environment. As such, the process is akin to 'replacement' in a new location. The displaced people are forced to change their social patterns, without getting any compensation for social costs and, thus, they are under pressure, causing a situation of socio-cultural stress (Advani, 1995).

Menezes (1991) highlights two fundamental reasons for displacement as a problem. First, it is compulsory and involuntary. Secondly, it is rare that fair compensation is paid. According to him, the current system fails to acknowledge that an oustee is deprived of the historical right of access to a large number of resources, an entire way of life, and is not given any opportunity to demand adequate price for this loss. Apart from his private land and cultural-historical heritage, an oustee holds several other livelihoods generating assets, which are not legally acknowledged. The report of the Commissioner for Scheduled Castes and Scheduled Tribes (1990) points out that when the land is acquired under the present law, only its property form is considered and the vital questions concerning the very survival of the displaced persons are settled on this basis.

Involuntary displacement creates the conditions of landlessness, homelessness and joblessness. Expropriation of land removes the main foundation upon which people's productive systems, commercial activities and livelihood are constructed. The loss of housing and shelter may be only temporary for many of the displaced, but for some, homelessness remains a chronic condition. In a broader cultural sense, homelessness is also placelessness, loss of a group's cultural space and identity. Due to both the above conditions, loss of wage employment occurs and those losing jobs are landless labourers, service workers, artisans and small businessmen. Resulting unemployment or underemployment among resettlers lingers long after physical relocation (Verma, 2004). The problem is aggravated because of the non-cooperative attitude of the officials, inappropriate compensation, agitations, family conflicts and court cases.

Involuntary displacement creates some specific problems like marginalization, increased morbidity and mortality, food insecurity, loss of access to common property etc. Marginalization occurs when family loses economic power and slides on a 'downward mobility' path. Relative marginalization may often begin long before the actual displacement; for instance, when lands are condemned for future flooding and are implicitly devalued, new public and private infrastructure investments are prohibited, and the expansion of social services are undercut. Serious decreases in health level result from displacement caused social stress, insecurity, and psychological trauma, and from the outbreak of relocation-related diseases (Verma, 2004). The displaced persons face problems at the relocation site. There are problems of adjustment and rifts over use of common property resources.

Displacement is associated with psychological stress that emerges out of the fear of relocation. An additional cause of the stress is the fear of abandoning the places of worship, which may invite the wrath of gods and goddesses. The result may be increased sickness, death and grief. The emotional stress is aggravated by a feeling of helplessness, as no amount of argument, plea or revolt can prevent the inevitable forced displacement (Agrawal, 1996). There is widespread ignorance about the problem of displacement. Majority of displaced persons belongs to lower socio-economic strata. They have to undergo a process of dispossession and disempowerment. Displacement disrupts the socio-cultural structures of the inhabitants, which include their production system and income sources.

Congenial environments, long established social standing and kinship linkages are broken. Thus, from social and cultural point of view, displacement is a disruptive process and it creates high risks of impoverishment among the displaced people.

Quantum of Displacement

The most noticeable aspect of displacement during the last four decades is the enormity of the problem. Though accurate figures are not available, but according to conservative estimates, about 15 million persons have been 'displaced' from the First Plan to the Sixth Plan, and the real figure may be as high as 36 million. Despite the enormity of the problem, the country lacks a reliable database on the situation of displaced people (Vyas, 1993).

The few estimates available put the number of displaced and project affected persons at a minimum of 21.3 million between 1951 and 1990 (Fernandes, 1998). By now, they must have crossed 35 millions. The estimate of total number of people displaced by planned development between 1951 to 1990 ranges from 110 to 185 lakh (Fernandes, 1989). According to another estimation, total of 213 lakh people have been displaced by various development projects (Fernandes and Paranjpye, 1997). Cernea (1996) estimates, "In 1990s about 10,000,000 people are displaced annually by infrastructure development programmes in some key sectors, a number much larger than the total number of refugees caused by wars and natural disasters".

Since independence, development projects under India's Five-Year Plans have displaced about 5,00,000 persons each year—evicted from their lands because of the direct administrative actions of government. This figure does not include those deprived of their livelihoods by the expansion of large estate mono-culture production, or those deprived of their livelihoods by project-related natural resource extraction, urban evictions, or by the relocation of other displacement victims. Estimates of the total number of those displaced by 'development' since independence reaches as high as 40 million people. India's recent thrust to open itself to the global economic system and to rely more on market forces will surely accelerate the displacement (Kothari, 1995).

Hydroelectric and irrigation projects are the major source of displacement. Maharashtra Irrigation II in Satara district and the Upper Krishana Irrigation Project in northern Karnataka resulted in displacement of over 4,50,000 persons (Parsuraman, 1999). The Sardar Sarovar Project has affected about 297 villages and displaced over two lakh persons. Fernandes (1998) indicates that by and large dams lower than 15 metres from the foundation built on streams in the plains, displace very few or none. Those in the hills displace around 1,000 each. Medium dams (say 15–30 m) displace 2,000 to 10,000 each. Some major dams like Tawa and Nagarjunsagar have displaced around 25,000 each and many others more than 100,000 and some above 100,000. Some like Upper Krishana have caused 2.5 lakh DPs (Guggenheim, 1990).

Another source of displacement is several mines and industries. The major coal companies displaced 32,751 families in 1981–85. The four steel plants displaced 1.25 lakh in 1950s and 60s (Government of India, 1985; Commissioner of SC & ST, 1961). Displacement due to urban development has not yet been assessed. But a few reports suggest that the number might have crossed the estimated quantum of those who have been displaced by the dams.

Types of Displacement

The types of displaced vary according to the causes, which range from environmental degradation to natural disasters and man-made disasters to internal conflicts. Further, displacement is caused because of the implementation of developmental project, outflows of migrants and external forces.

The following types of displacement are caused by various factors:

1. Natural disasters force many to leave their homeland. They move out of their region because of the earthquake, the cyclones, floods and droughts elsewhere. These are disaster-displaced persons.
2. People are displaced because of man-made disasters, e.g., gas disaster in the Union Carbide Factory, Bhopal.
3. People displaced from their habitat by wars, civil unrest, and social conflicts. They become refugees. For example, around 15 million persons migrated from India to Pakistan or from Pakistan to India during the partition of the country in 1947.
4. Many people leave their homelands when changes are introduced in the economic polices. In recent decades, lakhs of traditional fishing families, millions of tribals and Dalits have been rendered jobless by the economic activities. These are termed as process-displaced persons.
5. Millions of persons have been deprived of their livelihoods because their lands and other assets are acquired for development projects. These include displaced persons (DPs) and project affected persons (PAPs). DPs are those who are displaced, and PAPs are people whose livelihood is lost though they may stay where they are. Majority of them are displaced because of construction of large dams and development of water resources. Others include those displaced by development of highways, mining areas and urbanization. Land is also acquired for industrial areas, educational institutions and residential areas.
6. Displacement is caused when thousands of unauthorized constructions are demolished and some areas are cleared for urban development.
7. Many people from the ethnic minority communities are displaced from their original dwelling areas. For example, people from northern and eastern areas of the country have left for other cities within the country or in a neighbouring country. This is because of the uncertainty among these communities for peaceful living.

Development versus Displacement

Displacement claims the social and human costs of development that some citizens have to bear as best as they tend to promote the greater good of all. The evil (at least in the Benthamite sense as deliberative imposition of pain and suffering) is outweighed by the larger 'good' (welfare) arising from 'development' projects. Costs are simply inevitable; there is no development without displacement. All that developmental planning should do, we are constantly told, is to engage in cost-benefit analysis, especially factoring in social and human costs of displacement, and provide for measures of rehabilitation and compensation. Most Indian developmental projects, insofar as they affect the impoverished masses, ignore both these aspects (Baxi, 2003).

There were several struggles against rules of land acquisition and the changes made in the colonial times, the best known among them being the one of Mulshi-Peta near Pune in the 1920s (Bhuskute, 1997). The struggle was appropriated by the freedom fighters. But, though they opposed the colonial government on this particular issue, the nationalist leaders had themselves internalized much of the colonial value system including that of the eminent domain. So, the thinking behind development in India remains more or less unchanged even half a century after independence. When they became the decision-makers of independent India, the freedom fighters who had earlier supported the Mulshi-Peta struggle, continued to use the same colonial legislation to displace people in the name of national development (Murikan et al., 2003). There has been much greater displacement and many more struggles after independence, because of the policies adopted for the use of land, water, forests and other resources. Displacement has caused impoverishment of the already poor downtrodden. There has been an enormous increase in the number of DPs and PAPs. Despite this, no official database exists on the total number and the type of DPs/PAPs. The country does not have a uniform rehabilitation policy though millions have been deprived of their lands and livelihoods.

Resettlement and Rehabilitation

Resettlement of the displaced people is one-time relocation at a new site with payment of compensation for the land acquired and without other support such as jobs, training and welfare inputs to resettle in a new society and economic situation. Rehabilitation focuses on social and cultural factors and attempts to rebind the dispossessed livelihoods of the displaced and project-affected people. It is not limited to economic compensation but, goes beyond to include welfare approach.

Rehabilitation is more often understood as an economic rather than a psycho-sociological phenomenon resulting from displacement. It is normally perceived as a 'planned change effort'. In a strict sense, it implies that, the overall objective of the change is to restore the situation to its original condition (Franks, 1991). The nature of rehabilitation is quite different from other developmental processes. All developmental efforts imply planned change to improve existing conditions, whereas rehabilitation is designed to restore the status quo. This makes it imperative to understand the term rehabilitation in a much wider perspective, and its components, which make it different from other developmental processes (Sinha, 2006). However, rehabilitation should go beyond maintaining of the status quo and adopt welfare approach to improve the standard of living of the displaced population.

Components of Rehabilitation

Sinha (2006) discusses the components of rehabilitation. The bases of the antecedent conditions: Displacement and rehabilitation of people are required when certain antecedent conditions of the displaced, the cognitive state of the individuals and their affective state. He further describes their manifest and rehabilitation programme which includes allotment of land, house, occupation and many other facilities required for resettlement and consideration of further demands by people from the government.

The process of rehabilitation has to be carried out along with resettlement and it should restore the socio-economic status of the displaced. Land for land is considered as one of the ways of rehabilitation of the displaced persons, whose economy centres on agriculture. There are also other ways of rehabilitation, which include engagement in small scale and cottage industries, dairy, piggery, fishery, poultry, etc. PAPs have been demanding employment in the concerned project. The ways of rehabilitating are to be examined after proper assessment and exploration of new opportunities.

Cernea (1991) has identified eight main potential risks of impoverishment in case of the displaced persons. These are: (i) landlessness, (ii) joblessness, (iii) homelessness, (iv) marginalization, (v) increased morbidity and mortality, (vi) food insecurity, (vii) loss of access to common property, and (viii) social disintegration. Resettlement and rehabilitation (R&R) approach should focus on overcoming these risks. Social and cultural aspects should be well-considered in the process of rehabilitation.

Land-based rehabilitation is governed by:

1. Replacement of livelihood lost;
2. The ownership of the replaced means of production;
3. 'Quality of life' after rehabilitation;
4. Security/guarantee against future displacement or multiple displacement; and
5. 'Land for land' to be one of the main criteria for replacement of livelihood lost.

Income restoration is the basic objective of rehabilitation, the restoration activities should be based on the principle that no project-affected person shall be worse off than he shall or she was before the land acquisition. Restoration income is an important part of rehabilitating individuals, households, and socio-economic and cultural systems in affected communities.

To achieve this objective, preparation of income restoration (IR) programme could be approached as if they were economic development programme in their own right. Income restoration schemes could be designed in consultation with affected persons and they will explicitly approve programme designed to benefit them.

Income restoration entitlements are provided to the persons losing livelihood or suffering loss of income as a result of land acquisition in urban areas. These include land-based economic activities as well as non-land economic activities.

Individual income restoration schemes should consider the resource base of affected person and their socio-economic characteristics and preferences. These should consider their education level, skill possession and likely economic activities in the post-displacement period, extent of land left and extent of land purchased. Along with this, the suitability of economic activity to supplement the income and market potential and marketing facilities should be assessed.

Although it is widely recognized that the best option is to allow them to continue their former occupations, circumstances may not permit this option. When they elect to change activities, possible income restoration options could be explored. In addition, long-term socio-economic monitoring of the displaced is considered an important aspect of rehabilitation. It is evident that social support accompanied with sociological analysis helps in controlling social and cultural stress. The sociologists can play an important role in rehabilitation of the displaced (Advani, 1995).

Problem to be Investigated

Urban growth entails acquisition of land resulting into displacement of thousands of people every year in every city. The land is acquired by urban developmental bodies or purchased by property housing cooperative societies or dealers at a minimal cost from the agriculturists and it is developed and sold for housing commercial or other projects.

The process is continuous and mostly affects the people residing on the borderlines of cites. The rural areas are converted into the urban; the village agriculturists are pushed away from the city to a new locale, where they purchase lands from other agriculturists or engage themselves in alternative occupations. In this pursuit, they either misutilize the finances or fail to manage their socio-economic nexus. The change in their social structural network affects their lifestyle, family form, caste ties and community support. The joint families are broken and tendency of males residing away from the females increases. There is a greater flow of floating labour population. The women working outside the village are exposed to contractual labour and come in contact with urban population. The displaced are affected much more than the settled population. All this primarily changes their socio-occupational structure, population structure, and fertility and mortality levels.

The process of urbanization affects different groups differently. Some stand to gain, while others lose. Urbanization without some displacement is inconceivable, but those who are subjected to sacrifices for the larger good of the society are many a times left to fend for themselves.

Displacement is linked to socio-occupational aspects. When the agricultural land is acquired for housing projects, the farmers are paid financial compensation but the social costs are not calculated. In several cases, where the alternative agricultural land is not available, a change in their traditional occupational activity is inevitable. While the disruption due to displacement is commonly wide, it is the agriculturists that bear the burnt most of all. The dislocation to their life is total.

Displaced persons include owners of the land, tenants, share-croppers (continuously cropping for at least four years before first notification) and agricultural labourers (working since at least one year before notification). Besides this, it also includes displaced residents carrying on any trade or simply residing in the affected zone for a minimum period of one year before notification. The definition of PAP includes a person whose more than half of the land holding is affected by acquisition or who has to move on account of displacement process.

The key problem of the current system is that it focuses on a single aspect of displacement, i.e., acquired private land and property. It fails to acknowledge the historic rights of access to natural resources and an entire way of life. Resettlement in some cases include alter-native habitat, housing and the appurtenant support and infrastructure facilities but it fails to provide access to several livelihood resources which are traditionally availed in a typical Indian village community. The urbanization-related displacement is invariably associated with socio-economic impact on people facing displacement.

Rehabilitation of outees is one of least satisfactory aspects in the process of urbanization. The government authorities believe in giving cash compensation for the land and house acquired. They do not envisage any plan for compensation on loss of employment or disruption of livelihood and other ownership of land. The landless labourers, marginal farmers, sharecroppers, tenant cultivators, artisans, cattle grazers and the like who depend on the existing natural resources are not compensated for their loss. Thus, there are various facts of the displaced outees, which require sociological perspicuity.

Two

Features of Displacement and Methodology

Development has created a situation where more and more land is being acquired for urban development and lakhs of people are being displaced from their communities and traditional way of life. In the first part of the chapter, an attempt has been made to discuss the features of displacement, urban development and problems of displacement. In the second part, methodologies of resettlement and rehabilitation relevant to this study, areas of study and social background of sample population have been analyzed.

Features of Displacement

The fundamental feature of forced displacement is that it causes a profound unraveling of existing patterns of social organization. This unraveling occurs at many levels. When people are forcibly moved, production systems are dismantled. Long established residential communities and settlements are disorganized, while kinship groups and family systems are often scattered. Lives sustaining informal social networks that provide mutual help are rendered non-functional. Trade linkages between producers and their customer base are interrupted, and local labour markets are disrupted. Formal and informal associations, and self-organized services, are wiped out by the sudden scattering of their membership. Traditional management systems tend to lose their leaders. The coerced abandonment of symbolic markers (such as ancestral shrines and graves), or of spatial contexts (such as mountains and rivers considered holy, or sacred trails), cuts off some of the physical and psychological linkages with the past and saps at the roots of people's cultural identity (Cernea, 1996). This indicates change in social and cultural aspects of the displaced persons.

Majority of displaced persons are poor. They suffer most from displacement. It appears that development has made rich richer and the cost of development is borne by the displaced poor. Because of the developmental projects, lakhs of people are being displaced from their native places and traditional ways of life and most of them become victims of the process of development.

There are special features of the displaced population that make them even more vulnerable, unorganized and exploited. The majority of them are backward classes, Scheduled Castes and Scheduled Tribes. Because of displacement many of them became unemployed or under-employed labourers.

Women and adolescents constitute well over half among the displaced and the proportion of children may be about two-third. While women workers share all the vulnerabilities of men of their own class, they have added disadvantages, which make them doubly vulnerable. They have less assets, most of them are illiterate and unaware of their rights—as workers or as women—and the seasonality of rural employment makes them even more dependent on their employers as the source of work or loans in times of unemployment (Majumdar, 2003).

The living conditions of the majority of the displaced fall below the standard. Interestingly, the hardship does not show in their rating of life satisfaction. Despite their hardships in the urban areas, more than half of the people affected by land acquisition still feel satisfied with life. Too much of our thinking and social action on the issue of displacement and rehabilitation remains 'dam-centric' and ignores the happenings in contexts of industrial development-induced displacement (Dhagamwar et al., 2003). Other major cause of displacement is acquisition of land for urban development.

Planners and administrators invariably capitalize on and manipulate the relatively weaker socio-economic and political positions of most of the people facing displacement. Their numbers are underestimated, they are treated indifferently and only minimum cash compensation, it at all, is paid (Kothari, 1995).

In a village setting, the productive land is a collective source of livelihood not only to its owners but also to indirectly affected families like the agricultural labourers, village servants (carpenter, blacksmith, cobbler and so on). The directly affected, as per law, are entitled to compensation and other benefits as a part of resettlement and rehabilitation. However, the indirectly affected, who depended on the owners of land are left without any protection (Sharma, 2003).

The growing face of development under liberalization has increased the intensity of such displacement to the extent that communities living in their traditional setting are getting displaced with the loss of their traditional sources of livelihood. Once displaced, the PAPs are pushed into an open market situation as individuals competing for their survival in a hostile new environment. A majority of them prove to be losers in this new race of development (Sharma, 2003).

The displaced people undergo a process of disempowerment along with dispossession of assets. As such displacement dismantles and destroys social network and cultural structures of the inhabitants. When people move from their native places, their production systems get dismantled and their long established residential and caste groups get disorganized. The effects of displacement could be seen on religious practices, places and customs. They are so attached to their temples that they even refuse to move out of their home leaving the God behind. There are existential problems of leaving inhabitance. Loss of forest land during acquisition affects the livelihood of the dependent persons. It destabilizes the social and economic activities.

The next feature of displacement is the proportion of displaced persons (DPs) from the weaker sections, particularly tribals and Dalits. It has been high in the past and is increasing today. Most DPs/PAPs are assetless rural poor like landless labourers and small and marginal farmers. The tribals, who constitute 8.08 per cent of the country's population, are estimated to be more than 40 per cent of the DPs/PAPs of dams and mines, and 90 per cent of wildlife sanctuaries (Fernandes, 1998a: 265). Another 20 per cent are Dalits (Mahapatra, 1990). In urban areas, a big proportion of the displaced are poor. There is no uniform criterion for payment of compensation and rehabilitation.

Urban Development and Displacement

The importance of addressing the problem of urbanization-induced displacement in India where rapid economic development has resulted in the forced displacement of lakhs of people. It often produces social conflicts and within societies and results in involuntary displacement. It is observed that land acquisition for urban development benefits only certain segments of the population but negatively affects several people. There are inadequate efforts to address the needs of the oustees, although the risk of displacement may be detrimental to their human rights.

Urban displacement needs to be recognized as a critical concern as it is not well-addressed. It could have severe social, economic and political consequences. Many Indian cities experience substantial urban displacement. The affected people in India live under conditions of deprivation and hardship and these include a large proportion of women and children. Women and children are especially vulnerable. Several children do not enjoy the benefits of a normal family life.

As a result of urbanization, the number of people affected by land acquisition are multiplying to the point that their aggregate population displacement may surpass those affected by construction of dams. To analyze the displacement implications in urban development and to find better solutions to resolve social problems, monitoring of the problems is essential

The impact of urban displacement on basic social structure changes in family, caste system and community required systematic analysis. For this, an attempt has to be made to identify its effect on existing social organizations, kinship ties and cultural milieu. The social networks of local voluntary associations, social groups and their role in the displacement process has to be analyzed in the context of socio-demographic aspects as well as conflicts between the different classes of people. The areas under displacement include changes in value system, belief and culture of the oustees.

The people displaced because of urban development have multiple identities. Many of them belong to Scheduled Castes (SCs/Dalits), Scheduled Tribes (STs) and Other Backward Classes (OBCs). They might fall in categories of occupations like primary, secondary and tertiary sector workers, majority of the displaced are identified as disadvantaged social groups. One of the reasons of marginalization of SCs, STs and OBCs is that many of them have no legal entitlement or ownership of private property.

Problems of Displacement

The trauma of displacement begins well before the process itself actually takes place. As soon as the project is announced, all development work in the area comes to a halt. No one wants to invest in land that is to be submerged. Banks refuse to give loans, no new civic amenities like school and health centres are constructed. Even the withdrawal of existing facilities is not unknown (Thukral, 1996). Since the gestation period of land acquisition is long, the suffering of the people is also intense.

The effects of involuntary displacement are observed on the social structure of the society including family, caste and community. Family system receives a severe jolt. Family as a traditional system of production, changes into system of consumption. Consequently, caste system also loses its grip due to industrialization and, community system changes shape. Forced displacement tears apart the social fabric and the existing patterns of social organizations. Production systems are dismantled, kinship groups and family systems are often scattered, local labour markets are disrupted, and people's cultural identity is put at risk. Life sustaining informal social network of mutual help among people, common property resources, local voluntary associations, self-organized services arrangements, etc., are dispersed and rendered inactive. This unravelling represents a massive loss of social capital incurred by the uprooted people (Verma, 2004). Due to displacement and relocation, consequent change in values, beliefs, customs, traditions and culture is observed.

Development leading to displacement of people from their own land is inevitable. Land acquisition forces the otherwise stable, sedentary population to move away from their original places of home and work. It uproots people from their original lands and creates psycho-sociological stress leading to many dysfunctional consequences. More often, both social and economic benefits of such developmental projects are not shared equally by displaced population (Sinha, 2006). During the process of resettlement, relatively anonymous and new environment forces them to redefine their position. As such, displacement provides different types of experiences which are to be taken into account while analyzing the problem of displaced people. The size of different groups of displaced people varies enormously. There could be struggles for hegemony between sizeable and powerful groups and displaced population. Further, they have to undergo a process of impoverishment due to loss of basic resources of livelihood.

There are some specific problems resulting from the displacement which include marginalization, food insecurity, undernourishment, health status of old, women and children. Again, changes are observed in their income and expenditure pattern. There are problems of communication gap between the government authorities and the displaced population. In the absence of a national policy, there are variations in approach towards resettlement and rehabilitation.

There is a decline in the social economic position of the oustees due to loss of basic sources of livelihood, because of the loss of land. The loss of productive assets, and the loss of livelihood, shows a trend of downward mobility. Several middle income agriculturists become small landholders. In the case of farming families, full or partial land makes some of them non-viable.

In this process of displacement, women and children are considered as vulnerable groups. Displacement and relocation often changes the role of women who start working outside home. Several children are drafted into the labour market. The girls may become vulnerable.

Relevant Methodologies for R&R Studies

Most of the problems of displacement are relative to the approach or to the social situation. Hence, resettlement and rehabilitation (R&R) studies need a methodology, which, while providing a sufficiently satisfactory analysis of the problem gives us a clear-cut picture about it. Although, urban studies use the social survey method for different analyses, these are not action-oriented. The qualitative aspects are coded under the quantified categories, and results are presented in a quantified form. A general framework used in social survey is applied with slight modifications. Sometimes, a follow up study is undertaken to ascertain the changes.

Cernea (1996) and Kothari (1996) have emphasized social research in the areas of development. Cernea focuses on the role of social scientists in equipping government and public organizations with adequate practical and policy advice. The three-stage process includes understanding of macro processes and local factors, formulating of the basic principles and normative content of revenant policy, translating of knowledge and principles into a vocabulary of procedures. Kothari (1996) emphasizes scrutinizing of the desirability and justifiability of the execution of such projects.

Any research initiative designed to access all the data available on people displaced by development projects faces serious methodological problems. This is because displacement, R&R are not a one-time occurrence. It constitutes a prolonged and complex process with a number of stages and players involved. In fact, there are no strict rules regarding the time span after which the impact of displacement and rehabilitation could be accepted as apparent. An attempt of making accurate estimation of people displaced by developmental projects at national or state level becomes much more problematic because methodologies followed by different projects in presenting their data vary considerably from one project to another. Attaining an actual figure becomes difficult also because data is not available on all the parameters (Dhagamwar et al., 2003). The maintenance of old records in government offices is messy and to dig out relevant information from the land acquiring departments is a still more tedious job.

Movement or migration follows displacement to a new place on migration. A survey conducted by Gabriel Tati (2005) necessitated several site visits. The collection of data for this research heavily dwelt on the methodology of an ethnosurvey defined as a multi-method data-gathering technique that simultaneously applies ethnographic and survey methods within a single study. Massey (1993) emphasized the advantages of this methodology in the collection of information on the process of migration. He importantly argued that the methodology is particularly adopted when the research concerned is about the role played by the migrant networks. Thus, both quantitative and qualitative components are used separately, but these proceed simultaneously, to yield the necessary information. In such studies, in-depth interviews in the form of open-ended questions are discussed conversationally, in a predetermined sequence. The respondents are the key informants with information (and interpretation) on a variety of topics to be discussed. In qualitative data collection, the objective is to gather the insights in the views and experiences of concerned person.

In qualitative studies on resettlement and rehabilitation, information is collected about socio-demographic and family characteristics, events of displacement, housing conditions, individual assets, relocation, occupation, socio-economic status and community network. These data are collected from the sampled affected households. The responsible individuals staying in the households are interviewed, using a semi-structured questionnaire. Information at the community level consists of general field observations. The site observations help to elaborate a detailed description of the physical setting, activities pursued to gain a livelihood, the social setting, and contacts within or outside the community. Observations and discussions include descriptions of major events (meetings, agitations) and informal interactions. Informal conversation photos and vediography are used as parts of this information collection at the community level.

Cluster and network theories and their application in the form of Michael Porter's cluster model (1985) could be used in studies on urbanization, displacement, resettlement and rehabilitation. From a Porter's cluster model perspective, the theoretical foci are cluster model features; these include factor-input conditions, strategy and rivalry, demand conditions, related and supporting systems, government and local context. Porter's model can be supplemented by an analysis of the social network features. From an R&R network perspective, the theoretical units of analysis might include interconnections among the displaced and NGOs and GOs, and diversity of network linkages.

Cluster method is adopted in several surveys as the results obtained through this type of sampling are quite representative.

The R&R surveys mostly rely upon statistical data, as they are clear and handy for analysis. It prepares a set of computerized questionnaires, which are studied to the maximum extent. It is administered to the affected persons. Interviews are conducted by trained researchers. The collected data is classified, categorized and quantified. The qualitative aspects are also subsumed under the quantified categories and results or solutions are declared on the basis of the quantified picture such as a graph or a table. Sometimes, a general framework of methods is used to study connected problems by slight modifications. Sometimes, a follow-up study is undertaken to ascertain the changes.

Objectives of the Project

The project focuses on the resettlement and rehabilitation problems of the people affected by land acquisition (PALA) in urban areas. The following are the main objectives of the study:

1. Socio-economic profile of the displaced persons.
2. Process of acquisition of land and the process of payment of compensation
3. Utilization of compensation for purchase of alternative land, social obligations and occupational development.
4. Problems in movement from place of origin to place of destination and adjustment with host community.

5. Resettlement occupational change and rehabilitation at a new place.
6. Government policies for R&R and policy implications.
7. Sociological framework for urbanization, displacement resettlement and rehabilitation.

Hypotheses

1. Socio-physical situation of the people whose lands are acquired is disrupted because of shifting from the native place. The caste network supports them in resettlement at a new site.
2. Major portion of the compensation amount is spent on fulfilment of social needs, e.g., death feasts and social ceremonies. There is also tendency to purchase household equipments, transport vehicles and entertainment items.
3. Households receiving adequate compensation for acquired property and occupational guidance invest major share for improving their occupational status either by modernizing working conditions or through occupational entrepreneurship.
4. Those oustees, who have been engaged in agricultural activities and are illiterate, find it difficult to change their traditional occupation. The agriculturists suffer more than other groups because they neither find it easy to purchase alternative agricultural land nor they are capable of taking up other occupations.
5. During the process of displacement and rehabilitation, the number of domestic animals decreases but dependence on subsidiary occupation increases.
6. Women play a significant role in supporting the family during the process of resettlement and rehabilitation. They shift themselves from family/household role to supporting income roles (contractual labour activities) and start working for others.
7. Marriages are delayed and joint families are broken because of displacement and rehabilitation.

Research Design of the Study

Keeping in the background the methodologies that could be appropriate for R&R studies, exploratory and descriptive research design has been used. In the exploratory phase, main aspects of urbanization, displacement and rehabilitation have been identified. The situations analyzed through the studies carried out by several scholars have been reviewed. To explore it further, case studies, focus group discussions and situation analysis of affected areas were carried out.

For descriptive sample survey, standardized schedule included socio-economic status variables, before and after situations of the displacement and the relationship of social background with the management of displacement problems.

Area of the Study

The study has been carried out in Udaipur city and the surrounding areas in the district, which covered the people affected by land acquisition in six zones.

District Profile

Udaipur is one of the 33 districts of Rajasthan. It lies in the south-western part of the state and is spread over an area of 12,511 sq km; the district is divided into 11 blocks. Topographically, it portrays great natural diversity. The northern part has largely plateaus whereas the south is rocky with hilly areas and forests. The eastern part of the district has both slopes and plains while the Aravali range and hilly tract of the Mewar region dominate the west.

Dhariyavad is the farthest block from the district headquarters. The population and distance from district headquarters for the 11 blocks is given in Table 2.1.

Table 2.1
Population Distribution of Udaipur District

Blocks	*Total Population*	*Distances from District HQs. (in km)*
Kurabud	3,67,196	45
Sayra	1,59,070	70
Jhadol (F)	2,06,151	55
Kotda	1,87,065	125
Salumber	2,34,783	75
Jhadol (S)	2,40,937	65
Rishabdev	2,74,694	75
Dhariyavad	2,32,039	130
Kanode	2,49,380	75
Sanwad	2,25,964	65
Urban Area	4,84,221	—
Grand Total	28,61,500	

Source: Family Welfare and Reproductive, Child Health; District Action Plan, Office of Addl. CMHO (FW), Udaipur; 2004–05.

Udaipur is one of the most populous districts in Rajasthan with a population of over 28 lakh. The district has a large percentage of tribal population (36.8%) and seven of its eleven blocks are classified as tribal blocks. The decadal population growth of the district is 27 per cent, which is lower than the state average. The sex ratio in the district is 972 which is higher than that of the state average of 922. Literacy, both male and female, is marginally lower than the state average (Table 2.2).

Table 2.2

Basic Demographic Indicators of the District and Rajasthan

Particulars	*Udaipur*	*Rajasthan*
Population	27,28,895	5,78,84,950
Density of population	196	165
Decadal population growth	27.37	28.33
Per cent urban population	19.88	22.9
Per cent SC population	8.32	18.6
Per cent ST population	36.79	12
Sex ratio	972	922
Literacy Rate: Total	59.26	61.03
Male	74.47	76.46
Female	43.71	44.34

Source: Rajasthan Health Scenario, III IMR, 2001 (and www.udaipur.nic.in) (Source: Family Welfare and Reproductive Child Health; District Action Plan, Office of Ad. CMHO (FW), Udaipur; 2004–05).

Udaipur is known for having abundance of natural resources. However, it ranks as one of the poorest districts in Rajasthan in terms of development indices. Nearly 50 per cent of all the families involved in agriculture in the district cultivate land, which is less than one hectare in size. A majority of these small and marginal farmers are from tribal and other disadvantaged communities whose resource base is limited.

A large section of the population lacks basic amenities like electricity supply and toilet facility. Nearly two-thirds of the population lacks access to safe water supply. Table 2.3 lists the various development indicators and performance of Udaipur as well as the other districts with the best performance.

Table 2.3
Development Indicators and Performance of Udaipur District

Particulars	*HDR 2002 Udaipur*	*Best Index (HDR 2002)*	
		Value	*District*
Human Development Index*	0.503	0.656	Ganganagar
Health Index **	0.569	0.751	Ganganagar
Gender Related Development	0.465	0.5%	Ganganagar
Deprivation of electricity	68%	49.8%	Jaipur
Deprivation of toilet facility	86%	46.9%	Ganganagar
Deprivation of access to safe water	36%	24.2%	Kota and Baran
BPLHH: Total	11.8	10.57	
Per Capita Income	4038	7386	Ganganagar

*Composite index comprises of levles of human development in education, longevity or health, and in access to opportunities in per capita incomes.
**UNDP uses single criterion of Life Expectancy. Health Index = Target LE - Min LE.

Source: Human Development Report—Rajasthan 2002 and 1999 and Rajasthan Health TTM/FP UNDP Definitions (Human Development Report—Rajasthan 1999).

The district is plagued with a multitude of health-related concerns. The fertility, mortality and life expectancy indicators of Udaipur are well behind the better districts in the state. The Infant Mortality Rate, Crude Death Rate and Crude Birth Rate are poorer than the state average (Table 2.4).

Table 2.4
Fertility and Mortality Rates of Udaipur District and Rajasthan

Indicator	*District Udaipur*	*Best District*	*Rajasthan State*
Total Fertility Rate	4.6	3.9 (Ajmer)	4.9
GMFR	163	136 (Ajmer)	169
Crude Birth Rate	33.29	26.52 (Ajmer)	32.1
Life Expectancy	60.18	70.1 (Ganganagar)	61.36
Infant Mortality	91	46 (Bikaner)	85
Crude Death Rate	9.2	6.9 (Bikaner)	8.9

Source: Rajasthan Health Scenario, (IIHMR, 2001).

Udaipur has one tertiary care hospital with a medical college attached to it. The tertiary care hospital has two satellite hospitals within Udaipur. The district has 10 block primary health centres, community health centres (CHCs), 7 primary health centres (PHCs),

538 sub-centres, 11 Mother and Child Welfare (MCW) or Dai centres and one National AIDS Control Organization (NACO). Other facilities are shown in Table 2.5. In all, over 900 health institutions with more than 3,000 hospital beds are available in the district.

Table 2.5
Health Infrastructure: Udaipur District

Item	*No.*	*No. of Beds*
Allopathic Hospitals	12	2856
Ayurvedic and Unani Hospitals	192	221
Community Health Centres*	7	30
Primary Health Centres*	76	—
Urban Dispensaries*	10	—
Sub-Health Centres*	538	—
MCW/Dais Centres	11	
Private Hospitals	60	
NACO licensed Blood Bank	1	
Bloc PHC*	10	30–50/PHC
Satellite Hospitals*	2	50
Mobile Eye Units*	1	
TB Clinic*	1	12
Post-Partum Clinics*	4	—
Medical College*	1	Over 200
Rural Family Welfare Centres	10	—
MCH Centres	8	—
ESI Dispensaries	4	—

*CMHO Office Udaipur; March 2004 (Source: Family Welfare and Reproductive Child Health; District Action Plan; Office of Add. CMHO (FW), Udaipur; 2004–05)

Source: Rajasthan Health Scenario, IIHMR, 2001 and www.udaipur.nic.in

Udaipur is better than most districts in Rajasthan when it comes to the number of beds per lakh population. In fact, its figure of population per bed is better than the state average (Table 2.6).

Table 2.6
Population, Hospital, Beds Ratio in Udaipur

Particulars	*Best for the state*		*State Total*	*Udaipur*
	Value	*District*		
Beds in the Govt. Hospitals/per lakh	120	Ajmer	85	106
Population per Bed	696	Bikaner	1175	940

Source: Human Development Report 1999, Rajasthan, Original source: Directorate.

One-fifth of the villages within Udaipur district have a health facility within a distance of three kilometres but just over a quarter of the villages have some health facility within the village itself. This coupled with the fact that only 40 per cent of villages have public transportation and even lesser have telephone connectivity means that health services are not necessarily accessible to most people in times of emergency.

Table 2.7
Distribution of Villages by Available Services and Distance

Distance in km	*Health Facility*	*Bus*	*Railway*	*Post Office*	*Telephone*	*Dai Service*
Within Village	608	911	16	489	416	1783
1–3	987	596	127	1253	681	202
3–5	371	473	161	279	987	196
> =5 km	306	293	1944	252	189	92

Source: Family Welfare and Reproductive, Child Health; District Action Plan, Office of Addl. CMHO (FW), Udaipur; 2004-05.

Udaipur City

Udaipur city is situated in a valley surrounded by Aravali hills. It has an altitude of about 578 metres (1,896 ft) above the MSL and lies at 24°35′ north latitude and 73°42′ east longitude. It is a very important tourist centre of Rajasthan and is known as the 'City of Lakes'. It lies at a distance of about 435 km southwest of Jaipur, the state capital and about 250 km northeast of Ahmedabad, Delhi-Ahmedabad National Highway 8. passes through the city. State Highway 9, running eastwards, connects the city with Chittor. Major district road 13 passes through the city linking it with Mt. Abu to the northwest and Banswara to the southeast. Meter gauge railway line provides direct train connections to Jaipur, Jodhpur, Ahmedabad and Ratlam. Udaipur is thus very well connected both by road and rail. It has a civilian airport also near Dabok village (Sancheti and Singhivi, 2003).

Udaipur was founded in 1559 AD. The origin of Udaipur reminds of the glorious past of Indian history. After the downfall of Chittor by the hand of Mughal army, the place was no more considered a secure capital. Therefore, Maharana Udai Singh established his new capital at Udaipur, at a distance of about 110 km southwest of Chittor. The site was strategically located girdled by scenic hills and beautiful lakes. The city wall which is about six kilometres long and pierced by seven gates was constructed during 1620–1628 AD and the development took place only around the city palace during that period. Between 1628 and 1818 AD, relations with Mughals improved and peaceful conditions prevailed resulting in further growth of the city but well within the city walls. Brahampuri area was also established along the south of Pichhola Lake. Growth of Udaipur also got impetus due to linking of the city with Ahmedabad by a meter gauge railway line in 1966.

Up to late 1960s, around 25 different schemes were planned and developed by the Urban Improvement Trust. Expansion of the city towards the west, north and north-east was, however, restricted because of water bodies, hills and good agricultural lands. Development, thus, continued towards the south and the east. During the last decade, fast growth is experienced on Nathdwara road beyond Pullah and Bhuwna village due to establishment of RIICO industrial area and marble units (Sancheti, 2003).

Udaipur is an important tourist centre of Rajasthan. It is known as the 'City of Lakes' and also known as Kashmir of Rajasthan. The lakes and beauty of Udaipur attract a considerable number of tourists, both domestic and foreign. In the year 1993, a total of 5,10,365 tourists visited Udaipur, of which 44,527 were foreigners and 4,65,838 were home tourists. This was 16 per cent of the total tourists of Rajasthan. Udaipur shall continue to be the major tourist destination area of the state. In the year 1991, total tourists who visited Udaipur were 6,58,445. The flow of tourists has gradually increased. During 2005–06, a record number of tourists visited the city. In 2005, 5,60,076 domestic and 1,73,604 foreign tourists visited the city. It shows that more than seven lakh people visited the city. The city has a considerable load of floating population.

Population growth of Udaipur city can be traced back to 1881, when the first census was taken in India. The city had then recorded a population of 38,214. The population remained more or less constant till 1901. In 1911, the population decreased but after 1921 it again started rising. The maximum rise in population was between 1941 and 1951.

This was due to influx of displaced persons on account of partition of the country in 1947. According to 1981 and 1991 census,

Udaipur had a population of 2,32,588 and 3,08,571 respectively. During 1981–91, about 76,000 people were added to the city population. In 2001, the population variation was reduced about 6.5 points in comparison to 1991 because of slow growth of industrialization due to little rainfall. Simultaneously, population growth trend of the city is given in Table 2.8.

Table 2.8
Trends of Population Growth in Udaipur City, 1901–2001

Year	*Persons*	*Variation (Decadewise)*	*Percentage variation*
1901	45,976		—
1911	33,229	- 12,747	- 27.73
1921	34,789	+ 1,560	+ 4.69
1931	44,035	+ 9,24	+ 26.58
1941	59,648	+ 15,613	+ 35.46
1951	89,621	+ 29,973	+ 50.25
1961	1,11,139	+ 21,518	+ 24.01
1971	1,61,278	+ 50,139	+ 45.11
1981	2,32,588	+ 71,310	+ 44.22
1991	3,08,571	+ 75,983	+ 32.67
2001	3,89,438	+ 20,867	+ 26.21

Source: Census of India, Rajasthan Series 18, General Population Totals & Primary Census Abstract.

Udaipur city has a corporate body for its development. The local body Urban Improvement Trust (UIT) has a great deal of influence on the nature, extent and manner of development of the city. The local body has to coordinate various decisions to effect the physical development of the city. The local body requires some technical guidelines and legal backing to establish long range goals and short-term objectives for the orderly development of the city and its immediate environs in a planned and unified manner, and which can be continually referred to in making decisions on developmental issues.

Sampling

Cluster sampling is often conducted in multiple stages (O'Leary, 2004). This type of sampling is used when getting a full list of population could be really difficult. Second, when we want to do face to face interviews. Third, when we would like to cover all the areas of the study.

In multistage cluster sampling, we have to use a criterion to select geographical regions. Second, within these geographical clusters (zones) we then use a strategy to select a number of small clusters. Third, we either survey all the respondents in these clusters or employ yet another sampling strategy to select final respondents.

In this study, Udaipur city was selected as the area of study. Since the area of city is extended from time to time, the proposed area or lands to be acquired according to Master Plan were also included in the scope of study. In the first stage, the six zones were purposely selected keeping in view the areas where most of the lands were acquired for urban development and also the agency and the purpose for which the process of acquisition was executed. In the second stage, five clusters from each zone were selected for covering the major areas of land acquisitions. In the third stage, 10 persons affected by the land acquisition were identified through social networks and snowball method in each cluster. This is also termed as quota sampling. In all, 30 clusters were selected from Udaipur city covering a total of 300 respondents.

Major part of the land is acquired by the Urban Improvement Trust (UIT). Out of six zones, three covered the areas acquired by UIT for residential colonies, industrial development, educational institutions, offices, public grounds, parks and tourist places. Fourth zone covered the lands acquired by Public Works Development (PWD) and National Highways Authorities for development of roads. Fifth zone included areas developed through Rajasthan Housing Board (RHB) and Rajasthan State Industrial Development and Investment Corporation (RIICO). The sixth zone comprised of the land acquired through private dealers and colonizers. These six zones represent a variety of land acquired for various purposes. The details of sampling zones and clusters are given in Table 2.9.

Characteristics of Sample Households

The characteristics of the households included in the sample according to year of displacement and the size of land acquired are given in Table 2.10.

Table 2.9
Sampling Areas: Zone, Cluster Number and Number of Households

Zone	*Cluster No.*	*Area*	*No. of Households*
Zone I: North–East (UIT)			
	01	Chikalwas	10
	04	Bhuvana	10
	05	Shobhagpura	10
	12	Debari	10
	13	Dabok	10
Zone II: Central (UIT)			
	07	Pahada University	10
	18	Mali Colony	10
	19	Sub-City Centre	10
	17	Manwa Khera	10
	20	Savina-Gordhan Vilas	10
Zone III: South (UIT)			
	23	Titardi Phanda	10
	24	Savina Kheda	10
	26	Nela, Naya Ghar	10
	28	Suron Ka Phala	10
	29	Dewali, Gordhan Vilas	10
Zone IV: PWD Roads			
	02	Sukher	10
	03	Indira Colony	10
	09	Bedwas	10
	10	Bedwas NH	10
	30	Balicha	10
Zone V: Housing Board and RIICO			
	14	Madri Purohitan I (RIICO)	10
	15	Madri Purohitan II (RIICO)	10
	16	Madri – Goverdhan Vilas (HB)	10
	21	Goverdhan Vilas (HB)	10
	22	Savina Goverdhan Vilas (HB)	10
Zone VI: Property Dealers			
	06	Sobhagpura	10
	08	Dhikli	10
	11	Bedwas-Pratap Nagar	10
	25	Nela Village	10
	27	Jogi Ka Thala	10

Table 2.10
Zonewise Distribution of Households, Years of Displacement and Size of Land Acquired

Characteristics	*Zone*	*Zone*	*Zone*	*Zone*	*Zone*	*Zone*	*Total Number*	*Per cent*
Years of Displacement	*1*	*2*	*3*	*4*	*5*	*6*		
1990–93	06	13	32	09	37	21	118	39.3
1994–97	05	08	04	02	04	14	37	12.3
1998–01	09	10	10	33	04	10	76	25.3
2002–05	30	19	04	06	05	05	69	23.3
Land Acquired (Bigha)								
1–3	36	35	27	40	26	27	191	36.7
4–6	09	06	16	07	14	17	69	23.0
7–9	01	01	02	01	04	03	12	04.0
10 or more	04	08	05	02	06	03	28	09.3
Total	50	50	50	50	50	50	300	100

Tools and Techniques for Data Collection

Following tools and techniques have been used in this study for data collection:

- Interview Schedules
- Behavioural and Situational Change Scale.
- Office Records and Notifications.
- Local Media Reports.
- Situational Analysis Observation Schedule.
- Case Studies.
- Interview Guide for Leaders, Functionaries and Bureaucrats.
- Focus Group Discussion

Displaced households who have shifted from the place of origin to different places, residual households whose lands were not acquired, caste leaders in the neighbourhood having knowledge about the displaced were also interviewed to assess the problems. Further, land acquisition notifications and media reports have been analyzed to find out the problems of the displaced and their rehabilitation.

Present Living Conditions

Living conditions of the people affected by land acquisition have been adversely affected. The poor have become poorer and they have to lead a life of impoverishment. Their condition is shown in Table 2.11.

It is a matter of consolation that they have their own houses but nearly one half (49.3%) were squatters, without legal rights (*patta*) over the lands on which they lived. They are living in unauthorized houses and could be shifted to any other place. They reside in small houses and majority of them (n = 250) have a plot of less than 250 sq ft with constructed area of less than 200 sq ft. Thirty-three per cent have semi-*pacca* or *kachha* (mud) houses. About one-half of the house owners consider the quality of their house as medium or poor. Nearly one-fourth of the affected families reside in one or two small rooms. In majority of houses, the flooring is either cemented or covered with stone slabs and the walls are cemented. One-sixth of the houses have *Kelu* roofs and a little more than one-half have stone slab roofs. There is proper ventilation in about half of the houses.

Separate kitchen is available in 60 per cent of the houses; 53 per cent have a bathroom, but 54 per cent do not have toilet facility in their house. Electricity is available in 93 per cent of the houses and about 75 per cent have water connection.

The situation reveals that majority of the people affected by land acquisition in urban areas are living under conditions of impoverishment and they are further marginalized at the cause of urban development.

Table 2.11
Living Conditions of the People Affected by Land Acquisition in Udaipur City

	Household N = 300	*Percentage Total* 100%
1. House		
(a) Own house without patta	148	49.30
(b) Own house with patta	152	50.70
2. Area of plot (sq ft)		
(a) Less than 100	28	9.32
(b) 101–250	222	74.00
(c) 251–500	36	12.00

Cont'd...

Cont'd...

(d) 501–1000	10	3.35
(e) 1001 or more	4	1.33
3. Constructed area		
(a) Less than 100	84	28.00
(b) 101–200	168	56.00
(c) 201–400	34	11.33
(d) 401–600	7	02.33
(e) 601–1000 +	7	02.33
4. Type of house		
(a) Pacca	201	67.00
(b) Semi-pacca	80	26.70
(c) Kachha	19	6.30
5. Quality of structure		
(a) Good	153	51.00
(b) Medium	123	41.00
(c) Poor	24	8.00
6. No. of rooms		
(a) 1–2	75	25.00
(b) 2–3	160	53.34
(c) 5 and more	65	21.66
7. Flooring		
(a) Cement	139	46.33
(b) Slabs	122	40.67
(c) Mud	36	12.00
(d) Mixed	03	1.00
8. Walls		
(a) Mud	54	18.00
(b) Cement	241	80.34
(c) Mixed	5	1.66
9. Roof		
(a) Kelu	57	19.00
(b) Stone slabs	167	55.67
(c) RCC	69	23.00
(d) Other	7	2.33
10. Proper windows		
(a) Available	248	82.67
(b) Not available	52	17.33
11. Separate kitchen		
(a) Available	178	59.33
(b) Not available	122	40.67

Cont'd...

Cont'd...

12.	Bathroom		
	(a) Available	160	53.33
	(b) Not available	140	46.67
13.	Toilet in house		
	(a) Available	137	45.67
	(b) Not available	163	54.33
14	Fodder for cooking		
	(a) Wood	69	23.00
	(b) Kerosene	24	8.00
	(c) Gas	56	18.66
	(d) Wood and Gas	45	15.00
	(e) Wood and Kerosene	88	29.34
	(f) Kerosene and Gas	18	06.00
15	Electricity		
	(a) Available	280	93.30
	(b) Not available	20	06.70
16.	Water accessibility		
	(a) Water connection	172	57.30
	(b) Hand pump	87	29.00
	(c) Well	41	13.70
16.	(i) Everyday bath		
	(a) Yes	113	37.70
	(b) No	187	62.30
16.	(ii) Washing clothes		
	(a) Everyday	12	04.00
	(b) Once in a week	70	23.33
	(c) Twice in a week	188	62.67
	(d) Twice in a month or less	30	10.00

Background Characteristics and Living Conditions

The living conditions of the people affected by the acquisition of their land were further assessed on the following six background characteristics: (1) zone, (2) year of displacement, (3) size of land acquired, (4) caste, (5) class before acquisition, and (6) class after acquisition.

Most of important among the background characteristics is ownership of the house: (a) house without patta, and (b) house with patta. Patta is a legal document for land ownership. In the absence of a patta, the construction and occupation of the house land is unauthorized. As already noted, slightly more than one-half do not have the legal document. No significant difference is observed on account of the zone, year of displacement, size of land and caste. The association with class and occupation is shown in Table 2.12.

Table 2.12
Class and Ownership of House

Background Variable	*Ownership of house*		*Total %*	*N*	*Chi-Square*
	without patta	*with patta*			
Class Before					
Lower	67.5	32.5	100	77	20.71*
Lower Middle	50.6	48.4	100	164	
Middle	30.8	69.2	100	52	
Upper Middle	14.3	85.7	100	07	
Class After					
Lower	59.2	40.8	100	120	24.57*
Lower Middle	55.7	44.3	100	122	
Middle	19.6	80.4	100	51	
Upper Middle	42.9	57.1	100	07	
Total Number	152	148		300	
Percentage	50.7	49.3	100		

* Level of significance 0.01.

The difference of various categories of class before and after acquisition with patta (house ownership) is significant (Chi-square significant at 0.01 level).

In urban areas, the lower the class, less are the chances of possessing a legal document of the house. This is evident from the fact that 60 per cent of the lower class people affected by land acquisition are even now (after land acquisition) without the possession of a patta. The percentage of patta holders increases with the increase in the level of land losers.

Types of House

The types of house—pacca (solid), semi-pacca (semi-solid), kachha (mud house), varies with the urban zone, caste and occupation. There is no effect of year displacement, size of land and class. Significant effects of background characters are shown in Table 2.13.

Table 2.13
Zone, Caste and Occupation Differences and Type of Houses

Background Variable	*Pacca*	*Semi-pacca*	*Kachha*	*Total %*	*N*
Zone					
North East	58.00	32.00	10.00	100	50
Central	80.00	12.00	08.00	100	50
South	62.00	34.00	04.00	100	50
Roads	78.00	18.00	04.00	100	50
HB/RIICO	74.00	24.00	02.00	100	50
Dealers	50.00	40.00	10.00	100	50
Caste					
General	83.00	16.00	01.00	100	94
OBC	79.50	15.40	04.10	100	73
SC	42.90	42.90	14.20	100	14
ST	49.60	39.50	10.90	100	119
Class After					
Lower	64.20	31.7	04.2	100	120
Lower Middle	68.00	20.5	11.5	100	122
Middle	68.60	31.4	00	100	51
Upper Middle	85.70	14.3	00	100	07
Total	201	80	19		300
Percentage	67.00	26.70	06.30	100	

Percentage of the pacca households (74 to 80%) is higher in central roadside, Housing Board and RIICO zones than the percentage of houses in north-east, south and private dealer zones shows effect of zone on the type of house. It has also been observed that there are castewise differences in the type of houses. Majority of general caste (83%) and OBC (80%) have pacca houses, whereas majority Scheduled Castes (56%) have semi-pacca or kachha houses.

Another important character is the class of the affected people. Higher the class, greater are the changes of possessing a pacca house.

Quality of House Structure

The quality of 300 houses of the land losers observed was that 51 per cent houses were of good quality whereas 41 per cent were of medium quality. Table 2.14 shows that there were no significant differences according to the zone, year of displacement, size of land, class and occupation. It was revealing that the greater difference in the quality of house structure was associated with the caste factor. General caste and OBC had better houses than the Scheduled Caste and Scheduled Tribe people.

Table 2.14
Caste and the Quality of House Construction

Background Variable	*Good*	*Medium*	*Poor*	*Total %*	*N*
Caste					
General	57.40	41.50	01.10	100	94
OBC	71.20	24.70	04.10	100	73
SC	35.70	50.00	14.30	100	14
ST	35.30	49.60	15.10	100	119
Total	153	123	24		300
Percentage	51.00	41.00	08.00	100	

In rural areas, tribal households are generally scattered and situated on hills. In contrast it is not generally plausible; however, they choose outskirts with small land holdings. They have a tendency to reside in kachha houses with Kelu roofings. In rural areas, they have fear of moving from one place to another. In urban areas, although they look for permanent dwelling, the working situation shifts them from one place to another. They, therefore, build kachha houses with mud or poor material. The situation changes with their stability in city and they construct houses of medium quality.

Separate Kitchen

The families of all the castes consider kitchen as an important place in the house. Except for the period of the displacement, other background characteristics have a significant association with maintenance of a separate kitchen. Sixty per cent of the houses of the land losers have a separate kitchen.

Zonewise difference is observed in having a separate kitchen. About three-fourth of the houses in central zone, and houses of the most of the agriculturists (56%) who have disposed off their land through the dealers (zone 6) do not have a kitchen. So is the case with those who are of constructing a house. Majority of the houses, displaced during various of the years have a separate kitchen (55 to 65%) but, there are no significant differences among these categories. Size of the land lost does make a significant difference.

The caste aspect appears to be very significant (0.01 level) in having separate kitchen. General caste and OBC focus much more on this aspect in comparison to SC and ST. Only one-third of the Schedule Caste and Scheduled Tribe houses have a separate kitchen.

Higher the class, greater is the probability of having a separate kitchen. Displacement or acquisition of land does not matter much in this respect. Chi-square shows significant association (at 0.01 level) before land acquisition and also after it.

In urban areas, separate kitchen is seen as essential in higher castes and upper classes (Table 2.15).

Electricity

Electricity is available in all the areas. Ninety-four of those affected by land acquisition have electricity in their houses. Among those who are devoid of a regular connection, some use alternative or unauthorized ways of obtaining electricity. Because electricity is available in almost all the houses, no significant effect of zone, year of displacement or class is seen in the availability of electricity. Twelve per cent of the Scheduled Tribe houses do not have electricity connection (Table 2.16).

Bathroom in the House

It is observed that a separate bathroom is considered desirable in urban areas. Fifty-three per cent of the displaced persons had a bathroom in their house. There are significant differences according to zone, year of displacement and caste. The difference is also considerable according to class.

Toilet Facility

Most of the land acquired is for extension of the city. There were such outskirts, where agricultural land and open space was available for defecation. In some areas, public toilets were also available. Under this situation, the people who did not have a toilet in their house used such facilities. In all, only 45 per cent have a toilet (Table 2.18).

Table 2.15
Background Characteristics and Separate Kitchen in the House

Background Variable	*Available*	*Unavailable*	*Total %*	*N*	*Chi Square*
Zone					
North East	66	34	100	50	14.53*
Central	74	26	100	50	
South	46	54	100	50	
Roads	62	38	100	50	
HB/RIICO	64	36	100	50	
Dealers	44	56	100	50	
Year of Displacement					
1990–93	53.4	46.6	100	118	3.04
1994–97	62.2	37.8	100	37	
1998–01	61.8	38.2	100	76	
2002–05	65.2	34.8	100	69	
Size of Land (Bigha)					
Less than 3	64.9	35.1	100	191	8.75*
4 to 6	45.5	54.5	100	70	
7 to 9	66.7	33.3	100	12	
10 and above	51.9	48.1	100	27	
Caste					
General	75.5	24.5	100	94	53.97**
OBC	80.8	19.2	100	73	
SC	35.7	64.3	100	14	
ST	36.3	63.7	100	119	
Class Before					
Lower	39	61	100	77	N.A.
Lower Middle	61	39	100	164	
Middle	78	22	100	52	
Upper Middle	100	00	100	07	
Class After					
Lower	47.5	52.5	100	120	14.86*
Lower Middle	65.6	34.4	100	122	
Middle	66.7	33.3	100	51	
Upper Middle	100	00.0	100	07	
Total	178	122		300	
Percentage	59.3	40.7	100		

Level of significance *0.05, ** 0.01
N.A.—Not Applicable.

Table 2.16
Caste and Electricity in House

Background Variable	*Available*	*Unavailable*	*Total %*	*N*
Caste				
General	96.8	3.2	100	94
OBC	97.3	2.7	100	73
SC	92.9	7.1	100	14
ST	88.2	11.8	100	119
Total	280	20		300
Percentage	93.3	6.7	100	

Table 2.17
Background Characteristics and Bathroom in the House

Background Variable	*Available*	*Unavailable*	*Total %*	*N*	*Chi Square*
Zone					
North East	66	34	100	50	44.46**
Central	74	26	100	50	
South	32	68	100	50	
Roads	64	36	100	50	
HB/RIICO	62	38	100	50	
Dealers	22	78	100	50	
Year of Displacement					
1990–93	44.1	55.9	100	118	9.12*
1994–97	54.1	45.9	100	37	
1998–01	55.3	44.7	100	76	
2002–05	66.7	33.3	100	69	
Size of Land (bigha)					
Less than 3	56.0	44.0	100	191	4.70
4 to 6	42.9	57.1	100	70	
7 to 9	50.0	50.0	100	12	
10 and above	63.0	37.0	100	27	
Caste					
General	80.9	19.1	100	94	100.67**
OBC	76.7	23.3	100	73	
SC	28.6	71.4	100	14	
ST	20.2	79.8	100	119	

Cont'd...

Cont'd...

Class Before					
Lower	26.0	74.0	100	77	N.A.
Lower Middle	54.9	45.1	100	164	
Middle	82.7	17.3	100	52	
Upper Middle	100	00	100	07	
Class After					
Lower	38.3	61.7	100	120	N.A.
Lower Middle	59.8	40.2	100	122	
Middle	66.7	33.3	100	51	
Upper Middle	100	00	100	07	
Total	160	140		300	
Percentage	53.3	46.7	100		

Level of significance * 0.05, ** 0.01
N.A.: Not Applicable.

Table 2.18

Background Characteristics and Toilet Facility in the Houses

Background Variable	*Toilet Facility (%)*		*Total %*	*N*	*Chi Square*
	Yes	*No*			
Zone					
North East	50	50	100	50	38.59**
Central	70	30	100	50	
South	24	76	100	50	
Roads	54	46	100	50	
HB/RIICO	56	44	100	50	
Dealers	20	80	100	50	
Year of Displacement					
1990–93	40.7	59.3	100	118	5.78
1994–97	45.9	54.1	100	37	
1998–01	42.1	57.9	100	76	
2002–05	58.0	42.0	100	69	
Size of Land (bigha)					
Less than 3	50.3	49.7	100	191	8.13*
4 to 6	31.4	68.6	100	70	
7 to 9	58.3	41.7	100	12	
10 and above	44.4	55.6	100	27	

Cont'd...

Cont'd...

Caste					
General	70.2	29.8	100	94	82.75**
OBC	67.1	32.9	100	73	
SC	28.6	71.4	100	14	
ST	15.6	84.4	100	119	
Class Before					
Lower	22.1	77.9	100	77	N.A.
Lower Middle	47.0	53.0	100	164	
Middle	69.2	30.8	100	52	
Upper Middle	100	00	100	07	
Class After					
Lower	33.3	66.7	100	120	N.A.
Lower Middle	51.6	48.4	100	122	
Middle	52.9	47.1	100	51	
Upper Middle	100	00	100	07	
Total	137	163		300	
Percentage	45.7	54.3	100		

Level of significance * 0.05, ** 0.01
N.A. Not Applicable.

Toilet existed in 70 per cent houses of the central zone, whereas only in 20 per cent of the dealer zone. Year of displacement does not show any significant effect on the toilet facility. Size of the land significantly influences this aspect (significant at 0.05 level). Caste and class appear to be prominent factors affecting the toilet facility. Higher caste and class show positive association with possession of a toilet in the house. Similar situation is seen in the class category before and after the land acquisition. All the houses of upper class have a toilet in their houses, followed by a somewhat less percentage in middle class.

Living conditions of the people affected by land acquisition have been determined. Many of them do not have the legal rights for the land on which they are settled. Their houses could be termed as unauthorized and could be demolished. They now have smaller area of land at their disposal although their major concern has been to construct or renovate the house. Yet the majority have small houses which lack essential facilities.

Significance of the Study

Several aspects of urban life have been studied by sociologists yet little attention has been paid to the study of the problems of the people who are displaced because their lands have been acquired for urban development. Although the activities and social life of the 'displaced' are linked to the physical environment of the city.

Relevance to the Present-Day Problems

Urbanization has come to symbolize social and economic development reflected by peculiar types of human settlements, societal institutions and cultural forms. The growth of cities and urban development is a continuing process resulting in acquisition of land for various purposes. Thus, the people will be displaced in future also but the social costs of displacement are neither well recognized nor calculated for compensating the land losers. It is important to assess the social problems faced by these people during their resettlement. A study of short-term effects and long-term impact would help in analyzing various dimensions of the problems, which may become part of the resettlement and rehabilitation processes.

Contribution to Knowledge

How the way of life of the displaced households differs from that of city people and rural folk? Whether the change in residence and occupation has transformed their behavioural patterns? There are many such questions regarding the people whose lands have been acquired and whose entire lifestyle is affected at the cost of urban development. There are sociological studies on folk-urban continuum, characteristics of urban society, urban way of life, urban rural differences, city sub-culture and composite culture but surprisingly the studies on displacement due to urbanization are lacking. A theoretical framework on urbanization, displacement, resettlement and rehabilitation and their interlinkages would be a valuable contribution to Urban Sociology of Resettlement and Rehabilitation.

Three

Land Acquisition and Compensation

Laws for Land Acquisition

Land acquisition for public purpose began in India with the enactment of a new law—Regulation I of 1824 of Bengal Code. Its main aim was to make land available for salt pans and other purposes. In 1864, the forest laws were changed to suit British revenue needs to provide timber for railway sleepers and to build ships for colonial wars. "By one stroke of the executive pen (it) attempted to obliterate centuries of customary use by rural population all over India" (Gadgil and Guha, 1992).

Act VI of 1857 repealed the existing laws and it was made operative for whole of the British India. Act of 1870 was passed for doing away with the system of arbitration and for providing effective procedures. Land Acquisition Act, 1894 was enacted by the British government to remove all the difficulties. The Act is based on the doctrine of eminent domain, according to which the ultimate powers about the land are vested in the state. As such, the state could put the land to any use that it deemed necessary. Acquisition could be prevented only if the objective of public purposes could be justified. However, for all practical purposes, it cannot be achieved in a short period.

It is well known that the Land Acquisition Act, 1894 was passed by the colonial government to make it possible for the state to acquire private land for any public purpose. Yet, it provides procedures for settlement of certain disputes, e.g., right to make objections to the proposed acquisition, the right to represent in regard to quantum of compensation before the administrative authorities; and the right to agitate on the same issue before the civil courts. The procedure is an endorsement of the principles of legal justice.

The original Land Acquisition Act was enacted in 1894 by the British. Ninety years later, it was amended by Indian parliament and passed as a new Act. By and large, the new Act has the same objective and spirit as the old one. Although, few changes have been made in the new Act, but for all practical purposes, old Act continues to operate for acquisition of land in India.

The main objects and reasons for passing the Act I of 1894 were to remove the difficulties of the Act of 1870 and to make the Collector's award final, unless altered by the decree in a regular suit. This change in the procedure for determining the valuation of lands was taken up for public works and also to render it possible to dispense with the services of the assessors.

Act of 1894 has been amended several times. Following are important amended Acts:

1. Land Acquisition (Amendment) Act, 1919
2. Land Acquisition (Amendment) Act, 1921
3. Land Acquisition (Amendment) Act, 1923
4. Land Acquisition (Amendment) Act, 1933
5. State Acquisition of Lands for Union Purposes (Validation) Act, 1954
6. Land Acquisition (Amendment) Act, 1962
7. Land Acquisition (Amendment and Validation Act, 1967
8. Land Acquisition (Amendment) Act, 1984.

The amendment of 1984 is most important for modifications and additions. The definition of the 'public purpose' is so amended to include a longer illustrative list. Acquisition of land for non-government companies is made in pursuance of Part VII of the Act. A time limit of one year has been provided for completion of all formalities between issue of preliminary notification under Section 4(1) of the Act and the declaration for acquisition of specified land under 6(1) of the Act. It provides a period of two years from the date of publication of the declaration within which the Collector should make his award, failing which the entire proceedings for the acquisition of the land would lapse. Compensation payable at rate of 15 per cent of the market value of the land acquired in consideration of the compulsory nature of acquisition is to be increased to 30 per cent. It provides an opportunity to all the aggrieved parties to seek re-determination of compensation. It also provides for payment of simple interest at 10 per cent per annum on the amount of compensation for the period commencing from the date of notification to the date of payment of compensation awarded. The rate has been raised by amendments in Section 23 of the Act.

Several states have enacted their own Acts to extend the scope of Land Acquisition Act, 1984. There are Acts of Metropolitan cities, e.g., City of Bombay Municipal Act, 1888; Calcutta Municipal Corporation Act, 1980; Delhi Development Act, 1957; Madras City Improvement Trust, 1950. In Rajasthan, two Acts; Rajathan Land Acquisition Act, 1953 and Rajasthan Land Acquisition (Amendment and Validation) Act, 1966 have been enacted. Besides, Rajasthan Land Acquisition Rules have been passed in 1953. There are Acts for acquiring land for railways (Indian Railway Act, 1989, Metro Railway) and national highway. Other types includes Forest Acts, Slum Area Acts, Housing Areas Development Acts, Town and Country Planning Acts, Electricity Acts and Defence of India Act. These acts provide the government with a wide range of powers to acquired land for public purposes.

In spite of several amendments, the Land Acquisition Act, 1894 is still in operation. The 1984 Act was passed by the Indian parliament with several changes, yet this Act has the same objective and spirit as the old one. According to Dhagamwar (1989), by and large, the new Act is old wine in new bottle. A few changes generally for the worse have been made, the whole exercise not being fit to be called enactment of new law. The old Act can be said roughly like an Aristotelian syllogism. The premises of the doctrine of eminent domain allows the state ultimate control over land within its territory. The state plays stringent role in acquiring the land and accordingly the Act has provisions for the payment of compensation.

Procedure for Land Acquisition

Section 4 of the Land Acquisition Act necessities publication of notification for the acquisition and then empowers the government to order the survey and set up boundary of the land. The Act contemplates two types of acquisitions, one for the state and another for a company. The main purpose of the order under Section 4 of the Act and under Section 4(1) of the Rajasthan Land Acquisition Act is to undertake preliminary proceedings for the acquisition. The order is of exploratory nature and discloses tentative intention and considers objections of the interested parties.

It should be made clear whether the land has to be acquired for the public purpose or not. Criteria for determining the public purpose is that the land which is taken must be available to public at large or it should be in the general interest of the community.

Publication of notification before acquisition of the land and exercising the jurisdiction of the Collector in case where land is acquired for the public purpose.

Compensation

Compensation is determined on the basis of the market value of the property. Market value consists of not only of the land value but also other advantageous components including standing trees etc. Section 23 of the Act lays down the matters to be taken into consideration while determining the amount of compensation. The market value may be assessed according to the sale deed to the land sustained in vicinity and the comparable benefits and advantages. Where agricultural land has to be acquired, the compensation should be based on the use of land including its potentiality and nature of land. Sale instances of similar land with similar advantage could be considered as best evidence for valuation in the absence of which the market value could be determined in some other ways.

Under Section 23 of the Act, the statuary compensation includes the damages and incidental expenses for the standing crops or trees existing at the time of taking possession. If any other damages are caused to owner's property as an act of acquisition and for diminution of profit from land between final declaration and taking possession, these are also to be compensated.

The Act provides for the payment of mandatory solatium as a part of the compensation. The percentage of compensation has varied from time to time and place to place. After passing of amended Act in 1984, the solatium has been fixed at 30 per cent of the market value of the property. This amount is granted in lieu of the injury and distress caused to the feelings of the owners.

The Act also provides for payment of additional market value on the compensation. For the first 12 months, the interest is at nine per cent from the dated of award. For delays beyond 12 months from the declaration of the award, the rate of interest is 15 per cent.

The ownership of landed property is an essential condition before one could claim compensation. Everyone whose landed property has to be acquired is entitled to get compensation. However, those who do not have property or those who are indirectly dependent on it could not claim compensation.

Lacunae in the Scope of the Act

The major premises that the 1894 Act indicate are that ultimate powers about the land are vested in the state. The state could put the land to any use it deems necessary. Acquisition could be prevented only if the objective was not for public purpose, which however counts not be challenged in such a short period. Debashish Mukerji adds to this: "The Land Acquisition Act, 1894 is the single piece of legislation that governs the takeover of land for projects". Activists opined that this law remains heavily biased in favour of the state, allowing it to acquire land anywhere and every where in the public interest, providing only cash compensation.

Common Property Resources (CPRs) and Natural Resources (NRs) used by the affected population are not considered for compensation. There is no compensation for the basic amenities and infrastructure facilities. Their traditional rights are not recognized in the present legal framework.

Groups depending on CPRs or on the village as a community do not get compensation since these are guided exclusively by the Land Acquisition Act, 1894. It deals with individual patta holders (Vaswani, 1992) and has the market value of quantifiable commodities as the basis for compensation, though around 80 per cent of the DPs belong to the informal economy and very few have pattas. The loss of CPRs, the psychological trauma of forced displacement, the break up of community institutions and support structures are ignored in its calculation (Fernandes and Chatterji, 1995).

The compensation in each area is decided according to the market rate at which the land is being registered. But all land deals involve both 'white and black' money. The compensation amounts is paid on the white money (Mukerji, 1997)

The Land Acquisition Act does not give the victims any rights to prevent the acquisition of the land. One can only delay acquisition by raising objections. The government is empowered to acquire land for public purposes. Here, the term 'public purpose' is nowhere defined in the Act (Varma, 2004). It does not deal with the sufferings of categories of persons such as agricultural labourers, a share cropper, a rural artisan—all of whom may be dependent on land and community resources for their livelihoods.

Highlighting the lacunae of Land Acquisition Act of India, Fernandes says: "Land oustees do not own individual land but depend on Common Property Resources (CPRs) for their survival. The legal system, on the contrary, recognizes only individual property. The Land Acquisition Act, 1894 makes provision only for landowners. Its criteria for compensation is market value. These criteria are irrelevant to communities depending on CPRs and others whose livelihood depends on services rendered to the village as a community. The assumption behind the present criteria is that land is only a site for agriculture and building. It is forgotten that it is the livelihood not merely of owner but of a large number of others who depend on it."

The report of the Commissioner for Scheduled Castes and Scheduled Tribes (1990) points out that when the land is acquired and under the present law, only its property form is considered vital, questions concerning the very survival of the displaced persons are settled on this basis. Even those who are identified are very inadequately compensated. Lack of accurate data on such crucial issues, such as this, is itself an indication of both the Central and State Government degree of concern for the rehabilitation of oustees (Viegas, 1987).

Ganguly Thukral (1995) mentions about the gender insensitivity in the cases of land acquisition in India. She writes: "Land Acquisition Act 1984, the main law of acquisition reveals a gender bias which seems to reinforce the existing situation of women's lack of ownership of land and property". Similar lack of gender sensitivity is present in almost all the policies and plans that govern rehabilitation and resettlement.

The law of 1894 does not acknowledge traumatic overtones of displacement. It does not mention about resettlement, and social responsibility of rehabilitation. What could be said about a law which is not sensitive to human suffering.

That the Land Acquisition Act, 1894 is not adequate to deal with the problem of large scale and varieties of displacement. These are certain human settlements, which are excluded from its scope, e.g., households without legal rights, tenant households, landless households, households with land but not displaced.

Compensation is determined according to following types of lands: (a) khatedari land, (b) allotted land, (c) land under dispute, (d) encroachment land, (e) river bed land, (f) pasture land, and (g) mixed land.

Mathur (2004) has described various types of lands in detail:

1. *Khatedari land:* There are basically three types of khatedari lands and the compensation rates for each type is different from the other. The three types are: (i) irrigated or *chahi* land, (ii) unirrigated or *barani* land, and (iii) waste or *banjar* land. Khatedari rights are the basis for compensation, but land records seldom are up-to-date in the life time of a title holder cultivator. Land actually gets distributed in family, but the new owners usually do not get khatedari rights on paper. Land records and rates of compensation are two major problems regarding compensation for khatedari lands:
2. *Alloted land:* In the submergence area, all through the 1960s, 1970s and even up to 1986, allotment of government excess land took place. The allotments take place with some strings attached to it. In every village of the submergence area, there are families which were allotted land but were never given pattas to that land. Some of them, after the declaration of the dam, got their pattas by paying heavy bribes to tehsil staff. Most others have not received pattas and therefore no compensation has been paid though they are continuously cultivating this land.
3. *Land under dispute due to mistakes in land settlement work:* During land settlement, a few mistakes were committed. These are noticed in each village. It is a common practice to leave lands fallow by turns to improve their fertility. Lands that were kept fallow during settlement time were recorded as government lands in the land records by the settlement staff. Therefore, the owners of the land do not get compensation even though the land is theirs and they are cultivating it. Also, during settlement, land owned by one family was recorded as transferred to another family by mistake. As a result, the compensation goes to the wrong family.

4. *Encroached land:* Due to continuously expanding families and mechanization of agriculture, people undertake to cultivate government excess land. Such encroached lands make up anywhere between 25 per cent and 50 per cent of a family's total farm land. In villages under submergence, almost every family cultivates an average of two acres of government land. There is no provision of compensating such land, even though land of that amount has been contributing to a family's food supply. In Gujarat and Madhya Pradesh, even encroachers of forest land are allotted as much land as goes under submergence.
5. *River bed land:* The practice of cultivating river beds is age old. Both rabi crops like wheat and mustard are cultivated where there is good soil, and in sand, cultivation of melons is undertaken. Until 30 years ago, there was no administrative control over such land. Since then, the practice of allotment of such land by tehsil offices to cultivators on a three-years' term basis has started. The poorest of the people belonging to the Kheer, Kahar, Kewat and Bheel communities, cultivate such river beds. Some traditional irrigation methods are also used to irrigate such lands. Presently, no compensation for this land is being paid.
6. *Pasture land:* There are revenue pasture lands as well as forest pasture lands. Both are used for grazing purposes. Pastoral incomes contribute greatly to the total income of families. On an average, there are 5,000 animals in each village. In places where oustees are being resettled, there are no pasture lands.
7. *Mined lands:* Traditional mining is undertaken in the hills surrounding the dam to extract stone slabs used in building construction. Although the lands will not be submerged, displaced people will lose approach to these lands on account of being resettled in far away places. Presently, there is no provision of compensating for the loss of such land-based income.

Problems in Securing Compensation

A sample survey of the project affected households under the Sriramsagar and Srisailam projects was conducted to understand the problems faced by them in securing fair compensation. In addition, the findings of an earlier study by the Lokayan is also made use of. What follows here is the analysis of the problems faced by following five categories of households which do not come under the preview of the Land Acquisition Act, 1894.

1. Landed households with disputed legal rights.
2. Possessing lands without legal rights.
3. Households bypassed by the Land Acquisition Act, 1894 are the tenants.
4. Who do not stand a chance of any compensation under Land Acquisition Act are the landless households.

Land Acquisition in Urban Areas

In the process of expansion of cities, agricultural lands are being depleted for setting up urban development projects. The situation is aggravated because of major conversion of agricultural lands into urbanizable lands. There is no authentic data to ascertain the area of agricultural lands acquired and the number of people affected due to increasing urbanization in the country. With the expansion of cities, several surrounding villages are included within the enlarged area of such cities.

Nowadays, there is a growing awareness about the problems of people being displaced and acquisition of private lands and properties in 'public interest'. There are several cases of untold hardships and miseries caused to the affected people and social activists have started challenging the model of development that alienates people from their traditional sources of sustenance.

Characteristics of Compensation under the Land Acquisition Act, 1894

In urban areas, there are frequent land dealings through property dealers. In such transaction, the buyer and the seller negotiate the 'price'. The seller is willing to sell and the buyer is willing to buy. The price is determined on the basis of market conditions that vary from time to time. Contrarily, in the acquisition of private lands by the state, the landowner's consent is not necessary (Section 24) of the Land Acquisition Act.

While fixing the compensation amount, the land owner's objections could be heard (under Section 9 and 11 of the Land Acquisition Act), but it is not necessary that the amount quoted by him/her must be agreed to. The landowner loses the right of ownership and is bound to accept the compensation, which has been awarded. Thus, the compensation is just a consideration and not the price.

Methods of Acquiring Land

The basic element in deciding the amount of compensation is the market value (Section 23 of the Act). The market value is the price that a willing purchaser is ready to pay to a willing seller for a property, after all consideration and potential possibilities. Compensation determined on the basis of adequate market value is considered just and fair. It is, however, difficult to determine the accurate market value of a given property.

To gain possession of any land under Section 4(I) of the Land Acquisition Act of 1894, the very first thing the government would have to do is to publish a notice that the land in question is needed or may be needed for a public purpose or for a company. This does not mean that this land would be definitely acquired. This notice merely enables the government to survey this land to assess its suitability. It alerts the persons interested in such land and the people who are likely to be affected.

In Rajasthan, various departments of the government acquire the land. These include:

1. Urban Development Department, Jaipur
2. Home Department
3. Irrigation Department
4. Industries Department
5. Tourism and Civil Aviation Department
6. Urban and Development and Housing Department

The land is also acquired for Surface Transport and Highway Departments of the Government of India.

Rajasthan Urban Improvement Act, 1959 empowers government to order preparation of Master Plan in urban areas. According to Section (1) of Section 3 of the Act, civil surveys are carried out and a Master Plan is prepared by the Chief Town Planner and Architectural Advisor for the urban area. From time to time, several villages are notified to be included in the urban areas. In 1964, 65 surrounding villages were included in urban areas. Similarly, in 1969, 30 villages, in 1971 eight villages and in 1976 forty villages were included. In 1983, in supersession of the notification of 1976, the list was severed. The new list includes only 35 villages in urban areas of Udaipur. In 1999, the government authorized the Chief Town Planner to undertake survey of 62 villages for preparation of the Master Plan of Udaipur city. There has been an increase in the urban areas and the villages are covered under the scope of Master Plan, which results in acquisition of land for urban projects.

The Urban Improvement Department acquires land after obtaining permission from the Government of Rajasthan. In the same way, the Public Works Department also acquires land for development of roads and other works through the government.

Land Acquisition in Udaipur City

Urban Improvement Trust (UIT) is the main agency for acquiring land for urban development. The UIT has been established to resolve the problems of urban areas and to develop new areas for expansion of the city. It is functioning as an agency with administrative and legal powers assigned by the Government of Rajasthan. The agency has undertaken some important plans for development of Udaipur.

There are several plans for development of Udaipur city. Sancheti and Singhvi (1996) have highlighted some major problems of the city, These include shortage of houses, acute traffic congestion, lack of proper sanitation and other community facilities and amenities, haphazard commercial development, lack of tourist facilities. It became imperative to pay attention to these problems. Consequently, long range comprehensive plans have been undertaken. In view of the planned and orderly development, the State Town Planning Department has prepared a Draft Master Plan for the city. It provides guidelines for the future growth and development.

The local body has a great deal of influence on the nature, extent and manner of the development of the city. The Urban Improvement Trust (UIT) is the prime co-ordinating body for the city development. UIT has to co-ordinate various decisions to effect the physical development of the city. Under UIT Act and as per the Draft Master Plan proposals, UIT has prepared and executed a number of developmental schemes.

Keeping in view the Draft Master Plan proposals and new priorities, UIT has prepared an integrated development plan for the years 1994–2001. The plan could not be executed during the scheduled period. Varied nature of development schemes like residential, commercial, circulation, industrial, governmental, amenities and facilities and recreational have been included in the plan. Total project cost was about Rs 235 crore. Being nodel agency, UIT has prepared this integrated development project. Development works are being carried out by the concerned agencies of the project. Because of paucity of financial resources, various agencies are not able to carry out city level development works. Looking to the size of outline of development plan (financial) prepared for integrated development of Udaipur city as a whole, it was considered necessary to make provision for providing the seed capital of Rs 71 crore to take up the priority projects in a phased manner.

Problems

As the city is growing fast many problems have arisen, viz., shortage of housing, development of slums, haphazard development of commercial areas, increasing traffic congestion, improper road network, inadequate amenities and facilities, unplanned growth of industrial units and absence of mass transportation system etc.

For undertaking different development works, UIT does not have sufficient financial resources. Even UIT is unable to carry out some priority schemes. The integrated development programme of Udaipur city has been prepared for implementing the Draft Master Plan. The Draft Master Plan proposes to set up a unified authority to carry out urban development and co-ordinate the development works of the various other departments.

Developmental Schemes

Detailed estimates have been prepared for those schemes, which have been framed in detail. For the remaining schemes, forecast estimates have been prepared. These estimates have been based on certain assumptions, such as price index, cost of land acquisition and development, administrative and supervision charges and interest. The financial outlays have been worked out keeping in view the 1994 price as the base year. Acquisition in all the schemes would be involved.

Residential Schemes

Two residential schemes, namely, Pullan and Bhuwana, have been undertaken. These schemes are operating near already developed areas. Total area under these schemes would be about 2,366 acres.

Pullan

This scheme exists on Nathdwara road near Pullan village. Total area of the scheme is 118 acres. For acquisition of land the awards for whole of the area have already been issued. Some of the concerned Khatedars have gone to the High Court and taken stay against acquisition. Quick action is being taken by the UIT to vacate the stay. Detailed layout plan of this area has been prepared after conducting necessary physical surveys. The Town Planning Department has also approved the plan.

Bhuwana

This scheme area exists on Nathdwara road. Bypass Road is passing through this scheme area. Total area of the scheme is 1,136 acres. Scheme is divided in two phases, viz., I and II. The land has been acquired under Section (6). The land belonging to *Devesthan* and Panchayat Departments has been acquired. Part of this scheme under phase I is already under the possession of the UIT. Infrastructural development in this area has been done. UIT has also constructed about 100 LIG and EWS quarters. In this area, this scheme provides about 9,500 plots of different categories which are allotted or auctioned as per rule.

Commercial Schemes

Five commercial schemes have been under plan:

Sub City Centre

This is an important proposed commercial scheme of the southern area of the town. This scheme area falls on Salumber road in front of Krishi Upaj Mandi. Scheme of this area is prepared after conducting physical surveys of the area. Total area of the scheme is about 59 acres. Land acquisition process has been completed. Awards of the whole area have been issued. As per the government direction, 12 per cent developed area is given to concerned Khatedars in lieu of cash compensation.

Link Road-cum-Commercial Scheme

This areas lies near Udaiya Pole busstand. Total area of the scheme is about 13 acres. Proposed road link would directly connect Udaiya

Pole area to Chittor road. This scheme would ease out the traffic congestion being faced in Udaiya Pole and Suraj Pole area and would also provide direct access to Chittor road.

Almost whole of the land belongs to Agriculture University and is not being used for any purpose. Thus, it is easier to acquire the land.

Iron, Scrap, Stone and Timber Market

This scheme area lies on Bypass road, west of Transport Nagar, near Balicha village. This proposed scheme is taken up as per Draft Master Plan proposals. Total area of the scheme is about 115 acres.

District Centre Opposite Rana Pratap Nagar Railway Station

This scheme area falls opposite Rana Pratap Nagar Railway Station. This scheme is taken up as per the Master Plan proposals. Total area of this scheme is 18 acres. Almost whole area belongs to private khatedars, thus land would have to be acquired.

Hotel Complex

This scheme is also taken up as per the Draft Master Plan proposals. Scheme area lies near city railway station. Total area of scheme belongs to railway/army and therefore, it would be easier to acquire the land through negotiation. In lieu of compensation, land for land can be allotted. Total area of this proposed scheme is about 20 acres. Scheme would be framed after conducting necessary surveys. At present, scheme area is lying almost vacant. Total estimated cost of this project would be around Rs 135 Lakh.

Recreational Schemes

In addition to this, land is being required for governmental and industrial schemes.

Governmental Schemes

Bhuwana

This proposed area is located in Bhuwana Scheme Phase (I). Total area of the scheme is about 22 acres.

Chittor Road

Another office complex scheme as per Draft Master Plan proposals is taken up on Chittorgarh road in RCA campus. Total area of the scheme is about 40 acres.

Industrial Schemes

Areas under these schemes are be acquired by the RIICO/industries department. Following three areas as Master Plan have been included in the project:

	Location	*Area (acres)*
1. Eklingpura	On Eklingpura Road	100
2. Bedwas	Near Bedwas village	100
3. Purohitan Ki Madri	On Udai Sagar Road	40

Circulation Schemes

Road Widening

As town is growing, traffic is also increasing very fast, therefore, in view of the above, following important roads where huge traffic is plying have been taken for widening:

1. Paras Cinema to Sewasharam	8 km
2. University Road	3 km
3. Sukhadia Circle to Amberi and	10 km
4. Feteh Pura Choraya to Budgoan and Bedla village	6 km

Following proposed roads, as have been envisaged in the Draft Master Plan, have been taken to develop.

1. Proposed 100 ft wide road east of sector No 3, 4, 5, 6 to 9 area	2 km
2. Eastern Link road bypassing traffic on N.H. 8 to Nathdwara Road to Ahmedabad	5.5 km

Terminals

Transport Nagar near Goverdhan Vilas area, as envisaged in the Draft Master Plan is taken up. Total area of the scheme is 140 acres. Acquisition proceedings have been nearly completed. Awards have already been issued. In pursuance of the government order, 12 per cent developed land in the form of plots would be allotted to Khatedars in lieu of cash compensation.

Truck stand on Udai Sagar Road scheme exists on Udai Sagar road. Total area of the scheme is about 10 acres. This scheme is envisaged in the Master Plan. Because of the existence of industrial area and railway station there are huge loading and unloading activities being done in the area.

Bus stand for private buses near Udaiya Pole has to be developed. Land may be acquired through negotiation.

Multi-storey parking for commercial centres has been identified in: (i) Bapu Bazar, and (ii) Hathi Pole, Udaipur.

Table 3.1

Developmental Schemes of Udaipur City

	Nature of Scheme	*Area (in acre)*	*Estimated Development Cost (Rs in Lakh)*
1.	Residential	2,366	13,128
2.	Commercial	225	1,761
3.	Recreational	19	114
4.	Governmental	62	186
5.	Industrial	240	1,620
6.	Public and Semi-public	58	374
7	City Level Infrastructure		3,950
8.	Environmental		100
9.	Circulation		2,286
	Total		23,519

Present Position of Land Acquisition

Table 3.2 shows that the process of land acquisition in Udaipur city is quite lengthy. The proposals initiated in 1990 are not yet fully implemented. In Link Road-cum-Commercial Plan and Fatehpura Circle Plan, the notification under Article 32 was issued in 1996 but notification under Article 6 was issued in 1999 and 2002 respectively. Because of the political reasons, some plans (Swaran Jayanti Plan) remained recorded only in office files. However, action is faster in special plans like, ADB Plan Road land.

Table 3.2
Present Position of Land Acquisition

	Name of Plan	*Area (ha.)*	*Notification Sec. 32*	*Proposal for Notification Sec. 4 (1)*	*Notification Sec. 4 (1)*	*Notification Sec. 6*	*Present Status*
1.	Beautification and Park	0.26	8.1.90	12.12.96	8.1.98 Rev. 1.7.98	16.3.99 Rev. 22.7.99	Awards issued Payment made.
2.	Sukher Bypass	17.86	—	24.4.98	1.11.99	31.5.01	Awards issued, Payment made, Land acquired
3.	Swaran Jayanti	—	—	—	—	—	Demolition in process
4.	Link Road-cum-commercial	24.73	18.6.96	30.1.97	23.4.97	16.12.99	Awards issued, two cases in High Court
5.	Fatehsagar Lake area	0.88	—	8.5. 00	30.4. 01	—	Notification to be issued by state government
6.	Fatehpura Circle	14.60	18.1.96	18.5. 01	20.8. 01	19.2.02	Awards issued
7.	Shopping Centre, Syphon	0.97	—	18.5.01	20.8.01	19.2.02	Award in process
8.	District Centre Payada	7.34	—	26.6.00	1.11.02	—	—
9.	Drain, Road Public facility	0.64	—	16.10.01	—	—	—
10.	Sukher Bypass II	0.55	—	19.12.01	31.5.01	12.7.02	80% compensation determinate
11.	Sub-City Centre	44.88	—	31.12.01	18.10.02	31.7.03	Mutual agreement and acquisition
12.	ADB Plan Road land	19.59	—	27.4.03	30.7.02	37.7.03	—

There are some major plans of urban development in which land is being acquired. In Bhuwana Extension Plan, 1,040 hectares of land will be acquired for allotting plots and constructed houses to citizens. There are 907 cases of land acquisition. The awards were issued for 812 cases for acquiring 734.34 hectares of land with the total amount of

Rs 52 crore. The UIT has taken possession of about one-fourth of the land (see Box 3.1).

Box 3.1

Land Mafia in Bhuwana, Udaipur

In Bhuwana extension plan, the awards were issued under sender Section 6 of Land Acquisition Act. An appeal of 67 cases was admitted in the Rajasthan High Court. Consequently, the UIT has filed a special writ petition in the Supreme Court. Forty cases were pending in Jodhpur High Court, seventy-eight cases of land acquisition undecided. The UIT after having made payment of Rs 6.87 crore has taken possession of a part (68.87 hectors) of land.

It has been observed that in the Bhuwana plan, some Land Mafia was involved. They have had underhand dealings with the landowners. Several of the persons whose lands were to be acquired sold the land to the property dealers, who have been trying to develop colonies, sellers and manipulating with officers. Finely, the UIT has provided two options for the land under acquisition. In the first option, the landholders could surrender the land and, in lieu of it, obtain 20 per cent of residential and five per cent of commercial land. The second option was to get the land regularized at Rs 400 per square yard. Although, in the beginning, the landholders showed interest in the proposals but only few hundred turned out for surrounding the land. What the landholders suspected was the condition for regularization of constructed or semi-constructed area before the date of issue of the orders. Consequently people started construction and tried to finish it in a short period. It could be identified very easily that it was a new construction. The UIT is aware that large areas of land have been purchased by the property dealers from the agriculturists. The agriculture land is being converted to residential land. Thus it the dealers who would benefit more from such regulation of land.

Another major plan of Transport Nagar is being developed on 168.77 bigha private and 64.34 bigha government land. The payment had been made to the landholders for 100 bigha of land. The remaining landholders are being allotted 12 per cent of commercial and residential land at the reserve price.

It has been observed that those who surrendered land at the initial stage were in a disadvantageous position. Some of those who have been allotted residential land at reserved price have not deposited the amount in the hope that this will written off as and when required. Some have even constructed houses on roadsides without obtaining a legal permission or *patta*. Their plea was that these houses have been constructed on the agricultural land, which originally belonged to them.

Forcible Eviction

When the land is not evacuated, forcible methods are used by the local administration. The affected people oppose such eviction (see Box 3.2).

Box 3.2

Forcible Eviction

Badri Prasad Vaishnav was staying in Aavari Mata Kachhi Basti in a kachha house along with his family members. He did not possess a patta for his house. As such he was not entitled for compensation for the land and house in his possession. This land was to be acquired for a government complex.

One early morning, police knocked at his door and took him and his family members to the police station. His house was dismantled in his absence. He was released from the police station, when he gave an undertaking that he would shift to the alternative place. He said, when he returned he found his house dismantled and several things stolen. His four year child was also missing, who was located with the help of neighbours.

The demolition squad kept his remaining luggage in a vehicle and left him on a vacant plot in Verma Colony. He stayed there for few days but one day the real owner of the plot arrived and asked him to vacate. When he approached the UIT and some influential persons he was allotted a small house by the UIT on the condition that he would have to make full payment of Rs 84,000 in instalment of Rs 1,165 per month.

Several people stay in slum areas without proper land documents. They suffer much more when their lands are acquired and when they are forcibly evicted.

Issues about Payment of Compensation

During September 1990 and December 1997, an extra payment of Rs 4.08 crore was made by the Department of Irrigation, Rajasthan Industrial Development and Investment Corporation Ltd. (RIICO), Rajasthan Housing Board and Public Works Department in 51 cases for acquisition of 16,393 bighas of land. The extra cost of land and compensation included structures, trees, well, etc. in the market price of the land. Whether the government suffered a loss on this account is a moot question. The Auditor General, Government of Rajasthan, posed a query and development department clarified it with the definition of land in Article 3(A) of the Land Acquisition Act, 1944, in the following manner:

The expression land includes benefits arising out of land and things attached to the earth or permanently fastened anything attached to the earth.

Accordingly, the benefits attached to land and permanently attached things were included in the price of land. While determining the market value, the assessment of construction work has to be included in the market value of the land. Thus, there has been no mistake in calculation of the market value of the land. In this connection, the general and legal department took the advice. Thereafter, the things attended to land are considered to be included in the market price of the land.

Problems faced by UIT in acquisition of land

The following problems are faced by the Urban Improvement Trust, Udaipur in acquisition of land:

1. Stay orders of the courts and long time taken to resolve writ petitions.
2. Delay in publication of the land acquisition in government gazette.
3. Unauthorized and unplanned construction, even after the publication of land acquisition.
4. Implementing of the process of land acquisition without proper survey of the areas.
5. Delays in payment of compensation amount which gives rise to court cases.
6. Starting the process of land acquisition without properly assessing the financial resources of UIT.
7. Purchase of the agricultural land under acquisition and selling to public by the property dealers. The land is, thus, got registered in several names, which creates problems in acquisition. The dealers also get stay order from the courts and when several persons are involved and the houses are already constructed it become difficult to acquire the land for the planned purpose.

8. The delay in transfer of land in UIT records also creates problems.
9. Beginning of the process of the land acquisition without determining the priority of the schemes.
10. Demand and movements of the affected persons for more compensation for the acquired land.
11. Placing old colonies and already constructed houses in acquisition and adding more houses in the already sanctioned acquisition process.

The process of the land could be streamlined when preventives of the problem are pre-determined and notifications are timely published. The financial resources should be properly assessed before starting the process of land acquisition. There should be complete ban on construction activity after the issues of notification. Unauthorized construction should be banned. Court cases should be properly attended. The payment should be immediately made to the affected persons. Further efforts should be made for their resettlement and rehabilitation.

A conspicuous role is played by the property dealers in delaying and withholding the process of land acquisition. Land mafia is involved in the purchase and sale of land to be acquired. They get land a registered in several names. It has to be checked by the UIT that the land under acquisition is not transferred or registered in fictitious names. Efforts should be made to assess the situation of the area properly and not to disturb the colonies and houses which are already settled. Minimization of the land acquisition is a better option. Alternatively, full efforts are required for resettlement and rehabilitation.

Role of Property Dealers

Property dealers intervene in the process of land acquisition. As soon as they come to know about the area of land to be acquired, they start approaching the affected persons. They try to purchase the land from such persons by giving them some incentives. Sometimes, they cheat the affected people (see Box 3.3). After purchasing the land they demark the plots and start selling them. They try to get the agricultural land converted into residential and commercial land. They also obtain stay orders from the court and ultimately succeed in getting the land regularized. In this process, some of the agriculturists that sell their land through the property dealers are financially ruined (see Box 3.4).

Box 3.3

Bhil Cheated by Property Dealer in Process of Land Acquisition

The Urban Improvement Trust issued an award for acquisition of two bighas of agricultural land out of his four bigha possessed by Jagga Ram Bhil in Manwa Kheda. During the process of obtaining compensation, he expired. Jagga Ram's father Moti Ram Bhil (84 years) and son Gokul Ram Bhil are alive.

A property dealer, Ram Lal Patel approached Gokul Ram to sell remaining two bighas of land to him. He told him, these two bighas would also be acquired by the UIT. Gokul Ram agreed to sell one bigha for Rs 60,000. The deal was finalized and Ram Lal paid Rs 10,000 advance to Gokul Ram and assured him that the remaining amount will be paid when the land was transferred and registered it in his name.

After about three months, Gokul Ram approached, the dealer for payment of the balance amount. The dealer Ram Lal refused to pay anything. He told him that all the land was transferred in his name. He also told him to cut out the sugarcane crop standing in the field otherwise he would cut it. However, to satisfy him, the dealer paid him only Rs 8,000. Bhil was cheated. He lost his land, as well as compensation amount. He is left with no money to file a case in court.

Land mafia make huge profits in land deals. They give some advance money to the agriculturists. Sometimes, they give cash or even gold in transactions.

Such transactions create tensions among the family members (see Box 3.5).

Even though there are several problems involved in selling the land to the property dealers, there are possibilities of making a fortune out of it. In some areas, people have become rich (see Box 3.6).

It has been observed that the process of land acquisition is cumbersome. There are several formalities involved within the bureaucratic structure of the land acquisition. The planning takes a long time and the implementation even longer. The local Urban Improvement Trust takes certain decisions about the development of the city and acquisition of land without properly assessing the financial resources. They do not pay any attention to resettlement and rehabilitation aspects. The stringent procedures and delays create a situation whereby property dealers take advantage.

Box 3.4

Ruin in Sale of Agricultural Land

When Urban Improvement Trust issued notification for acquisition of land of Katarawala area (now known as a very posh locality—Nav Ratan Complex) the private dealers started approaching the agriculturists of this area to sell their land.

There were some lands of Dangis and Brahmins, which the property dealers were purchasing. In this area, the land of Prem Kumawat was also located. The dealers motivated Kumawat to sell his land. Out of his six bighas of land, he agreed to sell five bigha of land at Rs 4 lakh per bigha. He was paid an advance of Rs 5 lakh and was assured for payment of Rs 15 lakh after the registration of the land. Whenever Kumawat approached the dealers for payment of balance amount, they paid 10 or 15 thousand to satisfy him.

When Kumawat tried to force the dealer for payment of balance, they asked him to sell his remaining one bigha land. In lieu, they showed him 30 bigha land at a distance place. The dealers asked Kumawat to transfer one bigha and adjust balance amount of Rs 15 lakh. Kumawat transferred the remaining and took possession of the 30 bigha land.

After two months, Kumawat come to know that there was court case of family members pending for judgement about this land. The family member who won the case transferred the land in his mother's name and sold it to a third party. Now there were two owners of the land. Kumawat was asked by the dealers to file a petition in the court. Kumawat lost his case. He is now leading a life of poverty and his children are working as labourers.

It is observed that when notification for acquisition of land is issued, private dealers take advantage of the situation. They manipulate with government officials, file court cases, take possession of the land. They cheat the agriculturists.

Box 3.5

Land Acquisition by Land Mafia

Saligramji ki Bari, covering 70 bighas of land, was situated in a central area of the city. The agricultural land was divided in revenue records among the family members. Twelve bighas of land was in the name of Kamla Shankar son of Saligramji.

Out of the 12 bighas, Kamla Shankar had already sold seven bighas of land. In addition to this, he inherited 3.25 bighas of parental land which he wanted to dispose off. Three property dealers motivated him to sell this land to them for Rs 4,68,000. Keeping in view their influential background, Kamala Shankar agreed to sell it and accepted an advance of Rs 9 lakh. They agreed to pay him the remaining amount within six months.

The property dealer planned a colony and applied the conversion of agricultural land into residential land. They also started selling the plots. When Kamla Shankar asked for his balance amount, they told him to become a partner in development of the colony and provide rest of his land. Somehow, they motivated Kamla Shankar and the remaining land was to be added to the colony. When Kamla Shankar's family members come to know about all this, they tried to stop him. Kamla Shankar after having explored the market conditions realized that he was being cheated.

The family members claimed that they were partners in the land, as such all the dealings should be considered as illegal. Whereas the Land Mafia had already got the lands converted in their names. The parties have filed cases in the court. Kamla Shankar knows that he is fighting a lost battle.

Box 3.6

Problems and Prosperity in Private Land Deals

Lalu Ram Dangi inherited 17 bighas of agricultural land from his father. He was not interested in pursuing agricultural work. He purchased a tractor taking a loan from the bank. For paying instalment, he started selling the mud of his fields to brick manufactures. He was finding it difficult to pay the instalment and to look after his family.

When a property dealer approached him, he agreed to sell 12 bighas of land at Rs 7 lakh per bigha. He took advance of Rs 10 lakh. Dealer promised to pay the remaining amount in one year and started developing a residential colony. When the dealer delayed the payment, Lalu Ram booked a plot of one bigha in the colony which was developed on his land from the dealer. After a long notification, he obtained Rs 14 more lakh from the dealer. Thus, in all he received Rs 24 lakh. For remaining amount (Rs 50 lakh) dealer is paying him an interest of Rs 50,000 per month. The land has been registered and transferred but he has not received the notification amount.

Lalu Ram constructed a new house on main road and a showroom for which he is getting Rs 35,000 per month as rent and interest amount from the dealer. His three sons are engaged in marble industry. He has purchased a car and leading the life of prosperity.

Several people who have sold their lands to property dealers for development of residential colonies and commercial centres have become rich and are much more prosperous than the agricultural time when they were engaged in agriculture.

Four

Utilization of Compensation Amount

One of the major concerns in resettlement and rehabilitation is how the compensation received by the people affected through land acquisition, is utilized by them. Srivastava (1995), while analyzing the population dynamics and industrial development in Bhiwadi, Rajasthan, states that the amount received was utilized for improving their standard of living as follows:

- Most people constructed pucca houses in place of kutcha houses.
- The recent trends have been to buy motorcycles, scooters and cars.
- Some part of the compensation was used in fulfilling social obligations, like marriages, in their families.
- Some started sending their children outside for higher education, which they could afford now.
- Some used the money to buy more land.
- A part of the compensation was used by many to buy livestock, especially buffaloes, and some of them have set up dairies to supplement their income by sale of milk.
- A large number of them have bought trucks and earn their living by plying them. This group of oustees is quite prosperous.
- Some bought cars and vans and are plying them as taxis. After the development of the industrial area, they are doing a lucrative business.
- Some have built houses for rental purposes, which has also supplemented their income.
- A large number of people have set up general stores and outlets as building material suppliers.

- Very few were foresighted enough to set up an industrial unit with the compensation amount. A few who were better educated did so, and really have done well.

Contrarily, Shah et al. (1997) found that the compensation amount could also be misutilized. The effects of land loss could be dangerous. According to him, losing land is not easy. There is demographic roulette by which to lose—too many children, too many sons to educate, too many daughters to dower, too many mouths to feed, too few earning family members. One can lose in court cases filed by jealous neighbours and relatives or more distant rivals. One can blow it all in politics. Or have your business fail. As always, losing is more depressing and less interesting than winning.

The case of Navi Mumbai where people were being allotted some land in lieu of their acquired land is amusing. Many PAPs who got the allotment of lands (initial letter of intent) started selling them in the open market, even though there was a restriction on the transfer of land for a ten-year period. All such transactions started taking place under the power of attorney. As expected, PAPs did not get remunerative prices and were cheated by the builders. Most of the PAPs who got large areas of land allotted under the 12.5 per cent scheme were not able to retain it and they started to look out for the buyers. Similarly, small plot holders, who were unable to retain the plot due to financial or other problems, also resorted to selling. This created a situation where the PAPs, CIDCO and government were at a loss through the evasion of stamp duty as most of the transactions took place illegally. (CIDCO, 1991)

Ramaiah (1996) has also come out with a similar kind of observation in her study of several projects of India. She writes:

> Physical reproducible assets such as quality of housing and household assets were largely dependent upon the income levels of the household. A large number of PAPs had utilized parts of their compensation to construct better quality of houses and buy household assets such as transistor, radio, tape-recorder, etc. soon after resettlement. However, the 'economic prosperity' experienced by the PAPs immediately after resettlement could not be sustained, and, therefore, the 'standard of living' adopted by most PAPs soon after receiving compensation had declined. For example, several households were unable to afford basic

maintenance of the house and repairs of electronic goods after a few years of resettlement because of inadequate finances.

Mahapatra (1996) has made pertinent observations on the loss of compensation money. According to him, "It is usually seen that the tribal people are not always in a position to handle money in the way those well-versed with market economy do. They are supposed to be overwhelmed with the amount of cash when compensation money comes to their hand, and are apt to indulge in conspicuous consumption and in alcohol. They are usually amenable to sharing the money with close relatives, as is the tradition in tribal society." There are several instances where money received for the acquired land was misutilized by affected persons".

Advani (1990), in study for Hindustan Zinc Ltd., (HZL) Rampura Agucha Mines, analyzed the utilization of the compensation amount by four functionally stratified groups on the nature of their house (kachha, pacca). The payments were made to the displaced persons through account payee cheques which were to be deposited in their bank accounts. The compensatees were motivated to save the amount in fixed deposits. About 30 per cent of the amount was deposited in the bank. The major concerns in utilization were (1) Purchase of agricultural land and (2) Construction of houses. Only a few households were able to buy alternative land. Social ceremonies and repayment of loans had been their next priority.

When compensation amount is received by large numbers of people, the market value of agricultural land in the nearby vicinity is inflated, and the buyers have to pay more for the purchase of land. If there is a long gap between the loss of land and purchase of new land, difference in the price of land is alarming. The problem is aggravated when the displaced persons are uneducated and no assistance and guidance is provided to them.

While analyzing the problem of utilization of compensation amount by the evacuees affected by Gosunda Dam (Advani 1992), it was found that when payments were made through bank cheques, more than half of the amount was in the form of fixed deposits. Bank agents took extraordinary interest in motivating them for such an action. About 25 per cent of compensatees invested in procuring of alternative agricultural land. Since the evacuees were provided plots for construction of houses at a new location, some of them invested in construction of new houses. There was a tendency to invest money on buying vehicles of different kinds. Because of the assistance and guidance provided to them, the villagers utilized that amount rationally and gainfully. They purchased agricultural equipment and invested in occupational activities. Many compensatees cleared their debts.

In one more study on social and occupational aspects of evacuees at Agucha Mines (Advani and Sharma, 1993) it was found that the major portion of the compensation amount could not be utilized gainfully because of the illiteracy and poor socio-economic conditions. However, some people were able to utilize the amount properly for purchase of agricultural land and equipments. Some of the compensates have become entrepreneurs. Majority of the evacuees who could not purchase alternative land found it difficult to utilize the amount properly.

Training for occupational guidance helped in the process of resettlement and proper utilization of some part of the compensation amount. While studying R&R aspect of rural evacuees for the HZL, Advani (1993) found that the about 30 per cent compensatees purchased alternative land. About 25 per cent invested in construction of houses. Some of them purchased *charas* (water lifting system) for new wells. Other heads of expenditure included social ceremonies, household needs and alcoholism. Eleven per cent of the households purchased diesel engines. Few households purchased tractors and some brought motorcycles. After receipt of the compensation, the affected households faced the problem of distribution of amount among family members.

Utilization of Compensation Amount in Udaipur City

People affected by the acquisition of land in Udaipur city were asked how they utilized the amount received by them as compensation. They had not kept proper account of such amount. They could roughly estimate the amount spent on different heads of expenditure.

The main objective of this investigation was to understand the priorities of the people after land acquisition. The amount received by them is not correctly reported by them. Yet, whatever amount was received by them, they were told to narrate how they spent it. The amount is, thus, at the prevailing prices at the time of receipt of the compensation. Therefore, the expenditure could not be compared according to the period of displacement. Yet it could be compared according to the percentage of amount spent on different heads.

Table 4.1

Utilization of Compensation After Land Acquisition in Udaipur City

Expenditure Head	*Percentage Expenditure*	*Total Expenditure*	*Average Expenditure*
Land purchase	12.10	83,75,000	27,917
House	25.05	1,73,41,137	57,804
Agriculture equipment	1.51	10,48,000	3,493
Animals	0.21	1,42,800	476
Vehicles	7.05	48,80,944	16,270
Social needs	11.44	79,20,887	26,403
Division	20.29	1,40,47,252	46,824
Illness	0.63	4,29,600	1,432
Addiction	0.91	6,33,315	2,111
Savings	19.01	1,31,79,802	43,933
Others	1.77	12,28,100	4,094
Total (%)	100.00	6,92,26,837	2,30,756

Table 4.1 shows headwise percentage expenditure, total expenditure by 300 sample respondents and average expenditure. While analyzing the amount received as compensation for their acquired land, it was found that one-fourth of the amount has been used for purchase, construction or renovation of the house. It was followed by savings of various kinds. About one-fifth of the amount was in the form of savings. The third priority was to divide the compensation (22%) or other assets among the family members, generally brothers. Purchase of land was another head of expenditure on which about 12 per cent amount was spent.

When a lumpsum amount is received in compensation. social needs, e.g., marriages, *gaunna* (effective marriage), community feasts emerge for fulfilment of social responsibility; 11 per cent of the compensation amount is spent on such needs. Some of them also purchased vehicles, seven per cent of the amount was spent on this head of expenditure. In addition, the expenditure was incurred on other heads (1.77%), agriculture equipment (1.51%), addiction (0.91%), illness (0.62%) and purchase of animals (0.21%).

It has been observed that the people affected by acquisition of land give a considerable thought on how to spend the amount of compensation. The priorities of purchase of land, house and savings reveal that they are rational in their approach. Social needs was an area where they found it difficult to control their expenditure. In several cases, they have to resave their family tensions which resulted in division of compensation amount and their assets. Some of them have to agree with the wishes of their young children and buy vehicles for them. Other side of the picture revealed that several of the displaced were addicted to alcoholism, drugs, smoking, tobacco chewing which sometimes resulted in misutilization of expenditure. It created problems for the women in the affected households. The situation of the utilization of compensation could be further clarified when we compare the property of the affected householders before and after the acquisition of land.

Zonewise Utilization of Compensation

Land, house, division of amount, savings and social needs appear as main priorities in utilization of compensation. Table 4.2 shows the percentage of expenditure in each zone. Construction, purchase and renovation of house shows considerable zonewise variation. Whereas 43 per cent of the compensation amount is utilized for the house, it was only 20 to 24 per cent, where the land was acquired by the Urban Improvement Trust (UIT). Those affected by extension of roads have also spent 36 per cent of the amount on house. The percentage was lowest 19 per cent, where land was acquired for Housing Board or RIICO. It is revealing that in this zone, 30 per cent of the affected persons have given priority to purchase of land.

Division of the compensation amount among family members is an important issue. The zonewise percentage of utilized amount varied between 40 per cent to 10 per cent. The situation also varied considerably for social needs and savings from the compensation amount. Purchase of vehicles also appeared to vary according to zone.

Zonewise comparisons do reveal marked difference in utilization of expenditure according to area as well as the agency awarding the compensation. The situation mainly varies greatly where the land is acquired for roads or disposed of through the private dealers.

Table 4.2
Zonewise Utilization of Compensation in Udaipur City

Expenditure Head	*Zone 1*	*Zone 2*	*Zone 3*	*Zone 4*	*Zone 5*	*Zone 6*
Land purchase	11.45	1.35	4.64	3.32	29.81	3.91
House	22.06	24.83	20.12	35.79	18.89	43.23
Agriculture Equipment	1.39	0.64	0.25	4.98	2.39	0.00
Animals	1.02	0.05	0.00	0.82	0.05	0.00
Vehicles	9.97	16.11	3.63	8.76	5.32	0.61
Social needs	16.68	9.22	9.77	9.67	9.83	18.82
Division	22.45	14.93	39.58	13.47	15.52	9.62
Illness	1.30	0.79	0.71	0.66	0.14	0.83
Addiction	0.65	0.64	1.81	0.19	0.73	1.00
Saving	10.58	29.99	18.78	19.03	15.67	19.35
Others	2.45	1.44	0.72	3.31	1.64	2.64
Total (%)	100.00	100.00	100.00	100.00	100.00	100.00
Number	50	50	50	50	50	50
Average Expenditure (Rs in Thousand)	137	236	293	138	416	164

Yearwise Utilization of Compensation

The priorities of the people in urban areas vary according to the times. Those affected by land acquisition during 1990–93 have incurred more expenditure than those who are displaced after 2002. Table 4.3 shows the utilization of compensation according to four periods of displacement.

Table 4.3
Year of Displacement and Utilization of Compensation (N = 300)

Expenditure Head	*Year of Displacement*			
	1990–93	*1994–97*	*1998–01*	*2002–05*
Land purchase	20.18	0.00	4.53	6.28
House	19.21	36.42	37.73	18.10
Agriculture Equipment	1.93	1.97	1.28	0.50
Animals	0.12	0.35	0.13	0.48
Vehicles	5.95	3.65	3.09	17.04
Social needs	8.82	23.82	12.14	11.84
Division	24.56	9.81	9.17	28.92
Illness	0.38	1.06	0.91	0.67
Addiction	1.21	1.73	0.08	0.89
Savings	16.26	18.25	29.18	12.95
Others	1.38	2.94	1.75	2.33
Total (%)	100.00	100.00	100.00	100.00
Number	118	37	76	69
Average Expenditure (Rs)	285959	156220	226322	181204

Purchase of land, which was a priority area shows a declining trend. In contrast, expenditure on house construction appears as first priority during 1994–2001. The issue of division of compensation was less effective during this period. The division of property has become a major issue. Another change is observed in the amount spent on houses and vehicles which has considerably increased. With the result, lesser amount is left for the savings. Less amount is being spent on agricultural equipment. Twenty per cent of the amount was utilized for purchase of land during 1990–93 whereas, it was only six per cent during 2002–05.

The trend in utilization of compensation amount shows that the priorities of the affected households are changing. After the acquisition of land, people now find it difficult to buy alternative land. The cost of land has gone up. Moreover, the return from the agricultural land is not much rewarding. Many of the affected persons felt that agriculture is not a viable occupation in urban areas. The return from other sources could be more fruitful.

Size of Land and Utilization of Compensation

The size of land acquired influences the utilization of compensation amount. Table 4.4 shows variations in utilization.

Table 4.4
Size of Land Acquired and Utilization of Compensation (N = 300)

Expenditure Head	*Size of Land Acquired*			
	1–3	*4–6*	*7–9*	*above 10*
Land purchase	4.60	25.64	5.25	9.10
House	27.16	24.51	8.61	12.83
Agriculture Equipment	0.73	2.71	0.68	2.88
Animals	0.26	0.08	0.00	0.55
Vehicles	9.83	2.67	2.34	7.79
Social needs	13.11	6.47	9.76	28.22
Division	20.87	19.21	49.58	4.16
Illness	0.73	0.34	0.84	1.24
Addiction	0.92	0.45	7.40	0.52
Savings	19.46	17.07	15.54	30.25
Others	2.35	0.86	0.00	2.46
Total (%)	100.00	100.00	100.00	100.00
Number	191	70	12	27
Average Expenditure (Rs)	2,10,052	3,41,500	1,58,769	1,22,101

Displaced persons, whose land has been acquired between 4 and 6 *bighas*, spent about one-fourth of the amount on purchase of land. They also spent almost the same amount on house. Those who received compensation for small pieces of land (1–3 *bigha*) had comparatively spent higher percentage of amount on purchase of house.

Division of compensation amount is a major problem for those who have been awarded 7–9 *bigha* of land. They have spent 50 per cent of the amount on distribution among the family members. Social needs appeared to be a priority of those whose 10 or more *bighas* of land has been acquired. They have also kept 30 per cent of the amount as savings. Purchase of vehicles is another head of expenditure on such items. Other heads of expenditure reveal little difference. It has been observed that the size of land acquired varies according to other situations, e.g., land in possession after the acquisition. Economic status and education of the compensatees affects the ways of incurring compensation amount.

Castewise Utilization of Compensation

Pattern of the expenditure varies because of the social background. Table 4.5 shows how the utilization of amount of compensation differs according to caste categories.

Table 4.5

Castewise Utilization of Compensation (N =300)

Expenditure Head	*Caste*				
	Gen. %	*OBC %*	*SC %*	*ST %*	*Total %*
Land purchase	22.19	2.02	32.61	4.26	12.10
House	17.99	46.82	17.34	19.46	25.05
Agriculture Equipment	2.02	1.01	9.88	0.45	1.51
Animals	0.04	0.59	0.99	0.08	0.21
Vehicles	9.16	7.58	3.53	4.24	7.05
Social needs	14.85	11.07	11.13	7.30	11.44
Division	15.50	7.80	5.78	36.73	22.29
Illness	0.53	0.53	1.63	0.72	0.62
Addiction	0.17	0.24	0.20	2.43	0.91
Savings	16.70	21.57	14.20	20.73	19.04
Others	0.85	0.76	2.72	3.62	1.77
Total (%)	100.00	100.00	100.00	100.00	100.00
Number (n=300)	94	73	14	119	300
Average Expenditure	3,09,042	2,17,225	1,44,587	1,87,354	2,30,756

General (castes) and Scheduled Caste has spent a large sum of money on purchase of land. In contrast, Other Backward Class and Scheduled Tribes have paid less attention on this aspect. Among the OBC, 47 per cent have spent on construction or purchase of house. Expenditure on social needs is more in general caste. It appears that the higher the caste, more is the expenditure on social needs. The problem of division of compensation amount is dominant among Scheduled Tribes and considerable among general caste. STs have spent 37 per cent of amount on division among family members. OBCs and general castes reveal a tendency of more savings than the general and Scheduled Castes.

Since Scheduled Caste have spent more on land, they have also spent one-tenth of the amount on purchase of agriculture equipment. General and OBCs have spent more on purchase of vehicles in comparison to Scheduled Castes and Tribes. Addiction of various kinds is observed more among Scheduled Tribes. It is obvious that castewise difference is significant in utilization of compensation.

Class and Utilization of Compensation

Class of the people affected by land acquisition is based on their income, expenditure, occasional expenditure, occupation and economic status assessed by them. Here, class after the acquisition has been taken into consideration because this expenditure is after the land acquisition. Table 4.6 shows classwise differences in utilization of compensation amount in Udaipur city.

Table 4.6

Class-wise Utilization of Compensation (N =300)

Expenditure Head	*Class*			
	Lower	*Lower Middle*	*Middle*	*Upper Middle*
	Class I	*Class II*	*Class III*	*Class IV*
Land purchase	6.63	2.41	40.43	0.00
House	27.07	30.14	12.08	16.19
Agriculture Equipment	0.54	1.59	3.25	0.28
Animals	0.09	0.22	0.40	0.00
Vehicles	5.11	8.94	6.86	9.18
Social needs	9.46	11.32	15.70	6.92
Division	21.14	25.43	8.27	31.91
Illness	0.45	0.72	0.61	1.79
Addiction	1.57	0.71	0.05	1.51
Savings	25.54	16.12	11.13	32.32
Others	1.59	2.39	1.22	0.00
Total (%)	100.00	100.00	100.00	100.00
Number	120	122	51	07

Significant classwise difference is observed in purchase of land. The middle class have spent forty per cent of the amount on this head. Lower class and lower middle classes have spent 28 to 30 per cent on construction or purchase of house. Percentage of savings is predominantly more among lower and upper middle classes. Middle classes spent comparatively more on social needs. Division of compensation is a major head of expenditure in upper middle class, followed by lower middle class. Upper middle class have utilized about 10 per cent on purchase of vehicles. Lower and upper middle classes have spent 1.5 per cent of the amount on addiction.

The trend shows that there are marked classwise variations among various classes of the society in utilization of compensation in urban areas.

Box 4.1

Proper Utilization of Compensation Amount

In 1999, Bherulal Dangi came to know about the notification for acquisition of his land. He tried to save his land but failed. In 2001, his land was acquired. He received Rs 12.40 lakh as compensation for five bighas of land.

Bherulal had no son. His first priority was to get his one daughter married. He spent Rs 45,000 on her marriage and associated his son-in-law in new ventures. He purchased seven bighas of land in Rs 7 lakh in Lakawali, about 18 km from Udaipur.

Five bigha of land was fully irrigated and remaining two Bighas unirrigated. He constructed a house in Rs 2 lakh on the field and developed the land. He and his son-in-law established a dairy, with 12 cows and six buffaloes. He says, he has good income from agriculture. They also have additional income from dairy.

Bherulal was uneducated but his son-in-law is educated upto class VII. He, with the assistance of son-in-law, utilized the amount of compensation properly. He possesses a motorbike, television, furniture and necessary household amenities.

Bherulal is leading a happy life. He has forgotten the agonies of displacement.

Activities after Land Acquisition

The acquisition of land sets up some tasks for the affected people. Few of them obtained alternative land with government help, whereas some buy land in other areas. Those who were unable to procure land

Box 4.2

Naru Dangi's Entrepreneurship After Land Acquisition

According to notification of the Public Works Department Naru Dangi's land was to be acquired for a 150ft. wide bypass. In 1995 he received a notice for vacating the land. When he was trying to save his land, he received another notice from the Urban Improvement Trust that this land is being acquired for urban extension plan. In 1996 he was being paid Rs 16 lakh for his 10 bigha land by the UIT, which he refused to accept. The amount was deposited in the court. Finally, he got his Rs 16 lakh, without any interest. However, the UIT allotted him two plots of 40 × 60 ft. at reserved price. But he struggled for a long time to receive the compensation for his five bigha land which was acquired by the PWD for widening of the road.

Naru's fortune changed. He purchased 22 bigha land on Jaisamand Road, 20 km away from Udaipur. He paid nine lakh for the land and two lakh for a big farm house situated in the field. He purchased a tractor and other equipment. He diverted a nearby water channel in his field. The part of barren land was changed into irrigated cultivated land. He takes bank loan on the fixed deposits and developed the agricultural land. He has given part of the land (two bighas) for partnership cultivation. He is now recognized as a advanced farmer.

Naru has shifted his family to the farmhouse. He has divided the land among his three sons. But all are cultivating the land jointly and leading a happy and prosperous life.

engaged themselves in business or work as labourers. In order to explore the activities after land acquisition, the affected persons were asked, what they did after the acquisition of the land? It is quite revealing that only 13 per cent of the land oustees could buy alternative land. Government help was observed in very few cases (three per cent). Majority of them (47%) had to work as labourers. Table 4.7 provides information about their activities.

Zonewise differences were significant. Major variations could be observed in purchase of land and labour, which appear to be main alternatives in urban areas, followed by service. The situation of purchase of land is better for those who have disposed off their land through property dealers. Period of displacement does not appear to affect the difference in activities after land acquisition. The trend is almost similar during last 16 years. The size of land shows significant variation in responses. Only about 15 per cent of the small land losers were able to buy alternative land, whereas about 50 per cent losing land between 7 and 9 bighas were able to buy land. The land size effect is very obvious for small land losers. Over one half of them have to work as labourers.

Table 4.7
Activities After Land Acquisition in Udaipur City

Background Variable	*Land by Govt. Help*	*Purchase of Land*	*Labour*	*Service*	*Business*	*Other Work*	*Total %*	*N*
Zone								
North East	2	12	20	36	14	16	100	50
Central	4	06	16	36	24	14	100	50
South	4	16	02	62	04	12	100	50
Roads	2	16	18	42	16	06	100	50
HB/RIICO	2	08	14	54	04	18	100	50
Dealers	4	22	12	52	00	10	100	50
Year of Displacement								
1990–93	3.4	15.3	14.4	46.6	7.6	12.7	100	118
1994–97	5.4	10.8	16.2	48.6	5.4	13.5	100	37
1998–01	2.6	11.8	16.8	45.1	13.2	10.5	100	76
2002–05	1.4	13.0	13.0	43.5	14.5	14.5	100	69
Size of Land (Bigha)								
Less than 3	2.6	10.5	13.6	47.6	11.0	14.7	100	191
4 to 6	1.4	14.3	12.9	54.3	8.6	8.6	100	70
7 to 9	00	50.0	16.7	25.0	8.3	00	100	12
10 and above	11.1	14.8	14.8	33.3	11.3	14.8	100	27
Caste								
General	3.2	19.2	19.1	19.2	25.5	13.8	100	94
OBC	2.7	11.0	20.5	38.4	6.8	20.5	100	73
SC	00	14.3	00	42.9	7.1	35.9	100	14
ST	3.4	10.2	6.9	74.8	0.8	4.2	100	119
Class Before								
Lower	5.2	6.5	2.6	77.9	2.6	5.2	100	77
Lower Middle	3.0	17.7	13.4	40.9	7.3	17.7	100	164
Middle	00	7.7	28.8	26.9	26.9	9.7	100	52
Upper Middle	00	28.6	28.6	00	42.9	00	100	07
Class After								
Lower	3.3	11.7	1.9	71.7	4.2	7.5	100	120
Lower Middle	2.5	13.1	18.9	36.0	9.0	20.5	100	122
Middle	3.9	13.7	27.5	21.6	25.5	7.8	100	51
Upper Middle	00	42.9	28.6	00	28.6	00	100	07
Total	09	40	41	141	31	38		300
Percentage	3.0	13.3	13.7	47.0	10.3	12.7	100	

The difference appeared to be significant in caste, class and occupation characteristics. A large majority of higher castes and upper middle classes were engaged in business. Scheduled Castes, tribes and lower class were engaged in primary occupational activities, majority of them were compelled to work as labourers. It is found that in urban situation, the caste and the class are the main background characters making a significant difference in the activities of the land losers. The area of land acquired and the location (zone) are other factors influencing the activities of affected persons.

Place of Land Purchase

While analyzing the activities of those whose land has been acquired, we observed only 16 per cent of them have procured alternative land. Table 4.8 provides information about place where they got the land.

Eighty-four per cent of the persons affected by land acquisition (PALA) have not purchased the land, seven per cent have obtained land within or nearby the city and nine per cent in the rural areas. The purchase of land is difficult for the land losers, especially in urban areas. Zone, year of displacement and caste differences are not significant.

Size of the land holding, which is an important variable in background characteristic shows significant effect on the place of land purchased. More relevant is class before and after, which shows considerable effect in the place of purchase of land. We have also observed that caste linkages are not very helpful in searching the land for purchase. Here what matters is money and occupational linkages.

Adequacy of the Land and Occupation

Whether the available alternative land and engagement in occupation are adequate for survival after the acquisition of land, the responses are shown in Table 4.9. Nearly one half of the PALA consider the land and occupation as fully adequate. Nearly 15 per cent considered it less adequate, whereas about one-third assessed it insufficient. The situation was almost similar in all the zones. But the difference was very significant according to year of land acquisition. The period of displacement changes the situation of lifestyle in urban areas.

Table 4.8
Place of Alternative Land Purchased

Background Variable	*Inside of City*	*Near to City*	*Near to Village*	*Far to Village*	*Not Purchased*	*Total %*	*Number*
Zone							
North East	4	4	4	0	88	100	50
Central	0	8	6	0	86	100	50
South	4	8	8	0	80	100	50
Roads	4	2	4	10	80	100	50
HB/RIICO	0	2	4	2	92	100	50
Dealers	4	2	12	6	76	100	50
Year of Displacement							
1990–93	0.8	7.6	7.6	4.2	79.7	100	118
1994–97	00	5.4	8.1	0	86.5	100	37
1998–01	5.3	0	3.9	5.3	85.5	100	76
2002–05	4.5	2.9	5.8	00	87.0	100	69
Size of Land (bigha)							
Less than 3	3.7	3.1	4.2	3.1	85.9	100	191
4 to 6	00	5.7	7.2	2.9	84.3	100	70
7 to 9	8.3	16.7	25.0	00	50.0	100	12
10 and above	0	3.9	11.0	3.7	81.5	100	27
Caste							
General	3.2	6.4	7.4	6.4	76.6	100	94
OBC	4.1	4.2	4.2	1.4	86.3	100	73
ST	1.7	2.5	7.6	1.9	86.6	100	119
SC	00	7.1	00	00	92.9	100	14
Class Before							
Lower	00	1.3	10.4	2.6	85.6	100	77
Lower Middle	4.3	6.1	6.7	2.4	80.5	100	164
Middle	1.9	00	00	5.8	92.3	100	52
Upper Middle	00	28.6	00	00	71.4	100	07
Class After							
Lower	1.7	5.8	5.8	2.5	84.2	100	120
Lower Middle	4.1	2.5	8.2	0.8	84.4	100	122
Middle	2.0	00	3.9	9.8	84.3	100	51
Upper Middle	00	42.9	00	00	57.1	100	07
Total	8	1.3	19	9	251		300
Percentage	2.7	4.3	6.3	3.0	83.9	100	

Table 4.9
Adequacy of Land and Occupation for Survival After Land Acquisition

Background Variable	*Fully Adequate*	*Less Adequate*	*Not Adequate*	*Not Applicable*	*Total %*	*N*
Zone						
North East	40	08	48	4	100	50
Central	42	12	46	0	100	50
South	48	14	36	2	100	50
Roads	52	20	26	2	100	50
HB/RIICO	58	12	30	0	100	50
Dealers	50	20	26	4	100	50
Year of Displacement						
1990–93	54.2	15.3	30.5	0	100	118
1994–97	48.6	18.9	29.7	2.7	100	37
1998–01	52.6	14.5	27.6	5.3	100	76
2002–05	33.3	10.1	55.1	1.4	100	69
Size of Land (bigha)						
Less than 3	45.5	13.6	38.7	2.1	100	191
4 to 6	48.6	14.3	34.3	2.9	100	70
7 to 9	75.0	8.3	16.7	0	100	12
10 and above	55.6	22.2	22.2	0	100	27
Caste						
General	50.0	16.0	33.0	1.0	100	94
OBC	50.7	6.8	41.1	1.4	100	73
SC	50.0	00	50.0	0	100	14
ST	45.4	19.3	31.9	3.4	100	119
Class Before						
Lower	37.7	13.0	44.2	5.2	100	77
Lower Middle	53.0	17.7	28.7	0.6	100	164
Middle	55.8	5.8	36.5	1.9	100	52
Upper Middle	00	14.3	85.7	0	100	07
Class After						
Lower	45.0	9.2	42.5	3.3	100	120
Lower Middle	45.9	20.5	32.8	0.8	100	122
Middle	64.7	11.8	21.6	02	100	51
Upper Middle	28.6	14.3	57.1	00	100	07
Total	145	43	106	06		300
Percentage	48.5	14.3	35.3	2.0	100	

The size of land acquired and caste does not reveal any significant effect on available land and occupation. The class, which consists of their income, expenditure, occasional expenditure and occupational status, does makes marked difference. The effect of class is also seen after the land acquisition.

It has been observed that people displaced by acquisition of land are little affected by area, size of land and their caste. What makes significant difference is time period of displacement, the class before and after acquisition. Resettlement and resonance of economic status appear to be a long-term process for the people displaced because of the urban development.

It was further asked, if the land available to them and their occupation are not sufficient enough for leading a comfortable life, how do they take care of themselves? Forty-five per cent have no option but to accept the situation as it existed. Nearly thirty-one per cent said they would work as labourers. About ten per cent said that they would either do service or would start their business.

Desire for New Business or Occupation

When land is acquired, the affected persons have to look for alternative avenues. They were asked, whether they would like to start a new business or occupation? It is noteworthy that sixty per cent of them were willing for a new venture. However, 40 per cent wanted to continue with old way of life.

It is revealing that there is a great effect of the place (zone) and the class of displacement on their future desire. Zonewise difference is significant. Those affected by losing land due to the expansion of roads and those who had disposed off land through private dealers were less willing for a new option. In contrast, those who had surrendered land mainly for residential colonies and other development activity were looking for newer businesses and occupations in urban areas. There was no significant effect of the year of displacement, size of land acquired and caste on desire for new business. Desire for new business significantly associated with the class and occupation of the affected persons. Lower the class of the displaced, greater was the desire to pursue a new occupational activity in urban areas. The classwise affirmative responses show a decreasing trend from lower class to higher class. Almost similar trend is observed for class after the acquisition. The class background has significant effect on the newer occupation.

Table 4.10
New Business Scenario After Displacement

Background Variable	*Yes*	*No*	*Total %*	*Number*
Zone				
North East	56	44	100	50
Central	64	36	100	50
South	72	28	100	50
Roads	44	56	100	50
HB/RIICO	74	26	100	50
Dealers	46	54	100	50
Year of Displacement				
1990–93	58.5	41.5	100	118
1994–97	62.2	37.8	100	37
1998–01	56.6	43.4	100	76
2002–05	62.3	37.7	100	69
Size of Land (bigha)				
Less than 3	59.7	40.3	100	191
4 to 6	58.6	41.4	100	70
7 to 9	58.3	41.7	100	12
10 and above	59.3	40.7	100	27
Caste				
General	51.1	48.9	100	94
OBC	67.1	32.9	100	73
SC	42.9	57.1	100	14
ST	63.0	37.0	100	119
Class Before				
Lower	75.3	24.7	100	77
Lower Middle	56.1	43.9	100	164
Middle	48.1	51.9	100	52
Upper Middle	42.9	57.1	100	07
Class After				
Lower	78.3	21.7	100	120
Lower Middle	53.3	46.7	100	122
Middle	31.4	68.6	100	51
Upper Middle	42.9	57.1	100	07
Total	178	122		300
Percentage	59.3	40.7	100	

Purchase of Land

When the Urban Improvement Trust, Public Works Department or other agencies acquire land, the agriculturists might choose to purchase land somewhere at a distant place. The people affected by the land acquisition were, therefore asked, whether they were trying, purchase of alternative land. Since the nature of acquisition could vary according to zone, year of displacement, size of land, caste, class and occupation, the differences could be noticed in desire to purchase land.

In Udaipur, zonewise variations in desire to purchase new land are observed. Majority of the PALA (64 to 76%), whose land has been acquired by the UIT, Housing Board/RIICO were willing to purchase land. In contrast, whose lands were acquired for development of roads and those who had disposed off their land through property dealers (40 to 48%) were less interested in purchase of land. On the whole, zonewise difference is significant (Chi-square significant at 0.01 level). This reveals that those who have given land for expansion of roads tend to stay at roadside. Further, those who have sold land through dealers are also less interested in new land.

Another aspect, which could affect the desire to purchase, is the time period, i.e., the year of land acquisition. Although there are some variations according to years, but these are not significant. Similar results are obtained about the size of the land. Variation in size of land acquired does not reveal any significant effect on desire to purchase the land.

Castewise difference is significant. Majority of OBCs and STs wanted to purchase land. About one half of general caste were also interested in it. However, the Scheduled Castes, which were less in number, were less willing to purchase land. Chi-square is significant (0.05 level). Similarly, the class after the acquisition reveals significant difference. Lower and lower-middle classes were more interested in purchase of land than those who were in comparatively higher class after the acquisition of land.

When asked, what type of assistance they required in purchase of land, fifty per cent of the PALA wanted bank loan (n = 149), loan from District Industries Centre. Few others (n = 15) wanted some kind of training in occupational activities. About one-third (n = 106) did not require any assistance.

Table 4.11
Desire to Purchase New Land

Background Variable	*Yes*	*No*	*Total %*	*N*	*Chi-square*
Zone					
North East	64	36	100	50	20.31**
Central	66	34	100	50	
South	72	28	100	50	
Roads	40	60	100	50	
HB/RIICO	76	24	100	50	
Dealers	48	52	100	50	
Year of Displacement					
1990–93	59.3	40.7	100	118	6.42
1994–97	48.6	51.4	100	37	
1998–01	49.2	50.8	100	76	
2002–05	72.5	27.5	100	69	
Size of Land (bigha)					
Less than 3	61.8	38.2	100	191	1.54
4 to 6	58.6	41.4	100	70	
7 to 9	75.0	25.0	100	12	
10 and above	55.6	44.4	100	27	
Caste					
General	52.1	47.9	100	94	7.68**
OBC	65.8	34.2	100	73	
SC	42.9	57.1	100	14	
ST	67.2	32.8	100	119	
Class Before					
Lower	64.9	35.1	100	77	1.09
Lower Middle	58.5	41.5	100	164	
Middle	63.5	36.5	100	52	
Upper Middle	57.2	42.8	100	07	
Class After					
Lower	70.8	29.2	100	120	16.03**
Lower Middle	61.5	38.5	100	122	
Middle	39.2	60.8	100	51	
Upper Middle	42.9	57.1	100	07	
Total	183	117		300	
Percentage	61.0	39.0	100		

Level of significance **0.01, *0.05

The Present Situation

Displaced people are compensated for the acquired land in monetary terms. The money provided to them could be utilized according to their needs and comforts. The educated and knowledge persons may utilize the amount properly. On the other side, the poor uneducated agriculturists are likely to misutilize the amount. The priority of the affected has been construction of house and purchase of land, although some amount is spent for the family and social needs. There has been no proper accounting for utilization of the amount. Their activities are focused on social and occupational resettlement.

Five

Social Conflicts and Resettlement

When there is involuntary displacement and when affected households have to move from their place of origin to a place of relocation, conflicting situations arise because of disputes within the family with government officials and host community. The conflicts within the family are mainly about sharing of the compensation amount, purchase of land, alternative occupations, construction of new house, problems of women, education of children and problems of the widowers and the aged. Conflicts outside are related to dealing with official machinery, property dealers, court cases, and adaptation with people at a new site.

The conflicts within and outside the family are several times aggravated to take the shape of an agitation supported by leaders, non-governmental organizations (NGOs), political parties and vested interest groups. In this process, simple problems turn into complex struggles by which the affected population may either be partially benefited in resettlement or they may have to agitate for years together without any substantial benefit.

Displacement results in a conflict between the informal society to which most DPs belong and the formal one into which they are inserted. These societies are based on contradictory frameworks and value systems (Sharma, 1978).

Planning and Official Attitude

The initial source of dissatisfaction emerges from the approach of planning. The project authorities plan the financial and technical aspects meticulously, but make little effort to get a clear idea of the people to be affected by it or to plan their resettlement. In the few cases where rehabilitation is planned, the specificity of the problems faced by the disadvantaged groups is rarely attended to. In reality, the poor are displaced and left to fend for themselves. But, no compromise is made on the engineering and economic aspects of the project. In other words, economic growth gets priority over the people affected by it (Murickan et al., 2003). The approach is rather negative towards consideration of social aspects. The accumulated tensions are manifested in aggressive tendencies.

The problem becomes more chronic in the light of the fact that there is total communication gap between the project authorities and the project-affected persons. Ganguly Thukral and Singh (1995) assert: "The attitude of the authorities towards the oustees is apathetic, to say the least. Our findings clearly indicate that the level of information among the potential oustees about the dam, the submergence and rehabilitation was low. The authorities had made little effort to communicate the rehabilitation provisions to the people. The situation improved slightly after the movement against the dam under the banner of Narmada Bachao Andolan gained momentum. Until 1989, the situation had not changed much. None of the government officials visited villages to explain anything. The oustees were not aware of the policy as a whole." Regarding communication gap Fernandes (1996), states "It is not merely that they are not involved in the decision, but also that information about the project is kept away from them. Knowledge is power. The powerful project authorities render the affected populations further powerless by keeping them ignorant of their future situation".

Human perspective lacks in planning. There is no focus on the problems of the downtrodden masses. Complicated land acquisition act and complexities of compensation on procedures are far from the comprehension of the innocent people. After displacement, they find several people struggling to establish that they were the real heirs of their properties. The amount of compensation received by them was not adequate to reshape the lives of affected persons. Further, there are tensions or occupational change. There are also problems of landless and tribal dependents on the forest products. The planners do not take all these aspects into cognizance. Sometimes, the officials played a negative role and favoured the powerful, articulate persons with high-class background. There are changing parameters in payment of compensation.

Stress and Health Hazards

Studies have shown that some health problems are peculiar in displacement and resettlement. According to Mathur (2004), "Involuntary resettlement leads to increased stress, both psychological and socio-cultural and also heightens morbidity and mortality. Hazards to health are a common experience for those being resettled and of those with whom they come in contact in the process of resettlement. People who move take pathologies with them and the people among whom they settle are exposed to them and vice versa. One unfortunate outcome is the feeling of alienation, helplessness and powerlessness that overtakes the displaced. This stems from the way in which the people are uprooted from homes and occupations and brought to question their own values and behaviour, and the authority of their leaders. Such feelings persists for a long time."

The planners generally remain preoccupied with the pressing political and economic issues. They consider health matters only when they have to face crisis situation. Change in environment penetrated the health of residents as they fell ill due to various diseases.

It is now well-recognized that so called resettlement has often resulted in sheer dislocation, leading to urban migration and too commonly to homelessness and destitution. Relocation has also been accompanied by major public health hazards, by increased incidence of dysentery, measles, and encephalitis, by a rise in tropical diseases such as malaria and schiotosomiasis and sharp increases in mortality rates, particularly for the young and the elderly (Fahim, 1983). For example, Lumseden (1993), found that mortality rates for Nubians resettled as part of the Aswan Dam project increased from 13.6 per thousand in 1963 to 23.6 per thousand in 1965. Good (1994) focuses on mental health perspective, both for recognizing problems associated with resettlement and for designing policies that minimize sue problems and services that address those problems that arise, as efforts are made to move into a new era of resettlement practices.

Caste and Community Network

Settlement pattern in fringe area of city is generally caste-based. Change of residence affects the socio-cultural lives of the people. According to Ganguly Thukral (1995), "Dislocation and relocation, unless very carefully executed, means a breakdown in community network. Since the dependence of women on men is greater, breakdown of this network creates tremendous insecurity and trauma, which the women experience more than the men who are relatively more mobile". He further adds, "It is worth mentioning that the process of rehabilitation is itself leading to more displacement. The Gujarat government, in order to rehabilitate Sardar Sarovar oustees, is buying private land from absentee landlords willing to sell. But in the process, labourers, who were engaged in these fields for years, have been rendered jobless, as the oustees who have been allotted the lands are by and large tilling it themselve."

There are a number of caste-based issues which stand in the way of successful resettlement. It created problems in planning of resettlement colonies, moreover the affected people wanted government to provide everything for them, on the other side, the government also tended to see that they resettle at their own cost. The problems of dependency, entitlement and corruption were widespread. Experience in other places has shown the importance of resettling people taking their cultural traditions into account. Demographers describe 'push' and 'pull' factors in theories of migration. These could be seen in involuntary versus voluntary resettlement (see Box 5.1).

When people are displaced, production systems may be dismantled, kinship groupings disrupted, and long established residential settlements disorganized. People's lives are affected in very painful ways. Many jobs and assets are lost, health care tends to deteriorate. Links between producers and customers are often severed, and local labour markets are disrupted (World Bank, 1994). The displacement caused by land acquisition in urban areas, although intended for a larger social good, creates tensions and conflicts for a section of population. The problems of caste and community are observed at the place of relocation also.

Relocation and Hosts

Many displaced people have had a bitter experience with their hosts. In case of Pong dam, the oustees resettled in Rajasthan, for instance, were harassed, beaten up and their lands grabbed, many of them were even murdered. As a result, many of the resettlers returned to Himachal Pradesh (see Box 5.2).

Box 5.1
Involuntary versus Voluntary Resettlement

It is important to distinguish between involuntary and voluntary movements of populations at this stage. Anthropologists identify 'push' and 'pull' factors as influencing voluntary out-migration—the former forcing people out of their traditional localities, and the after attracting them to move to new ones. Therefore, levels of anxiety and insecurity are much higher among involuntary resettlers (Guggenheim and Cernea, 1993). Involuntary resettlement programmes, by contrast, are indiscriminate. Entire populations are bound to move, disrupting the diverse risk avoidance and social insurance mechanisms present in villages (Guggenheim and Cernea 1993). Involuntary resettlement consists of two closely related distinct processes: displacing people and rebuilding their livelihoods. The complexity of involuntary resettlement and the enormous diversity of project situations make achieving good resettlement a formidable task (World Bank, 1994).

Box 5.2
Return of Pong Oustees

The case of the Pong oustees is a good example. The states of Rajasthan and Himachal Pradesh were seen intent on playing a game of Ping-Pong with each other, forcing the oustees to shuttle between the two states looking for redressal in vain. While many were not rehabilitated, others, having lived their lives in the hills of Himachal Pradesh, found themselves unable to cope with the deserts of Rajasthan, where they had been offered resettlement. The affected population had been offered relocation in the command area where the promised waters of the project were destined to reach. But, in the meanwhile, they found the condition so inhospitable and alien that many were forced to return to Himachal Pradesh.

Government agencies make false promises to the poor and innocent and assure them of assistance in resettlement. Few affected persons agreed to vacate land but those who opposed and stuck to the belongings were forcibly thrown out of the house and land with the help of police and local administration. People affected by land acquisition had the problems of adjustment at a new location, which were aggravated when the host opposed their resettlement. The relocation affected their income-generating subsidiary occupations and living conditions. The search for new agricultural lands, social connections and symbolic identifications caries a long story of social tensions. The issues in resettlement were identified by Advani and Sharma in studies of Agucha Mines (Mathur, 1996) (see Box 5.3).

NGO Movement

Movements of NGOs has received a boost with approaches adopted by two major NGOs, the Arch Vahini and the Narmada Bachao Andolan. They took radically different stands on the consequences of the Sardar Sarovar projects for the affected people and the people of the region involved. What has not been sufficiently analyzed in this context is the entire process by which each group evolved, formed alliances, formulated differences and came into open conflict with each other (Dhagamwar, 1994).

Vidyut Joshi of the Arch Vahini, has described the processes by which NGOs in Gujarat first rejected the resettlement packages that were offered, then combined together to demand better resettlement packages and only after having wrested what are regarded to be appropriate deals from the government, agreed to be associated with the rehabilitation process.

Narmada Bachao Andolan, in addition to using courts of law, influencing international and national opinion, has also used the strategies of fasting and threats of collective suicide to stop governmental action on the Sardar project. While both movements see themselves as speaking on behalf of the affected groups, especially tribals, there are serious and urgent questions about their representation; about the relation between local and global knowledge in the description of events. There are questions about diverse and heterogeneous interests, especially those of the leaders and the followers, who are to be wielded together in the emergence of social practices.

The goals NGOs and their social movements should not be seen as poles apart from the interests of the state. In fact the differences in the attitude of the state governments of Gujarat and Madhya Pradesh

Box 5.3

Case of Mining Development at Agucha

The issues related to resettlement, however, took time to resolve. Anticipating difficulties that are inevitable in relocating people to new places, Hindustan Zinc Ltd., on the advice of its ODA social development consultant, engaged a local sociologist from Samaj Shastra Hindi Kenya Samiti (SHKS—a local NGO) as a consultant to help deal with this delicate human problem (Rew, 1994). The SHKS consultant carried out detailed social research on the local communities and on matters concerning their resettlement (Advani, 1990). A relocation plan based on this research proved helpful in moving people to the new location in a relatively smooth manner.

What are the main elements of this successful relocation plan and how was the reluctance of the affected people to leave Rampura eventually overcome? As the sociological research brought out, factors that facilitated resettlement included:

- Providing generous cash compensation for land, houses, and other property acquired by HZL.
- Giving assurances that HZL will provide jobs to one person from each affected family.
- Moving people to a location not far from Rampura so that those who still owned land there could look after it.
- Designing the relocation site so that it adhered to the original pattern in Rampura, with different castes and groups living in separate, well-marked areas.
- Naming the relocation site New Rampura so that it would remind resettlers of the old Rampura and help in developing the same deep attachment to their new settlement that they had for their old village.
- Promising that the new settlement would provide permanent roads, street lights, water supply system, and other facilities.
- Using a participatory approach that gives project-affected people a voice in decisions concerning their resettlement affairs
- Abiding by the ODA's insistence that international standards be followed in carrying out the resettlement operations.

Sociologists, who were engaged in the research project, feel emboldened and assert that, based on this experience, they can suggest approaches to resettlement that work. The elements of such an approach would include: micro planning for rebuilding lives of the displaced (not in an economic sense alone), assistance to the project-affected people during resettlement, occupational guidance, organization of groups for economic pursuits, resolution of social conflicts (including conflicts with hosts when necessary), respect for time-honoured socio-cultural patterns of living, consultative processes in management.

point to the fact that whether the industry is organized enough in a region to take advantage of a particular developmental project which would determine the extent of state support and political will to implement the project. Second, the fate of resettlement packages also depends upon the extent to which social support groups including NGO movements are developed enough to monitor the communication and implementation of these packages. As Ramchandra Guha (1985) has shown in relation to the history of forestry, the alliance between the state and different kinds of class interests cannot be defined in deterministic terms but shows elements of tactical alliances that have to be established through analysis of state policy and practice.

Possession of land is considered as a symbol of social status in Indian society. Acquisition of land not only impoverishes people by taking away their political source of livelihood it also disrupts their control on local social groups and other social institutions, and it increases their social marginalization. The affected people lose several resources and become impoverished. They lack knowledge and power to make their claims in the right perspective.

The pertinent question remains how to integrate resettled people into a powerful social and economic network so that they can put pressure on the government agencies to pay attention to their rehabilitation. Resettlement is socio-culturally a complex process. While a participatory, flexible and open-ended approach to planning and implementation may appear expensive but any other approach seems almost certain to fail in R&R and, in the end, to be much more costly overall (see Box 5.4).

Nature of Displacement and Conflicts

Acquisition of land affects the people in various ways. There are agriculturists whose total land has been acquired and they had to search an alternative place for resettlement. They are *relocated*. The second category is of *transient* people whose lands have been acquired but they have not yet moved from the place of origin—they continue to stay in the same house or nearby place. These people will have to move in future; they are in search of an alternative place. There is third category of the people termed as *stationary*. Their lands have been

Box 5.4

Case of Resettlement at Gosunda Dam, Chittorgarh District

Hindustan Zinc Ltd., Udaipur sponsored a sociological study and social work programme of the SHKS for the five villages affected by Gosunda Dam in Chittorgarh district. In carrying out the resettlement project, support and guidance was received from the Overseas Development Agency (ODA), UK.

Phase One: The first project at Gosunda Dam (Advani, 1992) began with a sociological study of the five affected villages—Panchdevla, Sarlai, Jetpura Khurd, Hazoorpura and Roopakheri. Household profiles of 290 families were recorded covering their socio-economic background (attitudes towards shifting to new localities), utilization of compensation amount, and problems in resettlement. The data were analyzed and three areas of social work assistance were identified as (i) assistance in shifting from old villages to new localities planned for their resettlement, (ii) counselling in family and social tensions, and (iii) providing education for alternative employment and job opportunities.

The whole process of this project has been an active and participatory investigative venture which involved qualified and devoted researchers and social workers who identified problems. The project was extended for one more year.

Phase Two: During the second phase of the project (Advani, 1993), more attention was paid to occupational training, and to resettlement in the new localities. Along with this, the earlier activities of monitoring and assisting every household, conducting sociological studies and social work continued. The evacuees were imparted training in household industries. They were also given direction and provided assistance in obtaining loans and facilities for small scale industries. About 40 evacuees were engaged in a fisheries project. Several others were engaged in poultry farming, sheep breeding, dairy farming and construction activities.

It was thus demonstrated that effective resettlement of displaced people should be done through sociological studies and social work programmes, covering family counselling, assistance in shifting, resolution of social tensions, occupational education and job training.

partially acquired; they need not move from their place—most of them are displaced due to construction of roads. The nature of people affected by land acquisition of land in Udaipur city is given in Table 5.1.

Table 5.1
Nature of Displacement and Resettlement in Udaipur

Category	*Number*	*Percentage*	*Description*
Relocated	102	34.00	Move to new location after land acquisition
Transient	40	13.30	Land acquired–In the process of moving– Future move
Stationary	158	52.70	Partial land acquisition. Likely to stay at same place.
Total	300	100.00	

Social Tensions and Reactions

Acquisition land causes tensions of various kinds among the affected families. There are worries about the compensation, occupation, relocation and resettlement. But, before all this begins, the first reaction is to make efforts to get the land acquisition orders cancelled and to continue occupying their land and house; where they and their ancestors have lived for a very long period of their lives.

After the publication of notification in the newspapers, they do not believe that they could be evacuated. They think such proposals hardly materialize. However, they start discussing the matter with other persons and in some cases, they find some leaders to support their cause. The leaders who occupy any official position do give some assurance initially but swing their tones as the time passes away. Following series of the conflicting situations have been observed in urban areas as the land is acquired.

- Rumours about the land acquisition.
- Discussion on Master Plan and presumptions about land acquisition.
- Publications of proposals for land acquisition.
- Formation of opposition groups or 'Sangarsh Samities' (Struggle groups).
- Intervention of private property dealers.
- Demonstration and meetings.
- Publication of notification for land acquisition.
- Issue of notices for land acquisition.
- Efforts for preventing the entry of officials.
- Struggle for preventing the takeover of the land and houses.

- Problems in obtaining compensation.
- Tensions and efforts for resettlement or relocation.
- Struggle for the change of occupation activity.
- Resettlement problems of women and children.
- Forget the past and lead life with consolation.

The social tensions and conflicts generally vary according to the area of displacement and agency dealing with payment of compensation; period and year of displacement; size of the land being acquired, caste, class and occupation. The organized struggles are observed more in the area where large chunk of land is acquired and when the amount of compensation—the land value is much less than the market and when the resettlement efforts are missing. In addition to economic issues, they are concerned about the community resources, temples and Devras. They are emotionally attached to their religious places.

In several cases, the people affected by land acquisition are squatters, they do not possess the authorized land document—patta of the land, which created tension in the family and problems in obtaining the compensation. Several times, they relocated themselves at an alternative place, constructed a house on an unauthorized land, for which again they did not possess a patta. Those who are displaced on roadside, search a place nearby roadside. But, the story of social conflicts continues, even when they obtain the compensation. The amount of compensation is gradually divided among the members of the joint family. This is either done by the land acquiring agencies or by the members themselves, which leads to breaking of joint families. The unity of years in the family is destroyed.

The issue of social conflicts among the displaced is specifically assessed on the basis of formation a 'Sangarsh Samities', desire to form a Sangarsh Samiti, organization of movement, and land property litigation cases.

Formation of Sangarsh Samiti

Table 5.2 shows the percentage of those who formed and participated in Sangarsh Samiti against the decision to acquire the land. In urban areas, the functioning of such Samitis is rather difficult. In Udaipur, 38 per cent of affected persons did form the Sangarsh Samiti.

Table 5.2
Formation of Sangarsh Samiti in Udaipur

Background Variable	*Yes*	*No*	*Total %*	*N*	*Chi-Square*
Zone					
North East	54.0	46.0	100	50	57.17**
Central	52.0	48.0	100	50	
South	42.0	58.0	100	50	
Roads	22.0	78.0	100	50	
HB/RIICO	58.0	42.0	100	50	
Dealers	02.0	98.0	100	50	
Year of Displacement					
1990–93	43.2	56.8	100	118	23.12**
1994–97	24.3	75.7	100	37	
1998–01	21.1	78.9	100	76	
2002–05	56.5	43.5	100	69	
Size of Land (bigha)					
Less than 3	43.5	56.5	100	191	6.87
4 to 6	32.9	67.1	100	70	
7 to 9	25.0	75.0	100	12	
10 and above	22.2	77.8	100	27	
Caste					
General	31.2	62.8	100	94	6.22
OBC	49.3	50.7	100	73	
SC	21.4	78.6	100	14	
ST	34.5	65.5	100	119	
Class Before					
Lower	32.5	67.5	100	77	6.86
Lower Middle	36	64	100	164	
Middle	53.8	46.2	100	52	
Upper Middle	42.9	57.1	100	07	
Class After					
Lower	49.2	50.8	100	120	10.37**
Lower Middle	30.3	69.7	100	122	
Middle	31.4	68.6	100	51	
Upper Middle	42.9	57.1	100	07	
Total	115	185		300	
Percentage	38.3	61.7	100		

Level of significance **0.01, *0.05.

Zonewise difference is significant in formation of the Sangarsh Samiti. Large area of land was acquired for Housing Board/RIICO (Zone 5). Fifty-eight per cent of the affected persons in this zone were organized to agitate through Sangarsh Samiti. Similar situation is observed north-east and central zones, where more than fifty per cent formed a Samiti to put forward their demands. In contrast, those displaced by acquisition of land on roadside were less organized (22%). The formation of such Samiti is negligible in case of those who disposed off their land through property dealers.

Year of displacement does significantly influence the formation of Sangarsh Samiti. Those displaced during 1990–2003 were more active than those affected in 1998–2001. The declining trend of formation Sangarsh Samitis was revived in 2002–05 as 67 per cent of the displaced have formatted Samitis. This appears to be due to growing knowledge about the displacement issues during the recent years.

Size of land acquired, caste or class does not significantly affect the formation of Sangarsh Samiti as majority of people do not participate in struggles. Yet, the class after acquisition of the affects significantly (0.05 level) as about 50 per cent of the lower class had formed such a committee and struggled to save their land.

Desire to Form a Sangarsh Samiti

The opinion of the displaced persons was sought to assess their desire on formation of committees to put forward their demands. They were asked, whether they would like to form a Sangarsh Samiti for the help of the displaced person? Majority of the displaced (66%) were willing to do so. Table 5.3 shows chi-square is significant at 0.01 level for zone, year of displacement and class after acquisition and significant at 0.05 level for caste. These background characters reveal significant effect on the desire to form the committee.

The desire for formation of the committees is observed more in the zones where large chunks or total land is acquired. It is comparatively less for the zones, where part of the land is acquired for roads. However, it is surprising that about one-third of the persons who have disposed off their land through the dealers also wish to form a Sangarsh Samiti. It has been observed that the private dealers have cheated several such people.

Table 5.3
Desire to form Sangarsh Samiti in Udaipur

Background Variable	*Yes*	*No*	*Total %*	*N*	*Chi-Square*
Zone					
North East	74.0	26.0	100	50	40.64**
Central	78.0	22.0	100	50	
South	80.0	20.0	100	50	
Roads	48.0	52.0	100	50	
HB/RIICO	80.0	20.0	100	50	
Dealers	36.0	64.0	100	50	
Year of Displacement					
1990–93	68.6	31.4	100	118	12.69**
1994–97	51.4	48.6	100	37	
1998–01	56.6	43.4	100	76	
2002–05	79.7	20.3	100	69	
Size of Land (bigha)					
Less than 3	70.2	29.8	100	191	5.67
4 to 6	57.1	42.9	100	70	
7 to 9	75.0	25.0	100	12	
10 and above	55.6	44.4	100	27	
Caste					
General	58.5	41.5	100	94	8.81*
OBC	79.5	20.5	100	73	
SC	57.1	42.9	100	14	
ST	64.7	35.3	100	119	
Class Before					
Lower	75.3	24.7	100	77	6.05
Lower Middle	61.0	39.0	100	164	
Middle	65.4	34.6	100	52	
Upper Middle	85.7	14.3	100	07	
Class After					
Lower	82.5	17.5	100	120	30.72**
Lower Middle	59.8	40.2	100	122	
Middle	41.2	58.8	100	51	
Upper Middle	71.4	28.6	100	07	
Total	198	102			300
Percentage	66.0	34.0	100		

Level of significance **0.01, *0.05

It is revealing that whose lands have been acquired in recent years are more conscious about their rights. Eighty per cent of them desire to form a Sangarsh Samiti. Similarly, eighty per cent of the other background classes are willing to form the Samiti. The desire to form a Sangarsh Samiti is predominantly greater among the lower class (8.3%) and upper middle class (71%). Size of land and class before land acquisition do not show significant effect on the desire for formation of the Sangarsh Samitis.

Movement Against Land Acquisition

Persons who are affected by land acquisition do not differ significantly on the basis of caste and class in the formation of Sangarsh Samitis for social movement. According to them, the organization of *Dharna* or procession is considered as a part of movement. Sometimes, few members of political parties support their cause, prominent among them are Communist parties.

Table 5.4 shows that nearly forty per cent of the persons affected by land acquisition participated in an movement, either for blocking the acquisition or for obtaining better compensation. Zone, year of displacement, size of land and occupation show significant differences in organization of movements. Larger the area of land acquisition, greater are the chances of a movement to withheld it. The movements were more during 1990–2003 and are revived again after 2002. Small farmers were more active in participation of the movements. General caste and OBC participations show that they are more knowledgeable and conscious of about their rights than the Scheduled Caste and Scheduled Tribes. Similar is the case for agriculturists who participate more in movements.

The movements are geared up by joint actions of leaders, members and their followers. Only 40 per cent of the displaced participated in organization of *Dharna*, raising slogans in procession.

Five per cent told they did *tor-phor* (breaking public property) and even threw stones towards those wanted to dismantle their house. About five per cent believed in joint organizational actions. It is revealing that sixty per cent did not participate in such movements. During such movements, they come in contact with leaders and lawyers who sometimes encouraged them adopt legal recourse for their rights.

Table 5.4
Movement Against Land Acquisition in Udaipur

Background Variable	*Yes*	*No*	*Total %*	*N*	*Chi-Square*
Zone					
North East	46.0	54.0	100	50	42.23**
Central	54.0	46.0	100	50	
South	46.0	54.0	100	50	
Roads	26.0	74.0	100	50	
HB/RIICO	56.0	44.0	100	50	
Dealers	04.0	96.0	100	50	
Year of Displacement					
1990–93	45.8	54.2	100	118	13.05**
1994–97	27.0	73.0	100	37	
1998–01	25.0	75.0	100	76	
2002–05	47.8	52.2	100	69	
Size of Land (bigha)					
Less than 3	45.0	55.0	100	191	8.49*
4 to 6	30.0	70.0	100	70	
7 to 9	25.0	75.0	100	12	
10 and above	22.2	77.8	100	27	
Caste					
General	40.4	59.6	100	94	3.76
OBC	45.2	54.8	100	73	
SC	21.4	78.6	100	14	
ST	35.3	64.7	100	119	
Class Before					
Lower	37.7	62.3	100	77	3.65
Lower Middle	35.4	64.6	100	164	
Middle	50.0	50.0	100	52	
Upper Middle	42.9	57.1	100	07	
Class After					
Lower	48.3	51.7	100	120	8.23
Lower Middle	32.0	68.0	100	122	
Middle	31.4	68.6	100	51	
Upper Middle	42.9	57.1	100	07	
Total	116	184		300	
Percentage	38.7	61.3	100		

Level of significance **0.01, *0.05.

Court Cases About Land and Property

In an effort to prevent acquisition or to obtain better compensation for the acquired, some of the affected persons opted for legal remedies. Some cases are also lodged for division of land and property among the family members and relatives. There are litigation cases among the village people about the legal rights of land. Sometimes, property dealers cheat them in sale of their property during the time of land acquisition. All these reasons entangle the affected persons in litigation, which becomes a main cause of tension in the family.

The persons affected by the acquisition of land were asked whether there were involved in any case about land or property. Only one-fifth of them replied affirmatively (Table 5.5). Chi-square shows significant difference according to zone, year of displacement and caste. In north-east and central zones, about one-third of the affected persons were involved in litigation. Yearwise difference was prominent, where about 30 per cent of the persons were involved in court cases. Almost similar percentage of other backward classes were having court cases. Size of the land acquired, class before and after acquisition does not reveal any association with the litigation process.

Assistance Rendered by Government and NGOs

The displaced people remain under stress during and after the acquisition of land. It is expected that some government or non-government organizations should come forward to resolve their social and psychological tensions. The affected persons were asked about the assistance provided to them by various agencies during their period of distress. Table 5.6 shows the association of size of land and class with assistance rendered by government and NGOs.

The affected persons (82%) reported that no assistance was being rendered to them by any government or non-government organizations. The difference in their opinion was not significant according to zone, year of displacement, caste and the class after land acquisition. Chi-square is significant for the size of land acquired and class before. A small number of persons (n = 17) who had more than seven *bighas* of the land could exert comparatively more influence and obtain some help from different agencies. The type of help received by these few people was related to raising of the demand for compensation and assistance in getting the compensation.

Table 5.5
Court Cases about Land and Property in Udaipur

Background Variable	*Yes*	*No*	*Total %*	*N*	*Chi-Square*
Zone					
North East	34	66	100	50	28.38**
Central	30	70	100	50	
South	12	88	100	50	
Roads	12	88	100	50	
HB/RIICO	28	72	100	50	
Dealers	04	96	100	50	
Year of Displacement					
1990–93	18.6	81.4	100	118	8.36*
1994–97	10.8	89.2	100	37	
1998–01	14.5	85.5	100	76	
2002–05	30.4	69.6	100	69	
Size of Land (bigha)					
Less than 3	17.3	82.7	100	191	2.62
4 to 6	20.0	80.0	100	70	
7 to 9	25.0	75.0	100	12	
10 and above	29.6	70.4	100	27	
Caste					
General	25.5	74.5	100	94	21.43**
OBC	31.5	68.5	100	73	
SC	21.4	78.6	100	14	
ST	06.7	93.3	100	119	
Class Before					
Lower	09.1	90.9	100	77	7.35
Lower Middle	22.0	78.0	100	164	
Middle	25.0	75.0	100	52	
Upper Middle	28.6	71.4	100	07	
Class After					
Lower	17.5	82.5	100	120	2.75
Lower Middle	18.7	80.3	100	122	
Middle	19.6	80.4	100	51	
Upper Middle	42.9	57.1	100	07	
Total	60	240		300	
Percentage	20.0	80.0	100		

Level of significance **0.01, *0.05.

Table 5.6
Assistance Rendered by the Government and Non-Government Organizations in Udaipur

Background Variable	*Yes*	*No*	*Total %*	*N*	*Chi-Square*
Size of Land (bigha)					
Less than 3	16.8	81.2	100	191	
4 to 6	7.1	92.9	100	70	
7 to 9	50.0	50.0	100	12	23.58**
10 and above	40.7	59.3	100	27	
Class Before					
Lower	23.4	76.6	100	77	
Lower Middle	20.7	99.3	100	164	
Middle	3.8	96.2	100	52	10.93*
Upper Middle	14.3	85.7	100	07	
Total	55	245		300	
Percentage	18.0	82.0	100		

Level of significance **0.01, *0.05.

Government Help in Resettlement

During the process of acquisition in urban areas, the main aim of government agencies was to get the land vacated by threats or use of force. They overlooked the problems of affected population. The affected persons were asked if they were provided any facilities, e.g., land, employment, assistance in shifting, health, education or community services. The results are shown in Table 5.7.

Table 5.7
Facilities Provided by Government in Udaipur

Facility	*Yes* (N = 300)*	*Percentage (100)*	*Observation*
Land	27	09.0	In RIICO area
Employment	35	11.7	In RIICO area
Shifting	01	00.3	Personal contact
Health	58	19.3	Existing facilities
Education	126	42.0	Existing facilities
Community	89	29.7	Existing facilities

* Multiple choice.

It is evident from the results that government assistance is negligible in resettlement. Some land plots have been allotted in colonies where the Rajasthan Industrial and Investment Corporation (RIICO) have acquired land. They have also provided employment to some deserving candidates. No assistance has been provided either in shifting of their luggage or resettlement. The affected people are utilizing the facilities of health and education already existing in the resettlement areas. No special community facilities have been created by the government—they are making use of the facilities which are existing for the public.

Chi-square revealed that differences in the facilities extended by the government were significant according zone and caste. There was no significant effect of the background characters in case of employment. The health facilities significantly differed according to to zone, period of displacement and class of the displaced before land acquisition. The facility of irrigation significantly differed according zone, caste and present class situation. Community facilities also varied significantly according to zone.

Type of Resettlement and Activities

After receiving compensation for the acquired land, the affected persons have a tough job of resettling themselves. Resettlement is mainly concerned with land and occupation. There are three types of resettlement (Relocation, Transient, Stationary) which could be associated with the obtaining of the land and planning for new occupation. (Table 5.8)

Relocation

First and foremost effort is to find out a place for relocation. Nearly one-third of the persons affected by land acquisition have been relocated to new sites. Among few persons who could get alternative land through the government, nearly two-third had shifted. Forty per cent of those who have purchased land have also moved. Thirty per cent of those engaged in service or working as labourers have also shifted. It is revealing that 52 per cent of the businessmen have *relocated* themselves.

Sixty two per cent of those who have purchased land within city and sixty nine per cent nearby city have relocated themselves. Fifty per cent, who have purchased in nearby village, have also moved.

Table 5.8
Type of Resettlement and Activities after Land Acquisition in Udaipur

Activities and Future Plan	*Resettlement After Land Acquisition*			*Total %*	*Number*
	Relocation	*Transient*	*Stationary*		
Activity After					
Land by Govt.	66.7	00.0	33.3	100.0	09
Land purchase	40.0	02.5	57.5	100.0	40
Service	29.3	07.3	63.4	100.0	41
Labour	29.8	17.7	52.5	100.0	141
Business	51.6	16.1	32.3	100.0	31
Other	26.3	15.8	57.9	100.0	38
Land Purchase					
Within city	62.5	00.0	37.5	100.0	08
Nearby city	69.2	00.0	30.8	100.0	13
Nearby village	52.6	00.0	47.4	100.0	19
Distant village	00.0	00.0	100.0	100.0	07
Not purchased	31.1	15.5	53.4	100.0	253
Undecided	00.0	50.0	50.0	100.0	02
Satisfaction With Land and Occupation					
Fully	35.9	13.1	51.0	100.0	145
Partially	27.9	14.0	58.1	100.0	43
Not	34.9	14.2	50.9	100.0	106
No response	16.7	00.0	83.3	100.0	06
Want to Buy New Land					
Yes	33.9	15.3	50.8	100.0	183
No	34.2	10.3	55.6	100.0	117
Want to Start New Occupation					
Yes	30.9	17.4	51.7	100.0	178
No	38.5	07.4	54.1	100.0	122
Total %	34.0	13.3	52.7	100	
Number	102	40	158		300

Among those who are relocated, thirty-six per cent are fully, twenty-eight per cent partially, and thirty-five per cent are not satisfied with their present status of land and occupation. Nearly thirty-four per cent want to buy alternative land and about thirty-one per cent of the relocated want to start a new occupation.

Transient

The second category in the resettlement comprises *transient* persons affected by land acquisition, who are planning to make a move to a new location. In the process of future move, they have carried out some activities. No assistance has been provided to them in resettlement. Very few persons have been able to purchase land. About 16 per cent of labourers, businessmen and others were in the transient situation. Among those who were fully satisfied, majority wanted to buy land or to start a new occupation, nearly five per cent were in a transient situation. While assessing the activities within the transient persons, it was noticed that 62.5 per cent were labourers and 12.5 per cent were businessmen. They have not been able to purchase land, although a large majority want to buy land or start a new business.

Stationary

The third category in resettlement is of those persons, who are stationary, having some piece of land and house. They are located in the place yet they have to buy land or start a new occupation. Nearly 57 per cent of the land purchasers, 63 per cent of service class and 52 per cent of the labourers are in stationary group. About one-third of these, who purchased land within a nearby village are residing in the same place. More than fifty per cent, who have not purchased land, are at the same place. It is estimated that within the stationary persons, 46.8 per cent are fully satisfied; 15.8 per cent are partially satisfied and 37.4 per cent are not satisfied. About 60 per cent of those residing at the old place wanted to buy land or to start a new business.

It is observed that the activities and aspiration of people affected by land acquisition vary considerably during the process of resettlement. Those who were staying in the old place were also suspicious of displacement in future. As several such people live in unauthorized colonies without a land authorization (patta) so they could be evacuated. Because of difficult situations in obtaining alternative land and also of starting new work in the absence of agriculture, they tend to stay at the same in a portion of land which has not been acquired. Some of them have occupied a nearby piece of land in an unauthorized way or have constructed a house on a non-converted land (agricultural land).

Resettlement and Struggle

In majority of land acquisitions, people react aggressively and form struggle committees (Sangarsh Samiti) with an object to withhold the acquisition proceedings and to obtain better compensation and rehabilitation package. The people affected in urban area were asked whether they formed a struggle committee? The responses are related to the type of resettlement.

Table 5.9

Type of Resettlement and Struggle Committee in Udaipur

Resettlement		*Struggle Committee*		*Total %*	*Number*
		Yes	*No*		
Relocated	R	39.2	60.8	100.0	102
	C	*34.8*	*33.5*	*34.0*	
Transient	R	45.0	55.0	100.0	40
	C	*15.7*	*11.9*	*13.3*	
Stationary	R	36.1	63.9	100.0	158
	C	*49.6*	*54.6*	*52.7*	
Total	R	38.3	61.7	100.0	300
	C	*100.0*	*100.0*	*100.0*	
Number		115	185		

R: Row Percentage; *C: Column Percentage.*

Table 5.9 shows that fifty per cent of the persons affected, who formed struggle committees are *stationary*, although 16 per cent are *transient*, likely to move in future. Only 34 per cent have been relocated. Among the *relocated*, 61 per cent have not formed or participated in struggle committee. Surprisingly within the *stationary* also 64 per cent have not formed any struggle committee. The situation is fluid in the *transient* category, in which 45 per cent have committee. This suggests struggles may delay the process of relocation but they do not install the process of resettlement. There is no significant effect of struggles on the process of resettlement.

Resettlement and Compensating Agencies

The rates of compensation and the policies of resettlement vary according to the agencies acquiring land for urban development.

Urban Improvement Trust (UIT) paid only cash compensation; but its rates were higher than the Public Works Department (PWD). The land acquired for Housing Board Colonies were in connivance with UIT and other development agencies. Although the rates of compensation were according to government specification, yet the mode of payment and procedures adopted were somewhat different. The land acquired by the Rajasthan Industrial Development and Investment Corporation (RIICO) is for development of industrial areas, yet residential colonies for officers and commercial centres were also created. In this case, the authorities had to face violent opposition from the affected population. With the result, few house plots were allotted for the resettlement. The cases of those who have disposed off their land through the private dealers, because of the fear of land being acquired by the government agency, have a peculiar pattern of displacement. They are indirectly displaced as most of them are cheated by the land mafia, who offer higher rates for their land, scare them that their land will be acquired for urban development; and later on cheat them in payment procedures.

Table 5.10 shows how the variation in agency making payment influences the resettlement. Forty-six per cent of the persons affected by land acquisition through UIT (46%) were relocated at a new site,

Table 5.10

Type of Resettlement and Land Acquiring Agency in Udaipur

Resettlement		*Agency Compensating*				*Total %*	*Number*
		UIT	*PWD*	*HB/RIICO*	*Dealers*		
Relocated	R	67.6	06.9	14.7	10.8	100.0	102
	C	*46.0*	*14.0*	*30.0*	*22.0*	*34.0*	
Transient	R	42.5	22.5	22.5	12.5	100.0	40
	C	*11.3*	*18.0*	*18.0*	*10.0*	*13.3*	
Stationary	R	40.5	21.5	16.5	21.5	100.0	158
	C	*42.7*	*68.0*	*52.0*	*68.0*	*52.7*	
Total	R	50.0	16.7	16.7	16.7	100.0	300
	C	*100.0*	*100.0*	*100.0*	*100.0*	*100.0*	
Number		150	50	50	50	300	

R: Row Percentage; *C: Column Percentage.*

and 43 per cent, who were in a transient situation, were likely to make a move in the future. Majority of persons (68%) who were paid compensation by the PWD were stationary. Similarly, majority of the persons who were paid by dealers were also stationary. Among the relocated, majority (46%) were compensated by the UIT and majority in the transient category were also affected through UIT. This reveals that the Urban Improvement Trust, which is the main agency for land acquisition, displaced more people than those who were affected by other agencies. Chi-square shows a significant association between the type of agencies and the extent of resettlement.

Resettlement and Displacement Year

Forty per cent of the total persons affected by land acquisition during 1990–93 are *relocated*, whereas only 23 per cent affected during 2002–05 come under the same category. However, only 12 per cent affected during 1994–97 are *relocated*. Among the relocated, 40 per cent were displaced during 1990–93. Similarly, among the *transient* category, majority were affected during 1990–93. But there is no uniform trend. It does not reveal significant effect of the year of displacement on type of resettlement (Table 5.11).

Table 5.11

Year of Displacement and Type of Resettlement in Udaipur

Resettlement		*Year of Displacement*				*Total %*	*Number*
		90–93	*94–97*	*98–01*	*02–05*		
Relocated	R	40.2	15.7	18.6	25.5	100.0	102
	C	*34.7*	*43.2*	*25.0*	*37.7*	*34.0*	
Transient	R	55.0	05.0	22.5	17.5	100.0	40
	C	*18.6*	*05.4*	*11.8*	*10.1*	*13.3*	
Stationary	R	34.8	12.0	30.4	22.8	100.0	158
	C	*46.6*	*51.4*	*63.2*	*52.2*	*52.7*	
Total	R	39.3	12.3	25.3	23.0	100.0	300
	C	*100.0*	*100.0*	*100.0*	*100.0*	*100.0*	
Number		150	50	50	50	300	

R: Row Percentage; *C: Column Percentage.*

Resettlement and Size of Land Acquired

Fifty-three per cent of the people affected by land acquisition have resettled themselves at the same location. Thirty-four per cent were relocated and another 13 per cent were in the *transient* process. Among the small land losers, majority were stationary. Those whose 10 or more bigha land was acquired, 57 per cent were relocated. The trend shows larger the size of land acquired, greater are the chances of relocation at a new site. Among the transient persons, majority belong to small land acquired category; same is the position of this category in stationary type. Chi-square does not reveal significant effect, yet Linear by Linear Association is significant at 0.018 level. Table 5.12 shows the situation of resettlement is different according to the size of land acquired.

Table 5.12
Resettlement and Size of Land Acquired in Udaipur

Resettlement		*Size of Land – Bigha*				*Total %*	*Number*
		1–3	*4–6*	*7–9*	*10 +*		
Relocated	R	55.9	24.5	04.9	14.7	100.0	102
	C	*29.8*	*35.7*	*41.7*	*55.6*	*34.0*	
Transient	R	67.5	27.5	00.0	05.0	100.0	40
	C	*14.1*	*15.7*	*00.0*	*07.4*	*13.3*	
Stationary	R	67.7	21.5	04.4	06.3	100.0	158
	C	*56.0*	*48.6*	*58.3*	*37.0*	*52.7*	
Total	R	63.7	23.3	04.0	09.0	100.0	
	C	*100.0*	*100.0*	*100.0*	*100.0*	*100.0*	
Number		150	50	50	50	300	300

R: Row Percentage; *C: Column Percentage.*

Resettlement According Zones

Fifty-three per cent of the people affected by land acquisition have chosen to stay at the place of origin, hence they are considered as stationary. Thirty-four per cent have moved to a place of relocation. Thirteen per cent are in transient situation—planning to move a new location. Chi-square shows that the zonewise difference is significant at 0.01 level indicating the significant association between zonewise displacement and nature of resettlement.

Table 5.13 shows resettlement according to nature of zone in Udaipur. Among those affected by land acquisition for roads, 68 per cent are stationary; only 14 per cent are relocated and 18 per cent are likely to move in future. Difference is also found in first three zones (UIT). More than one-half of zone 2 and 3 were relocated, whereas 56 per cent of zone 1 were stationary. Forty-two per cent of Housing Board and RIICO affected are also staying as the same place. Among the relocated, only seven per cent of the people living on roadside who were affected have shifted, although 23 per cent will make a move in future. Within the stationary category, majority (21.5%) were affected through private dealers.

Table 5.13

Resettlement According to Zones in Udaipur

Resettlement		*Zone*						*Total %*	*Number*
		1	*2*	*3*	*4*	*5*	*6*		
Relocated	R	16.7	26.5	24.5	06.9	14.7	10.8	100.0	102
	C	*34.0*	*54.0*	*50.0*	*14.0*	*30.0*	*22.0*	*34.0*	
Transient	R	12.5	17.5	12.5	22.5	22.5	12.5	100.0	40
	C	*10.0*	*14.0*	*10.0*	*18.0*	*18.0*	*10.0*	*13.3*	
Stationary	R	17.7	10.1	12.7	21.5	16.5	21.5	100.0	158
	C	*56.0*	*32.0*	*40.0*	*68.0*	*52.0*	*68.0*	*52.7*	
Total	R	16.7	16.7	16.7	16.7	16.7	16.7	100.0	
	C	*100.0*	*100.0*	*100.0*	*100.0*	*100.0*	*100.0*	*100.0*	
Number		50	50	50	50	50	50	300	300

R: Row Percentage; *C: Column Percentage.*

Zones

1. North-East, 2. Central, 3. South, 4. Roads, 5. Housing Board/RIICO, 6. Private Dealers.

Zonewise differences in movement of people to a new site occur because of the location of residence, the size of land acquired and the years of displacement. In majority of cases, the affected persons find to difficult to relocate themselves, whereas in other cases they find a smaller place to readjust themselves at the same place.

Six

Social and Occupation Change

Displaced persons find it difficult to adapt themselves to the new production pattern into which they are inserted without any psychological or socio-cultural preparation. As a result, they often turn out to be 'undisciplined' workers and take to alcohol and even to crime as a way out of their trauma. Many of them lose their job, because of these problems.

Moreover, the social pollution aspect, for example, the introduction of new diseases, because of the change of the environment and the introduction of exotic species, is ignored (Baboo, 1991; Mahapatra, 1990). The process of land acquisition in urban areas poses several problems for the affected people. With the result, several social and occupational changes occur in their social structure.

Urbanization and Social Change

Undesirable outcomes that have also reached alarming proportions with urbanization are denial of access to safe drinking water, sanitation, and adequate waste management for a substantial portion of the country's urban households. According to India's Union Urban Development Ministry, 20 per cent of the country's urban households are denied access to safe drinking water, 58 per cent do not have safe sanitation, and more than 40 per cent of garbage generated is left uncollected for want of proper waste management. While the problems highlighted by Urban Development Ministry imply that there are probably too many immigrants into the city, the problems could well be due to the fact that migrants do not compensate for the social costs they create.

Urbanization is a natural consequence of economic changes that take place as a country develops. At the same time, urbanization helps to contribute to the growth process at large. But the latter is not always true. The positive role of urbanization is often overshadowed by the evident deterioration in the physical environment and quality of life in the urban areas caused by the widening gap between demand and supply of essential services and infrastructure. This results from increasing population pressure on urban centres, most of which are financially and organizationally ill-equipped to respond to infrastructural needs (Prasad, 2003). With the development of the country, urban population is increasing. There is a trend to rural to urban migration. Many rural areas are included in the expanding areas of the cities.

The cities in India face many and increasing problems as they grow—those of resources, organization, social and technological difficulties. However, there has been significant cultural efflorescence brought about in the urban settlements due to the very factors of wealth, contiguity and education. On the other hand, the malaise of an impoverished urban environment has brought about an awareness of cultural gaps, lack of contact with nature and unhappy disparities. The economics of the crisis also has grown (Prasad, 2003). The problems of urbanization in India are more related to poverty and unemployment. The rural areas lack occupational avenues. There is wider gap between upper and lower classes in cities.

The National Commission on Urbanization (NCU) presented its report in August 1988. The report is quite exhaustive and penetrating in its analysis of trends and problems of urbanization in India. However, except for the pattern of rural-urban migration, it has paid absolutely no attention to growing rural-urban dichotomies (Prasad, 2003). There is no concern for the people who are to be displaced and affected because of the urban development projects.

Displacement and Impoverishment

Displacement in urban areas revealed the story of impoverishment as in case of other type of displacement. There was no uniformity in terms of resettlement. There were negligible efforts for resettlement of the people with varying socio-economic and cultural backgrounds. The people get resettled by their own efforts. The motion of rehabilitation does not prevail for land acquisition in urban areas. With the result, poor people and agriculturists have to struggle and they become poorer. While the agricultural bases have been virtually eroded, in urban areas there are families who have tried to hold on to their traditional occupation and have tried to purchase land in the areas away from the city. The affected people who are poor having less contact with the formal sector than most other citizens, are pushed into a new economy. A large number of DPs pushed them into a new economy without any preparation and they were unable to cope with the new changes.

The consequence of all these factors is impoverishment and marginalization of most of the persons affected by land acquisition. Impoverishment refers to their status as individuals and communities after loss of livelihood and not to economic poverty that may have been their state prior to it. The consequences of deprival of livelihood are felt differentially. Some PAPs, from the better off sections of the high castes living in the 'advanced' districts, may improve their livelihood by getting a somewhat high price for their not very fertile land. But, most tribals and Dalits experience deterioration in their financial, social and cultural status (Fernandes and Raj, 1992: 142–143). In every category, particularly among the disadvantaged sections, women are the worst hit and pay the highest price of development (Ganguly Thukral and Singh, 1995).

The people affected by land acquisition who are engaged in agriculture, uneducated and traditional in their approach are not aware about the systems of accounting and handling large amount of money. Neither source of their livelihood is recognized, compensated or replaced. Those who limit their analysis to monetary income and marketable commodities, exclude from their calculation what the DPs/PAPs used to get from the informal economy. They ignore the fact that even when monetary income rises after displacement, they are often impoverished also in economic terms, because the CPRs and other sources of their non-monetized livelihood are not replaced (Murickan, 2003).

There are certain changes, which occur in the social and cultural life of people displaced by urban development. These changes deprive them of the very motivation required for improvement of their status. The DPs and other marginalized categories internalize a sense of helplessness and powerlessness, because of their encounter with the powerful external world they are pushed into without adequate preparation. They also internalize the value system of the formal society that does not recognize their economy and culture, and begin to consider their own society and culture of little value. Such internalization makes it impossible for them to rebuild their lives, leave alone improve their lifestyle (Fernandes, 1996). Their standard of living deteriorates, so do their social status and self-esteem, as social status is also linked to the possession of land.

Impoverishment

Consequences of displacement have mainly been discussed in terms of impoverishment risks. Cernea (1999) has described following impoverishment risks:

1. *Landlessness:* Expropriation of land removes the main foundation upon which people's productive systems, commercial activities and livelihoods are constructed. This is the principal form of decapitalization and pauperization of the displaced people, as they lose both physical and man-made capital.
2. *Joblessness:* Loss of wage employment occurs both in urban displacement and in rural areas, and those losing jobs are landless labourers, enterprise or service workers, artisans and small businessmen. But creating new jobs is difficult and requires substantial investments. Resulting unemployment or underemployment among resettlers lingers long after physical relocation.
3. *Homelessness:* Loss of housing and shelter may be only temporary for many displacees, but for some homelessness remains a chronic condition. In a broader cultural sense, homelessness is also placelessness, loss of a group, cultural space and identity, or cultural impoverishment.
4. *Marginalization:* It occurs when families lose economic power and slide on a downward mobility path; middle income farm-households do not become landless, but become small landholders; small shopkeepers and craftsmen are downsized and slip below poverty thresholds. Relative marginalization may often begin long before the actual displacement; for instance, when lands are condemned for future flooding and are implicitly devalued, new public and private infrastructure investments are prohibited, and the expansion of social services is undercut.

5. *Increased Morbidity and Mortality:* Serious decrease in health levels result from displacement-caused social stress, insecurity, and psychological traumas, and outbreak of relocation-related diseases. Unsafe water supply and poor sewerage systems heighten vulnerability to epidemics. The weakest of the demographic segment—infants, children and the elderly—are affected the most.
6. *Food Insecurity:* Forced uprooting increases the risk that people will fall into chronic undernourishment and food insecurity, defined as calorie-protein intake levels below the minimum necessity for normal growth and work.
7. *Loss of Access to Common Property:* Loss of access to common property assets belonging to communities that are relocated, represents a major form of income and livelihood deterioration. Typically, such lost resources remain uncompensated by the government relocation schemes.
8. *Social Disintegration:* It tears apart the social fabric and the existing patterns of social organization. Production systems are dismantled, kinship groups and family systems are often scattered, local labour markets are disrupted, and people's cultural identity is put at risk. Life-sustaining informal social networks of mutual help among people, local voluntary associations, self-organized service arrangements etc. are dispersed and rendered inactive. This unraveling represents a massive loss of social capital incurred by the uprooted people, yet a loss that remains unquantified and uncompensated. Such elusive disintegration process undermines livelihoods in ways unaccounted for by planners.

Some other findings on risks of impoverishment emerging from this study in Rajasthan are also noteworthy. There was enough evidence to suggest that while displacement affects the whole community, people who happen to be poor often bear its brunt most of all; this is particularly true of tribal people, women, and female children. Uprooted from their lands and livelihoods, they see no hope of returning to their previous standard of living. On the other hand, the impoverishment effect of displacement on affluent people generally is limited. With the right connections, affluent people are in a position to turn displacement into an opportunity to get even richer than they are (Mathur, 2004). In an another study of projects in Rajasthan (Mathur, 1996) that involve resettlement attempted to find out whether the characteristics of eight risks that make up for Cernea's impoverishment model were all present there, too. He observed that in addition to the eightfold model envisaged by Cernea, there exists one more in the form of 'loss of access to basic public services'.

In this context, Fernandes (1996) observes, "The situation that results from the loss of social and psychological infrastructure may be summarized as economic pauperization, political disempowerment and cultural alienation. Their impoverishment thus has economic, social, cultural and psychological components." But very few have studied their long term consequences. The whole exercise should be seen as a positive effort in the direction of reestablishment of displaced people.

There are few quantitative methods which could be applied for assessing the level of impoverishment but these may not be adequate. Fernandes (1996) states, "They calculate losses and gains on the basis of monetary income alone. Often they conclude that the status of the DPs has improved after displacement since in many cases their monetary income rises. In this assessment they ignore the fact that much of the livelihood of the DPs/PAPs before their displacement belongs to the non-magnetized informal economy".

Family and Community

Loss of traditional livelihoods is generally accompanied by movement from one place to other in search of wage employment. It sometimes leads to breakdown of the joint families. Generally, the young and energetic male persons move or migrate. The women are left behind to take care of young children. In several cases, the women also move out to work as labourers as household servants. In urban areas, the tendency of commuting to the place of work is more prevalent than that of the migration.

In the process of resettlement, the people affected by the land acquisition, especially tribals, may be open to adopting certain ways of urban life, but they like to maintain the identify of their community. In this context, Hakim (1999), found that most of the Vasavas' apprehensions are related to the fear of losing their self-sufficiency, introduction and consumption, which to them represents the core of their identity. The move to the plains involves a change in production and hence consumption patterns. The community is apprehensive about resettlement, which involves the adoption of the *deshi* mode of market dependent production and consumption. Then, it no longer appears inconsistent, that while they are very open, even eager to adopt many aspects of religious and social behaviour (such as rites and dress) of communities in the new sites, they are very apprehensive about adjusting their behaviour, in terms of production and consumption, to the demands of the new land.

The agricultural mode of production had the strength to bind and feed a joint family together under the same roof, as it required several persons to work in the agricultural ground. As such, a large proportion of family members were depending on single kitchen for food. But, the acquisition of land and traditional spacious houses has brought the same family into a state of misery. Now, they lacked food, space and resources to fulfil the basic needs of the family members (Verma, 2004). It has been observed that during the process of resettlement several joint families are broken because of the lack of space and change in occupational activities.

The community network of the affected people is a culturally set. The people of same caste or tribe who lived together for generations are scattered. Even for those who find outside people with different orientations in their locality, place their traditional structure under turmoil.

From the network perspective, the people affected in urban areas used their occupational networks more than their caste or tribe networks to overcome their problems. Although such networks were found outside clusters and were not limited by space. There were several opportunities of intervention by the local and state government officials to extend help to the affected people but these were limited to those who work within the vicious circle. It was found that the close-knit community networks were turned into scattered semi-formal network. The data also confirmed that interconnection between these scattered groups was lacking.

Shahpur Jat Village: A Case Study

The points which emerge from the study of Shahpur Jat village (MARG, 1998) are relevant for our study. In their efforts of resettlement, the people affected by land acquisition in urban areas faced the situation on their own as no assistance for rehabilitating them was available. The family members change their occupational activities; instead of working on agricultural fields, they work as labourers or as maid servants in nearby homes. Children also feel their responsibility, many young children start working (see Box 6.1).

Box 6.1

Shahpur, Jat Villagers' Self Rehabilitation

1. The villagers stand on their own feet without any assistance from the government
2. As their residential areas were not acquired, they had a foothold in the ongoing developmental process, which they have used very well.
3. Better financial position and the influence of urbanization have improved the condition of women and scheduled castes.
4. Social evils like untouchability and the purdah system are not publicly practised. A scheduled caste person can enter a tea shop, though one is not sure about his being able to enter the temple.
5. Improved educational status brings the villagers closer to the mainstream. The literacy rate has improved but not the motivation to go in for vocational or higher studies.
6. Earlier every boy as he grew up and every girl when she married, automatically joined the family's occupation. While now there is more choices which require training, aptitude and competitiveness. For lack of all these, large number of unemployed young men have been playing cards. Development has yet again proved itself to be a Pandora's Box.

Even so, one can safely say that this study of Shahpur Jat has established that in any displacement situation, if the local people are not driven away and are given a chance to remain at close proximity to the developmental project and also made a part of it, there are better chances of their survival than if they were driven away from their home and hearth.

MARG, 1998

Entrepreneurship at Highway

When people are affected by acquisition of land for development of roads, e.g., bypass or national highway, some people take advantage of the situation. When a part of their agricultural land is acquired, they tend to turn their residential land which is close to the road, into a commercial land. They do not bother to get the land converted but construct shops and houses on the roadside (see Box 6.2).

Box 6.2

Enterprising Farmers on Highway

The Delhi-Jaipur part of National Highway No. 8, which passes through the Rajasthan territory for about 150 km, currently is being widened into a four-lane highway. The Asian Development Bank funded this project. In order to widen the existing highway, the acquisition of small strips of land from farmers on both sides became unavoidable. The land acquired so far has affected 442 families. They did not lose their lands completely, but it has reduced their productive capacity. It has taken a long time to complete this project. Work that started in 1989 is proceeding very slowly. The reason is that some project-affected people have chosen to challenge in the courts the amount of compensation. This underlines the need to resolve resettlement and rehabilitation (R&R) issues before embarking on construction of the project, even if the dimensions of R&R appear small.

Although the loss of land has meant some reduction in agricultural income, the project has brought forth benefits for the affected people. Land values have gone up and are continuing to go up. Some enterprising farmers have opened teashops along the highway that are doing a flourishing business. Others have invested their compensation in trucks, and they, too, are doing well. Apparently, the effect of this project has not been too adverse. Therefore, people generally are not opposed to it. However, there has been mixed reaction to its operation. The highway is used by many truck drivers known for their reckless driving. They do not hesitate to run over village cattle and strike down anybody they regard as coming in their way. It is becoming dangerous to travel on the highway. Diseases, such as Acquired Immune Deficiency Syndrome (AIDS) unknown in the area previously, have affected roadside villages, and truck drivers are their houses and believed to be their speedy carriers.

Status of Women

- Changes were observed in the life pattern and in the economy of the people affected by land acquisition. There has been deterioration in their standard of living and increase in the work burden. Lower class women have to earn their livelihood by working as casual labourers and household servants. Some are even exposed to prostitution.

- Some household requirements of fuel and fodder were available free of cost. There was place for grazing of the animals. Now, they have to pay for such requirements.
- In the process of resettlement, the purchasing capacity is reduced and the women are unable to buy commodities for basic needs. There is little amount available for education, health care, electricity and transportation. More than fifty per cent of the members of families move out every day in search of livelihood.
- The loss of agriculture land has also resulted in loss of income from subsidiary occupations. Changes in food habits and dispossession of animals have brought in changes in traditional systems and food habits. Many women feel humiliated and disgusted with the dependence on others for their necessities and work. Displacement places some families into a debt cycle. They have difficulties in fulfilment of social needs. It becomes difficult to get loans from financial institutions. Lack of assets has also resulted in lack of social security for the women.
- When the affected families shift to a new place, they have to adjust to the new environment. Their participation in social and political activities is restricted. Lack of basic infrastructure facilities make them dependent, leading to marginalization in various spheres of life.

The displacement affecting women varies in situation of violence. This is evident from the study of displaced women in Baroda city (see Box 6.3).

It was observed that many women who were earlier engaged in agriculture work had to settle for unskilled wage labour, which was often irregular and underpaid. In urban areas the community and family network were very important support systems for the affected women. A breakdown in such networks created insecurity among them. Yet they had to become more mobile and link themselves to new networks. Because of the increase in alcoholism by men, the status of women was affected by way of

Box 6.3

Suffering of Women due to Displacement

At some level, displacement meant deskilling for women as well as reduction in social status. During the 1990s, there were some incidences of communal violence in Baroda, and some women were displaced due to the violence. These women feel that the secularizing factor does not operate all the time because caste demarcations remain very clear in new areas (Srinivasan, 1996). Studies on the impact of displacement on women have found that the women have suffered more than men due to displacement. The key impacts identified are given below:

Single women had to suffer more as all the support structures collapsed with displacement.

Many women felt that there are more economic opportunities in urban areas compared to rural areas. However, they also felt the loss of traditional skills, social support—especially for social occasions, and sometimes, economic support. Under the greater economic pressures, most women take up unskilled jobs and very few have the opportunity to train in other skills.

Surprisingly, many men could get the benefit of government schemes, while despite their awareness, the women could not benefit from them.

violence inflicted on them. In some cases, there were incidences of sexual assault, exploitation and becoming sex workers.

While analyzing the problems of women, Ganguly Thukral (1995) states, "Because women in India are much less mobile than men, the breakdown of village and social units affects them much more severely. The fact that she might be leaving relatives and friends behind, or may never again meet her daughter who is married into a village which will not be displaced, is a great cause of concern for the women, a fear that cannot be brushed aside."

It was observed that there was more negative impact on women than on men. Even in labour work, men are preferred more than women. As a result, women who had some control in their own agriculture activities, now work for others in lower level jobs. Tribal women were the more vulnerable to the loss of the household resource base. The loss of agriculture, natural resources and common property resources affected their way of life. The increasing burden on the women, is also transferred to the children. There was increase in school dropout girls and induction of more children into labour.

Social Change among Tribals

"Nowhere are the effects of displacement more disastrous than in the case of the tribal people whose very survival is already at stake", Mathur (1995). When tribal families are scattered from tribal hamlets, acquired for urban development, there is cultural shock for them and their way of life falls apart. Many displaced tribals stay in the city as slum dwellers.

The expansion of urban area of Udaipur city has witnessed large scale acquisition of the land of the tribal people. On one side they are deprived of their agricultural land and on other there are employment avenues in construction and industry. But the increasing industrialization and urbanization of the region and diversification of the economy have been of little use to the tribes.

Urban displacement does not disperse the tribals to rural areas, rather it scatters them in and around the city. This provides them an opportunity for changing their occupational activities.

Analyzing the situation of powerless class and tribals, Fernandes (1996) observes, "In Asia a majority among those deprived of their livelihood belong to the powerless classes, and get further marginalized by displacement since their specificity is ignored while planning the project and rehabilitation". For example, a substantial number of the DPs/PAPs in India are tribal, depending on the CPRs as their livelihood. But the Land Acquisition Act 1894 does not require the project authorities to compensate this loss or rehabilitate them.

Occupational Change

Acquisition of land in urban areas signifies occupational shifts. The affected people are generally forced to shift from the type of occupation they were engaged in before displacement to a different type of occupation after displacement. The change is evident because agriculture becomes no more viable for them. It exposes them to manual work in industrial and construction activity and subjects them to lead a scattered life.

Consequences

1. The people affected by land acquisition generally move in unplanned human settlements, which are form of slums. Besides,

contrasting lifestyles of local people and outsiders generate frustration among displaced communities, something which results into social deviance.

2. When villages are transformed into urban, the administrative system is changed. As a result, they lose their participation in Panchayati Raj institutions, which offered them easy access to the authorities. Apart from this, people are expected to follow the new official system while getting any work done (Dhagamwar et al., 2003).
3. It is difficult for the illiterate agriculturists to take up new or technical jobs. However, they have been getting manual work. It is difficult for traditional artisans to adjust in new environment.
4. Drunkenness is often a mode of coping with the trauma linked to forced displacement and to the inability to cope with the new economy. It is, therefore, well known that if care is not taken, the resettlement and rehabilitation packages of development projects become nominal relief, and are not steps towards rehabilitation (Fernandes and Raj, 1992).
5. Changes in land use, acquisition of land for urban growth and loss of livelihood have also led to environmental degradation and pollution.
6. These consequences vary with local circumstances, but the ultimate common factor underlying the displacement is impoverishment. This occurs along the following crucial dimensions: landlessness. homelessness, joblessness, food insecurity, social disarticulation, loss of common property, morbidity and mortality (Cernea, 1990).
7. Tribal regions are more particularly affected in this process of development. A significant number of displaced tribals have historically been dependent on natural and common resources for their subsistence. Their displacement on a massive scale adds a serious dimension to the problem (Fernandes, 1994).

Change in Class Characters

Land acquisition in urban areas causes certain changes in the class characteristics of the affected persons. Certain changes are observed not only in the size of land but also in their income, expenditure, occasional expenditure, occupation and self-assessment of status. These indicators, combined together are considered as class characteristics. The respondents were apprehensive of reporting current income or expenditure. In spite of it, the percentage in each category reflects information about the change in the class characters after the acquisition of their land (Table 6.1).

Table 6.1
Change in Class Characters after Land Acquisition in Udaipur

Background Character	*Land Acquisition*			
	Before		*After*	
	f	%	*f*	%
Size of Land (Bigha)				
1. 1–3	120	40.00	239	79.67
2. 4–6	83	27.67	27	9.00
3. 7–9	43	14.33	16	5.33
4. Above 10	54	18.00	18	6.00
Monthly Income (Rs)				
1. 0–3000	164	54.67	187	62.33
2. 3001–6000	99	33.00	80	26.66
3. 6001–9000	19	06.33	18	06.00
4. Above 9001	18	06.00	15	05.00
Monthly Expenditure				
1. 0–3000	172	57.33	127	42.33
2. 3001–6000	98	32.66	124	41.33
3. 6001–9000	21	07.00	34	11.33
4. Above 9001	09	03.00	15	05.00
Occasional Expenditure				
1. 0–25000	197	65.66	169	56.33
2. 25001–50000	55	18.33	63	21.00
3. 50001–75000	19	06.33	13	04.33
4. Above 75001	29	09.66	55	18.33
Main Occupation				
1. Labour	104	34.66	141	47.00
2. Agriculture	117	39.00	66	22.00
3. Service	52	17.33	59	19.66
4. Business	27	09.00	34	11.33
Total	300	100.00	300	100.00

Number of persons with small land holdings (1–3 bigha) increased from 40 per cent to 80 per cent; consequently the percentage of persons having land, four or more bighas has decreased. The effect of acquisition is evident on the size of land holdings. Similarly, the percentage of persons with income of Rs 0–3,000 has increased and percentage of higher income groups has decreased. Same trend has been found about the monthly expenditure.

Social needs demand increasing of expenditure on special occasions. Occasional expenditure is incurred in such situations. The percentage of persons has slightly declined in the expenditure category of Rs 0–25,000. Majority of persons, who fall in this category find it somewhat difficult to incur expenditure on special occasions. In contrast, the percentage of persons spending more than Rs 75,000 has nearly doubled. It appears that for majority of the affected persons, it has become slightly difficult to spend on special occasions, whereas a small number tend to spend more on such occasions.

The change in main occupation is significant. The number of persons in labour class has increased. There is marked decline in persons engaged in agriculture. There is slight increase in the number of persons in service or business. It is found that land acquisition mostly change the occupational class of labourers and agriculturists.

The sixth background character of the class was considered as own assessment of the economic status of the persons affected by land acquisition.

Change in Economic Status

Acquisition of land in urban areas should indicate change in the economic status of the affected persons. The respondents were asked to assess their own economic status, before and after the land acquisition in six categories. However, nobody reported himself belonging to very high status. Only five categories shown in Table 6.2 were retained.

About 50 per cent of the displaced persons assessed their economic status as very low or low before the acquisition of their land. Their percentage increased to sixty per cent after the land acquisition. The percentage of medium economic status also declined from 41 per cent to 36 per cent. Thus, the effect of land acquisition is obvious, the economic situation is further examined according to background characters.

Table 6.2
Economic Status Before and After Land Acquisition (N= 300)

Economic Status	*Before Acquisition*		*After Acquisition*	
	f	%	*f*	%
Very Low	34	11.3	93	31.0
Low	115	38.3	86	28.7
Medium	123	40.4	108	36.0
Upper Medium	25	8.3	7	2.3
High	5	1.7	6	2.0
Total	300	100.0	300	100.0

Economic Status before Land Acquisition

The differences according to zone, year of displacement, size of land, caste, class before and after the acquisition of land are shown in Table 6.3.

It is revealing that the difference in all the six background variables are significant. This implies that the change in economic status is associated with the zone, year of displacement, size of land, caste, class before and class after land acquisition.

Majority of the displaced persons with very low and low economic status were found in south (68%) and dealer (52%) zones. Year of displacement also shows significant difference (at 0.05 level) in economic status. Yearwise comparison shows that the percentage of very low and low economic status appears to decline from 1990–93 (53.47%) to 2002–04 (44.97%). Majority of displaced persons whose 10 or more bigha of land has been acquired, had gone into medium economic status.

Castewise difference is significant (Chi-square) at 0.05 level. Majority of affected persons in general and other background caste had medium and higher economic status. In contrast, Schedule Castes and Tribes had confirmatively lower economic status, classwise difference between before and after situation shows declining economic status because acquisition of land.

Table 6.3
Economic Status Before Land Acquisition

Background Variable	*Lower*	*Lower Middle*	*Middle*	*Upper Middle*	*Upper*	*Total %*	*N*
Zone							
North East	0	46	38	14	2	100	50
Central	16	30	32	20	2	100	50
South	22	46	30	2	0	100	50
Roads	2	42	48	6	2	100	50
HB/RIICO	0	42	46	8	4	100	50
Dealers	28	24	48	0	0	100	50
Year of Displacement							
1990–93	7.6	45.8	39	5.9	1.7	100	118
1994–97	18.9	32.4	43.2	2.7	2.7	100	37
1998–2001	17.1	30.3	46.1	6.6	0	100	76
2002–05	7.2	37.7	34.8	17.4	2.9	100	69
Size of Land (in bigha)							
Less than	9.9	42.4	34.6	11.5	1.6	100	191
4 to 6	15.7	35.7	45.7	2.9	0	100	70
7 to 9	16.7	41.7	25.0	8.3	8.3	100	12
10 and above	7.4	14.8	74.1	0	3.7	100	27
Caste							
General	1.1	24.5	57.4	13.8	3.2	100	94
OBC	5.5	35.6	43.8	12.3	2.7	100	73
SC	28.6	21.4	35.7	14.3	0	100	14
ST	21.0	52.9	25.2	0.8	0	100	119
Class Before							
Lower	35.1	53.2	11.7	0	0	100	77
Lower Middle	4.3	39.0	50.6	4.9	1.2	100	164
Middle	0	19.2	51.9	25.0	3.8	100	52
Upper Middle	0	0	28.6	57.1	14.3	100	07
Class After							
Lower	16.7	61.7	21.6	0	0	100	120
Lower Middle	10.7	27.9	50.8	8.2	2.5	100	122
Middle	2.0	13.7	56.9	25.5	2.0	100	51
Upper Middle	0	0	57.1	28.6	14.3	100	07
Total	34	115	121	25	05		300
Percentage	11.3	38.3	40.3	08.3	1.7	100	

Economic Status after Land Acquisition

It has already been shown in Table 6.4 that the economic status of the persons whose land is acquired declines after the acquisition. The difference according background characters is shown in Table 6.4. All the six background variables show significant association with change in economic status after land acquisition.

Zonewise differences were noticed. Majority (more than 60%) of persons with very low and low economic status were found in zone 1 to 3 and zone 4. Year of displacement also shows considerable difference. The percentage of persons with lower economic status appears to decline with proceeding years. Lower the size of land lower was the economic status.

In the same way, the economic status of the Scheduled Castes and Tribes was lower than the status of general and other backward castes. Class before and after the acquisition of the land also revealed significant association with economic status. The economic status declined after the acquisition of land in urban areas.

Pattern of Expenditure

The acquisition of land has shown some decline in the income of majority of affected persons. This could result in changes in the pattern of monthly expenditure. Table 6.5 shows the percentage of itemwise expenditure incurred by them.

It has been estimated on prevailing prices, but the percentages would reveal the change in the pattern of expenditure. Percentage expenditure has increased on fuel, education, treatment, sanitation, travel and loan repayment. It has decreased on house rent, food, addiction, festivals, maintenance, entertainment, savings, liquor and other expenditure.

The pattern of change shows marked increase in repayment of loans and decrease in savings. The percentage of expenditure on education has increased from 3.29 to 7.81. In contrast, other expenses have decreased from 17.51 per cent to 13.77 per cent. There are little changes in other items of expenditure.

It has been observed that after the acquisition of the land, affected persons have to invest on either purchase of land or construction or purchase of a house. Some of them have to change occupation to fulfil social needs. This results in reduction of savings and obtaining of loans from banks or other sources, for which they have to pay instalment and interest.

Table 6.4
Economic Status after Land Acquisition in Udaipur

Background Variable	*Lower*	*Lower Middle*	*Middle*	*Upper Middle*	*Upper*	*Total%*	*N*
Zone							
North East	28	40	28	0	4	100	50
Central	32	20	44	4	0	100	50
South	50	24	24	0	2	100	50
Roads	26	28	34	8	4	100	50
HB/RIICO	42	20	36	0	2	100	50
Dealers	08	40	50	2	0	100	50
Year of Displacement							
1990–93	40.7	22.0	35.1	2.5	1.7	100	118
1994–97	16.2	40.5	40.5	00	2.7	100	37
1998–2001	30.3	21.1	40.8	5.3	2.6	100	76
2002–05	23.2	42.0	33.3	00	1.4	100	69
Size of Land (bigha)							
Less than 3	35.1	29.9	30.9	2.3	1.6	100	191
4 to 6	31.4	28.6	38.6	1.4	00	100	70
7 to 9	16.7	8.3	66.7	00	8.3	100	12
10 and above	7.4	29.6	51.9	3.7	7.4	100	27
Caste							
General	19.1	20.2	56.4	1.1	3.2	100	94
OBC	24.7	38.4	28.8	5.5	2.7	100	73
SC	42.9	7.1	50.0	00	00	100	119
ST	42.9	31.9	22.7	1.7	0.8	100	14
Class Before							
Lower	49.4	33.8	15.6	00	1.3	100	77
Lower Middle	28.7	26.8	39.0	3.7	1.8	100	164
Middle	15.4	28.8	50.0	1.9	3.8	100	52
Upper Middle	00	14.5	85.7	00	00	100	07
Class After							
Lower	58.4	28.3	13.3	00	00	100	120
Lower Middle	18.0	32.0	44.3	4.1	1.6	100	122
Middle	2.0	23.5	66.7	2.0	5.9	100	51
Upper Middle	00	14.3	57.1	14.3	14.3	100	07
Total	93	86	108	07	06		300
Percentage	31.0	28.7	36.0	2.3	2.0	100	

Table 6.5
Land Acquisition and Average Monthly Expenditure in Udaipur

Itemwise Average Monthly Expenditure	*Before Acquisition*		*After Acquisition*	
	Amount	%	*Amount*	%
House Rent	11,000	1.60	10,070	1.03
Food	1,62,890	23.66	2,23,720	22.80
Fuel	45,010	6.54	66,830	6.81
Education	22,640	3.29	75,090	7.65
Treatment	18,510	2.69	33,920	3.46
Sanitation	5,290	0.77	8,810	0.90
Travel	36,760	5.34	57,150	5.82
Addiction	33,010	4.79	45,700	4.66
Festival	25,340	3.68	33,320	3.40
Maintenance	17,670	2.57	11,100	1.13
Entertainment	15,370	2.23	21,440	2.18
Loan Repayment	3,150	0.46	1,04,285	10.63
Saving	1,18,550	17.22	81,800	8.33
Liquor	52,750	7.66	73,100	7.45
Others	1,20,550	17.51	1,35,100	13.77
Total	6,88,490	100.0	9,81,435	100.0

Occasional Expenditure

The expenditure incurred on special occasions is not a regular expenditure. Families save and look forward to occasions like marriages and birth ceremonies when they could spend lavishly. The changes in such expenditure are shown in Table 6.6.

Majority of the persons (69%) affected by land acquisition had spent large sum of amount on marriage before land acquisition. Their percentage has declined to 57 per cent after the acquisition. The amount spent on death feast has also declined. Besides, birth ceremonies and religious rituals, there are other occasions, when more expenditure is incurred. Expenditure on such occasions has significantly increased, from 4.42 to 23.40 per cent. There are minor changes in other items also.

Table 6.6
Land Acquisition and Average Occasional Expenditure in Udaipur

Items of Expenditure	*Before Acquisition*		*After Acquisition*	
	Amount	%	*Amount*	%
Jewellery	3,29,820	3.48	2,80,900	2.44
Gauna	1,79,050	1.89	2,00,300	1.74
Boy Birth Ceremony	2,18,640	2.31	2,42,040	2.10
Girl Birth Ceremony	2,46,720	2.60	2,53,740	2.20
Marriage	65,32,100	68.89	65,15,600	56.59
Religious Travelling	4,57,500	4.83	4,91,900	4.27
Death Feast	10,99,000	11.59	8,34,500	7.25
Others	4,18,670	4.42	26,93,940	23.40
Total	94,81,500	100.0	1,15,12,920	100.0

It has been observed that during the period of resettlement, marriages are postponed and death feasts receive little less attention. Jewellery purchase is decreased but birth ceremonies of children are celebrated as usual.

Occupational Changes

Acquisition of land results in certain changes in the situations related to the occupation of the affected people. It was appropriate to limit the assessment to only the persons who received the compensation, therefore the occupational activities of other family members have also been shifted.

Table 6.7 shows that before the acquisition of land, 81 per cent of the family members were non-workers, whereas their percentage has declined to 78 per cent. Thus, there is some decrease in the percentage of dependent persons in the families. The percentage of members engaged in agriculture has decreased. The percentage has significantly increased in labour class. Some new persons have entered in business.

There are certain changes in the place of work. More number of persons now go towards main city area for work. There is about 50 per cent decline in the number of those working in agriculture field. There is some increase in the number of those who go to labour stand or market.

Table 6.7
Land Acquisition and Occupational Changes in Place of Work and Commuting in Udaipur

Family members' characteristics	*Before Acquisition*		*After Acquisition*	
	N	%	*N*	%
Main Occupation				
Labour	166	6.92	261	10.88
Agriculture	166	6.92	101	4.21
Service	86	3.58	113	4.71
Business	34	1.42	44	1.84
Non-worker	1,948	81.16	1,881	78.38
Place of Work				
Main city	276	11.50	336	14.00
Rural area	70	2.92	75	3.13
Labour market	51	2.13	63	2.63
Agriculture field	25	1.04	13	0.54
Near house	21	0.87	19	0.79
Other	19	0.79	13	0.54
Not applicable	1,948	81.17	1,881	78.37
Distance (km)				
Upto 2	112	4.37	43	1.79
3–4	63	2.63	45	1.87
5–6	94	3.91	130	5.42
7–8	84	3.50	143	5.96
9–10	41	1.71	65	2.71
11–12 and above	37	1.54	64	2.67
Uncertain	21	0.87	29	1.21
Not Applicable	1,948	81.17	1,881	78.37
Means of Commuting				
By foot	97	4.05	80	3.33
Cycle	215	8.95	227	9.47
Two wheeler	110	4.58	165	6.88
Jeep/car	19	0.38	18	0.76
Bus	15	0.20	02	0.08
Tempo	16	0.67	27	1.13
Not applicable	1,948	81.17	1,881	78.37
Total	2,400	100.0	2,400	100.0

The percentage of those who travel more than four kilometre to reach their place of work has consistently increased after the land acquisition. On an average, those going for work had to travel nearly four kilometre, which has increased to about seven kilometres after the land acquisition.

The percentage of persons commuting to place of work by cycle, two-wheelers (motorbike, scooter) and four-wheeler (car, jeep) has increased. The percentage of persons travelling by public transport (tempo) has also increased.

It has been observed that there are marked changes in the occupational life of the people affected by the land acquisition. The percentage of workers has increased. This may also be due to increasing age of the young persons. In several places, women who used to assist in agriculture and animal husbandry have now started working in the houses of other people. There is significant decline in agricultural activity because of reduction in availability of land for this purpose. Those who are aged and illiterate, now find it difficult to engage themselves in alternative work. When they are idle, other young members start working. Some young members discontinue their education and start working as labourers. It is generally observed that those who are devoid of agricultural activity now tend to work as labourers mainly for house construction.

Resettlement and Occupation Change

During the process of resettlement, some people are relocated at a new place, whereas the others are likely to move and thus are in transient situation. Nearly 53 per cent are stationary and 13 per cent have plans to move. The varying situations have affected their occupation.

Occupation before Acquisition

The change in occupation could be revealed when we compare the situation before and after the land acquisition.

Table 6.8 shows that about 70 per cent in relocation category were agriculturists and labourers. A slightly higher percentage of these people was found in the transient and stationary categories. Less numbers of people were engaged in service and business. Nearly 54 per cent of the persons engaged in labour, agriculture and service were stationary and one-third pursuing such occupations have been relocated. Those in business found it easier to relocate themselves.

Table 6.8
Resettlement and Occupation Before Land Acquisition in Udaipur

Resettlement		*Occupation Before Land Acquisition*				*Total %*	*Number*
		Labour	*Agriculture*	*Service*	*Business*		
Relocated	R	31.4	39.2	16.7	12.7	100.0	102
	C	*30.8*	*34.2*	*32.7*	*48.1*	*34.0*	
Transient	R	37.5	35.0	17.5	10.0	100.0	40
	C	*14.4*	*12.0*	*13.5*	*14.8*	*13.3*	
Stationary	R	36.1	39.9	17.7	06.3	100.0	158
	C	*54.8*	*53.8*	*53.8*	*37.0*	*52.7*	
Total	R	34.7	39.0	17.3	09.0	100.0	
	C	*100.0*	*100.0*	*100.0*	*100.0*	*100.0*	300
Number		104	117	52	27	300	

R = Row percentage, C = *Column percentage.*

Resettlement and Occupation after Land Acquisition

The type of resettlement and occupation after the acquisition of land does not reveal any significant association because the majority of affected persons were labourers or agriculturists. Considerable difference could be observed when we compare the situation 'before' and 'after' the land acquisition (Table 6.8 and 6.9).

Table 6.9
Resettlement and Occupation after Land Acquisition in Udaipur

Resettlement		*Occupation After Land Acquisition*				*Total %*	*Number*
		Labour	*Agriculture*	*Service*	*Business*		
Relocated	R	49.0	19.6	14.7	16.7	100.0	102
	C	*35.5*	*30.3*	*25.4*	*50.0*	*34.0*	
Transient	R	47.5	27.5	12.5	12.5	100.0	40
	C	*13.5*	*16.7*	*08.5*	*14.7*	*13.3*	
Stationary	R	45.6	22.2	24.7	07.6	100.0	158
	C	*51.1*	*53.0*	*66.1*	*35.3*	*52.7*	
Total	R	47.0	22.0	19.7	11.3	100.0	300
	C	*100.0*	*100.0*	*100.0*	*100.0*	*100.0*	
Number		141	66	59	34	300	

R = Row percentage, C = *Column percentage.*

Among those who were relocated, there were 31 per cent labourers before, while their percentage has risen to 49 per cent after the land acquisition. In contrast, the percentage of agriculturists has declined from 39 per cent to 20 per cent. There is some increase in percentage of persons doing business. While comparing the situation of transient persons, the percentage of labour class increased from 37 to 47 per cent. Similar trend could also be seen in stationary category. Overall situation indicates that percentage of agriculturists has declined and several agriculturists have started working as labourers.

Resettlement and Change in Class

Class situation discussed here is based on composite score of income, expenditure, occasional expenditure, occupation and self-assessed economic status before and after the land acquisition. Resettlement represents the position of relocated, transient and stationary persons. Nearly 55 per cent persons belong to lower middle class; 53 per cent are stationary. It is revealing that 53 per cent are staying at the same place even after the land acquisition.

Class before Resettlement

Among those who are relocated, 57 per cent belonged to lower middle class and 24 per cent to lower class. Similar trend was observed in

Table 6.10

Resettlement and Class before Land Acquisition in Udaipur

Resettlement		*Class Before Land Acquisition*				*Total %*	*Number*
		Lower	*Lower Middle*	*Middle*	*Upper Middle*		
Relocated	R	23.5	56.9	18.6	01.0	100.0	102
	C	*31.2*	*35.4*	*36.5*	*14.3*	*34.0*	
Transient	R	35.0	47.5	12.5	05.0	100.0	40
	C	*18.2*	*11.6*	*09.6*	*28.6*	*13.3*	
Stationary	R	24.7	55.1	17.7	02.5	100.0	158
	C	*50.6*	*53.0*	*53.8*	*57.1*	*52.7*	
Total	R	25.7	54.7	17.3	02.3	100.0	300
	C	*100.0*	*100.0*	*100.0*	*100.0*	*100.0*	
Number		77	164	52	07	300	

R = Row percentage, C = *Column percentage.*

'transient' and 'stationary' categories as majority belonged to lower middle followed by lower class. About one-third of the lower and lower middle class persons have been relocated. Those who are planning to shift include 35 per cent of lower and 48 per cent of the lower middle class. Only 14 per cent of the upper-middle class were relocated, although five per cent planned to move. Fifty-eight per cent of upper-middle class were stationary. Resettlement did show significant effect on class before and after land acquisition.

Class after Resettlement

Class situation after the acquisition of land shows similar trend during the process of resettlement. But considerable difference could be noticed when we compare the situation before and after the land acquisition. The percentage of lower class in the relocation category has increased from 23 per cent to 39 per cent. Lower class also increased from 35 per cent to 58 per cent in transient category. About one-fifth of the lower classes were planning to make a move to a new location. It is revealing that 52 per cent wanted to stay at their previously settled place (Table 6.11) As such the resettlement does not affect the class situation. But there are changes because of physical or occupation displacement, which are seen while comparing the class situation before and after the acquisition of land.

Table 6.11
Resettlement and Class after Land Acquisition in Udaipur

Resettlement		*Class After Land Acquisition*				*Total %*	*Number*
		Lower	*Lower Middle*	*Middle*	*Upper Middle*		
Relocated	R	39.2	44.1	16.7	00.0	100.0	102
	C	*33.3*	*36.9*	*33.3*	*00.0*	*34.0*	
Transient	R	57.5	30.0	07.5	05.0	100.0	40
	C	*19.2*	*09.8*	*05.9*	*28.6*	*13.3*	
Stationary	R	36.1	41.1	19.6	03.2	100.0	158
	C	*47.5*	*53.3*	*60.8*	*71.4*	*52.7*	
Total	R	40.0	40.7	17.0	. 02.3	100.0	
	C	*100.0*	*100.0*	*100.0*	*100.0*	*100.0*	300
Number		77	164	52	07	300	

R = Row percentage, C = *Column percentage.*

Change in Movable Assets

Situation of the possession of movable assets changes because of the acquisition of land when agricultural land acquired, the affected persons are left with no land or little land at their disposal. In a small position of land, they cannot pursue their occupational activities in the similar way and their way of life changes the type of requirements and possessions.

Table 6.12 shows some changes in keeping agricultural equipment, a marked decline in livestock and increase in household assets. The availability per 100 households, before and after the acquisition of land, reveals the difference in such items. Although the change in tractors is negligible, the number of pumps and motors for irrigation has declined significantly. There is increase in other items, such as general multipurpose equipment which could be used for other purposes, e.g., construction work. The requirement for equipment used for agriculture work has decreased. After the acquisition of land, the intensity of the technology for agriculture has declined.

With the decrease in size of agricultural land, it becomes difficult to maintain the animals and therefore there is a significant decline in their livestock. Major change could be noticed in possession of cows and goat and sheep. The decrease in number of bullocks and buffaloes is also considerable. On the whole, there is marked decline in the number of animals used for saving the income of the affected households.

It is revealing that there is increase in possession of household items. The numbers of gas/stove, fans, television, scooters/motorcycles and other things have increased. The change in radio/transistors, television shows that there is significant increase in means of entertainment and mass communication. So is the case for scooters and motorbikes.

Before the acquisition of land, the status of family could be assessed by the size of land under their possession. The status indicators are being replaced by the means of entertainment and communication. Young persons having motorcycles, not only reveal fashion, but also their economic status. It also shows increasing penetration of technology in urban areas.

Table 6.12
Land Acquisition and Change in Movable Assets

Type of Assets	*Number (N= 300)*		*Availability per 100 Household*		
	Before	*After*	*Before*	*After*	*Differences*
Agricultural Equipment					
Tractor	07	06	02.3	2.0	- 00.3
Pump/Motor	116	77	38.7	25.7	- 13.0
Other	15	68	05.0	22.6	+ 17.6
Livestock					
Cows	763	391	254.3	130.3	- 124.0
Bullocks	221	41	73.7	13.7	+ 60.0
She-Bullocks	287	159	95.7	53.0	- 42.7
Buffaloes	148	54	49.3	18.0	- 31.3
Goat and Sheep	1130	536	376.7	178.7	- 198.0
Poultry Birds	166	89	55.3	29.7	- 25.6
Donkeys	14	01	04.7	00.3	- 04.4
Household					
Gas/stove	177	279	59.0	93.0	+ 34.0
Fan	414	676	138.0	225.3	- 112.7
Radio/Transistor	138	198	46.0	66.0	+ 20.0
Music System	14	33	04.7	11.0	+ 06.3
Television	89	201	29.7	67.0	+ 37.3
VCR/CD Players	11	26	03.7	08.7	+ 05.0
Mixture	20	70	06.7	23.3	+ 16.6
Scooter/Motorcycle	79	184	26.3	61.3	+ 35.0
Cycle	259	277	86.3	92.3	+ 06.0
Other	29	43	09.7	14.3	+ 04.6

Behavioural Change

Some behavioural changes were observed among the people affected by land acquisition in urban areas. The changes were multi-dimensional and empirically verifiable. In order to measure it, a five-point Likert type scale was used. The respondents were asked to rate the extent of change which occurred because of the displacement. The change could be positive or negative. Yet these have been further clarified by their comments and observations. In all, the scale included 73 items. For analysis, these have been classified according to behavioural aspects related to family, marriage, women, diet and nutrition, caste and religion and family conflicts and problems. Mean weightage of each item is presented for comparisons. The minimum score being 5, mean score 2.5 was taken as midpoint base. It was assumed that the behaviour would change to some extent between scores 2.5 and 3.5. Score 3.5 and above indicates great change in the behavioural patterns.

Behavioural Change in Family

Table 6.13 shows the assessment of people affected by land acquisition about the changes in family because of the displacement. The affection in family appears same as before the acquisition. But, some change was

Table 6. 13

Behavioural Change in the Family Because of the Displacement in Udaipur (N = 300)

Items: Family	*Extent of change*	
	Mean	*Extent*
Affection in family	2.45	
Obeying parents	2.66	*
Dispute among brothers	3.60	**
Brother-sister quarrel	3.59	**
Disintegration of family	3.77	**
Number of children	3.34	*
Size of family	2.85	*
Status of family	2.55	*
Service of aged	2.73	*
Respect to aged	2.73	*
Problems of aged	3.38	*
Problems of children	3.48	*
Education of children	3.57	**
Education of girls	3.43	**
Birth of children	3.41	**
Travelling	3.92	**
Shifting	3.89	**
Migration	3.90	**
Outgoing of males	3.70	**
Watching television	3.74	**
Reading newspaper	3.33	*
Listening radio	3.20	*
Standard of living	3.14	*
Problems of widows	3.25	*

* Some extent, ** Great extent.

reported in the obeying the parents, service to the aged, respect to aged and in problems of the aged, widows and the children. Such change was also found in newspaper reading and radio listening. Disputes and quarrels increased to a great extent resulting in disintegration of families. Education of children was affected. There appeared a great change in movement from place to place and in migration.

Changes in Marriage Patterns

The changes related to the marital aspects are shown in Table 6.14.

Table 6.14
Changes in Marital Aspects (N = 300)

Items: Marriage	*Extent of change*	
	Mean	*Extent*
Child marriage	2.45	
Effective marriage (Gauna)	3.20	*
Late marriage	3.86	**
Inter-caste marriage	3.54	**
Expenditure on marriage	4.11	**
Problems of marriage	3.64	**
Divorce	3.61	**
Remarriage	3.34	**
Polygany	2.12	
Alliance (Nata)	3.27	*

* Some extent, ** Great extent.

Although the situation of child marriage appears to be the same as before displacement; the effective marriages (*gauna*) are delayed. To some extend, there was an increase in alliance, *nata* which is prevalent in their tribal region. The marriages are delayed; the expenditure and problems of marriage and inter-caste marriages revealed an increasing trend after the acquisition of land.

Change in women

The changing behavioural aspects of women are shown in Table 6.15.

Table 6.15
Behavioural Change among Women (N = 300)

Items: Women	*Extent of Change*	
	Mean	*Extent*
Domestic work of women	3.64	**
Work outside home	3.22	*
Beating of women	2.27	*
Women morbidity	3.12	*
Women labour	3.51	**
Illness of women	3.27	*
Clothing of women	3.31	*
Jewellery of women	3.09	*
Women mortality	2.88	*
Mobility of women	3.86	**
Prostitution	2.72	*
Problems of widows	3.31	*

* Some extent, ** Great extent.

There appeared a considerable increase in their domestic work, labour and mobility of the women. To some extent, they had work outside home. It was resulting in increase in their illness and morbidity and mortality. The problems of the widows have increased. There were some indications of prevalence of prostitution.

Changes in Food, Addiction and Illness

Table 6.16 shows changes in consumption of food, alcoholism and addiction and illness, treatment and child mortality.

Changes were observed in behaviours relating to eating and drinking patterns because of land acquisition. To a great extent, change was revealed in consumption of vegetarian diet, alcoholism, smoking and drug addiction which were observed as increasing, the increase in illness and treatment and more expenses on medicines also occurred. Comparatively, lesser change was found in consumption of fruits, gambling and child mortality.

Table 6.16
Changes in Food, Addiction and Illness (N = 300)

Items: Food, Addiction and Illness	*Extent of Change*	
	Mean	*Extent*
Consumption of vegetables	2.96	*
Consumption of fruits	2.87	*
Non-vegetarian diet	3.30	*
Vegetarian diet	3.60	**
Eating and drinking	3.10	*
Alcoholism	3.87	**
Smoking	3.92	**
Drug addiction	3.61	**
Gambling	2.88	*
Illness	3.58	**
Treatment	3.62	**
Expenses on medicines	3.61	**
Child mortality	2.58	*

* Some extent, **Great extent.

Social and Religious aspects

Table 6.17 shows the behavioural changes in social and religious aspects.

Table 6.17
Change in Social and Religious Aspects (N = 300)

Items: Social and Religious	*Extent of Change*	
	Mean	*Extent*
Caste unity	2.92	*
Distance in caste ceremonies	3.32	*
Death feast	2.67	*
Social feast	2.33	*
Religious journey feast	2.60	*
Son birth rituals	3.59	**
Daughter birth rituals	3.63	**
Going to temple	3.25	*
Religious group singing	3.25	*
Boy-girl friendship	3.13	*
Friendship among boys	3.06	*
Friendship among girls	3.10	*
Friendship among aged	2.83	*
Friendship among youth	3.04	*

* Some extent, ** Great extent.

There was great change in observing rituals of the birth of children and expenses on it. There was a marked decline in it. Some changes were observed in organization of feast and attending religious ceremonies. Friendship patterns have changed to some extent. The problems of resettlement leave less scope for such activities.

Factor Analysis of Behavioural Components

Using Principal Component Method for factor analysis of 73 variables included in Behavioural Change Scale was carried out. Variables with high factor loadings in the rotated factor analysis matrix are given in Table 6.18

Factor I: Marriage and Migration

First factor explains largest amount of variance in the rotated output (26%). The variables with high loadings are given in Table 6.18

Table 6. 18
Marriage and Migration: Factor Analysis

Variables	*Factor loading*
Expenditure on marriage	0.878
Travelling	0.873
Shifting	0.821
Problems of marriage	0.783
Migration	0.748

Although marriage and migration appear as two different problems of displacement but these are interrelated in this context. There are maximum variations in the responses about the expenditure on marriage. It appears that those who get large sum of money as compensation spend more on marriage ceremony. On the other side, who get meagre amount, spend less than the usual amount. Yet, the problems of finding a suitable match and organizing marriage are increased. The process of resettlement is associated with more travelling, shifting and migration. This type of movement is further related to increased problems of organization of marriages.

Factor II: Living Condition

The second factor of living conditions explains 16 per cent of the total variance in the rotated matrix. The variables having high loading are given in Table 6.19.

It is interesting to find that the factor of living conditions reveals a combination of the patterns of diet, standard of living and friendship. The level of variation in this dimension determines nature of interactions during the process of displacement and resettlement.

Table 6.19
Living Conditions: Factor Analysis

Variables	*Factor Loading*
Consumptions of vegetables	0.825
Consumptions of fruits	0.813
Eating and drinking	0.793
Boy-girl friendship	0.757
Standard of living	0.757
Friendship among boys	0.740

Factor III: Status Symbol

The third factor includes such variables, which are considered as status symbols for most of the agriculturists whose lands are acquired. These are shown in Table 6.20.

Table 6.20
Status Symbols: Factor Analysis

Variables	*Factor Loading*
Listening radio	0.696
Religious journey feast	0.524
Reading newspaper	0.522
Respecting aged	0.498
Women's jewellery	0.482
Service to aged	0.449

Variables like listening radio/transistor/tape recorder, organization of feast after the religious journeys, reading daily newspaper, respecting and providing service to the aged who generally receive the compensation amount and purchasing jewellery for the women appear as status symbols during the transitional period of resettlement.

Factor IV: Morbidity

Some increase in morbidity has been observed after the acquisition of land. The variables clustered in the morbidity relate to medical expenditure, illness and medicines (Table 6.21).

Table 6.21
Morbidity: Factor Analysis

Variables	*Factor Loading*
Treatment	0.725
Illness	0.670
Expenses on medicines	0.580

Displacement reveals the signs of mental and social tensions. It also necessitates extra efforts on the part of affected persons. With the result, morbidity appears as one of the important dimensions among this people. Therefore, there appears to be greater need for the treatment of illness and of spending more amounts on medicines.

Factor V: Addiction

Fifth factor relates to addiction. The variables appearing with high factor loadings are shown in Table 6.22

Table 6.22
Addiction: Factor Analysis

Variables	*Factor Loading*
Alcoholism	0.650
Non-vegetarian diet	0.559
Drug addiction	0.535
Smoking	0.516
Gambling	0.459

Some kind of deviation in the behaviour of the people has been observed in urban areas when their land is acquired. This also shows more intake of alcohol and non-vegetarian diet. These are also linked to drug addiction, smoking and gambling. It is revealing to find these variables are clustering together. It indicates as an important dimension of the problem of displacement.

Other factors

Three other factors were communication, family, and social and religious ceremonies. These variables although important did not account to much variance. When we consider all the eight dimensions, these cover about 50 per cent of the variance in the rotated solution of the factor analysis.

Seven

Resettlement and Rehabilitation: Policy Implications

Resettlement of the displaced people has become a problem of national concern. Displacement is now viewed as a multidimensional phenomenon, affecting people's lives in their entirety. It encompasses not only the economic but also the social-cultural and psychological spheres, all of which are intermingled. Earlier, displacement was defined very narrowly; i.e., physical transfer of the project affected population. Many other aspects related to displacement were not included in the resettlement and rehabilitation processes. Changes in economic activities, land-use, ownership of assets, accessibility to natural resources and common property resources, loss of livelihood, social disruption and the psychological trauma of the affected persons are the main concerns of human rights and R&R policies.

Because of the increasing trauma of the displaced people, as is being witnessed in almost all parts of the world, displacement is redefined. Its resettlement and rehabilitation are understood as the humane concerns and in the context of social justice, guidelines are given for betterment of the displaced persons. The present view necessitates change in norms for compensation, calculating non-monetized items, common property resources and natural resources. In the absence of it, the disadvantaged social groups will continue to suffer because of inhumane policies. The government policies should recognize customary rights and traditional practices of the people who have been dependent on natural and common resources. In the process of rehabilitation, reconstruction of the livelihood should be the main objective. It should improve the quality of life of the displaced population. This could be possible only by change in policies, which adopt a welfare approach in the process of rehabilitation.

Displacement has both positive and negative impacts. However, the negative impacts generally overshadow the positive impacts because majority of the displaced people experience a process of dispossession and disempowerment. The oustees face major impoverishment and dispossession risks. Not only the economic hazards of displacement but also the social, cultural, political, psychological and environmental impacts mark the risks that the oustees face. The most vulnerable groups like the assetless rural and urban poor, the tribals, women and children are the worst affected. There are cases of complete loss of their source of livelihood.

UN Guiding Principles

The UN guiding principles about the internally displaced persons, have been summarized by Paula Banerjee et al. (2005), as under:

1. These guiding principles address the specific needs of internally-displaced persons worldwide. They identify rights and guarantees relevant to the protection of persons from forced displacement and to their protection and assistance during displacement as well as during return or resettlement and reintegration.
2. For the purposes of these principles, internally-displaced persons are persons or groups of persons who have been forced or obliged to flee or to leave their homes or places of habitual residence, in particular, as a result of or in order to avoid the effects of armed conflict, situations of generalized violence, violations of human rights or natural or human-made disasters, and who have not crossed an internationally recognized state border.
3. These principles reflect and are consistent with International Human Rights Law and International Humanitarian Law. They provide guidance to:
   (i) The representative of the Secretary-General on internally-displaced persons in carrying out his mandate;
   (ii) States when faced with the phenomenon of internal displacement;
   (iii) All other authorities, groups and persons in their relations with internally-displaced persons; and
   (iv) Intergovernmental and non-governmental organizations when addressing internal displacement.

4. These guiding principles should be disseminated and applied as widely as possible.

Assessing the present status of R&R policies and by emphasizing on compensation package, Cernea (1996) says: "Sometimes borrowing agencies propose cash compensation only, in lieu of resettlement facilities. Experience with the resettlement of large population tends to show that the payment of cash compensation alone is often a very inadequate strategy for dealing with the displaced".

Principles of World Bank Policy

World Bank is the first global agency to experience the aftermath of development in the form of resettlement and rehabilitation. So, being sensitive towards the growing problems, it was the World Bank, which took the first steps in formulating an approach to the resettlement question. In 1980, the Bank issued for its staff a statement outlining a policy to guide operations in this sensitive and difficult area with the aim of protecting the interests of the populations displaced by the development projects. This was the first time that any major development agency instituted a policy to deal specifically with the problems of involuntary resettlement. Since then, the Asian Development Bank, the Inter-American Development Bank and the Organization for Economic Cooperation and Development laid down policies for projects requiring resettlement. As a result, every part of the globe is slowly sensitizing towards the lives of millions as natural atonement of development.

The Bank policy rests on a collection of basic principles, such as, minimizing displacement, government responsibility towards the relocated, participation of stakeholders, the rights of victims of displacement, protection of host populace interests, a forward-looking definition of objectives of resettlement and so on. Embedded largely in anthropological research, inference and other social science knowledge, the policy on resettlement was fabricated by a Bank staff group consisting of Michael Cernea, David Butcher, Deborah Robin and Lois Gram. Many studies that helped shape the policy include those by Chambers on Volta Dam in Ghana, by Colson on the Gwembe Tonga reservoir, by Thayer Scudder on man-made lakes especially in Africa (Verma, 2004).

As per World Bank guidelines, the very nature of involuntary resettlement gives rise to special social and technical problems which are to a great extent different from, and usually more severe than, those encountered in cases of voluntary resettlement. A feeling of powerlessness and alienation is often engendered in those who are relocated especially when entire communities are uprooted from familiar surroundings. To the extent that pre-existing community structure and social networks disintegrate, and tightly-knit kin groups are dispersed to new locations, social cohesion is weakened, and the potential for productive group action is diminished. Thus, the oustees find themselves in a position of helplessness, powerlessness, landlessness, placelessness, alienation and most importantly, joblessness which diminishes the chance of a sustainable livelihood (Verma, 2004).

Further, emphasizing the sociological nature of involuntary resettlement, the guidelines caution against viewing resettlement as a mere environmental issue. Frequently, involuntary resettlement is dealt with by governments, consulting firms, the media, etc., under the rubric of 'environmental problems'. But by its very nature, resettlement is a socio-cultural/economic process that happens first to people, rather than to their environment. Therefore, the correct understanding of the sociological nature of involuntary resettlement—with its cultural, economic and psychological ramifications that much exceed the environmental aspects. It leads to a different course of action on addressing resettlement than if it is regarded only as an environmental problem.

The Bank policy recognizes that in any involuntary resettlement situation, some human suffering is inevitable. As its very first requirement, the policy therefore states that involuntary resettlement must be avoided wherever possible. When it is unavoidable, it must be minimized. Emphasis is on providing resettled people with new and better economic opportunities. The policy states that the families affected by a bank-financed project should share in benefits from the project and, as a result, be better off than before. The idea is that since involuntary resettlement dismantles the existing production system, all resettlement programmes must at the same time be development programmes. Emphasis on the policy on preparation of resettlement plans in advance is intended to ensure that the people affected by projects are helped effectively in their rehabilitation. Specifically, the plans are to provide for compensation in full before departure to the new locations; assistance in moving to the relocation site and support during the transition period; and assistance in efforts to improve their living standards.

It is a matter of great concern that the projects designed and appraised in the past had no provision for resettlement and rehabilitation in their guidelines. Subsequently, when it was discovered that resettlement would be necessary, the lack of resources for the purpose only complicated the implementation of otherwise sound projects. In order to prevent recurrence of such cases, the Bank guidelines insist that initial planning of any project construction should accompany the budget of R&R and other development activities.

As resettlement planning decisions impinge on the lives of the displaced groups, agencies concerned are enjoined to encourage community participation on planning and implementing resettlement. A related recommendation concerns the involvement of local groups and non-governmental organizations (NGOs). Being closer to the people, they are in a better position to articulate resettlers' needs and defend their rights.

The Bank policy regards as of particular importance the welfare and development of the indigenous groups, ethnic minorities, pastoralists and other marginalized groups, such as women. Even without legal title, these adversely affected groups are eligible for full compensation as well as resettlement.

World Bank Revised Policy

The World Bank policy on resettlement has undergone several revisions since it first came into existence. Its first revision took place in 1986. A new version of the policy document appeared in 1988. This, too, underwent some revisions lately and an updated operational directive has been in effect since 1990. Current resettlement policy governing funding of development agencies takes the element of policy guideline from the last amended and most recent policy of 1990.

Paranjpye and Kewalramani (1997) list out following salient features of the World Bank Policy.

1. The Policy demands the avoidance or minimization, whenever feasible, of involuntary displacement by conducting a

comprehensive assessment of alternatives and selecting the least displacing alternative within the economic and technical parameters.

2. The Policy states that wherever displacement is unavoidable, the Bank will assist the displaced persons in their effort to improve or at least restore their former living standards and earning capacity. The means to achieve this objective consists of the preparation and execution of resettlement plans as if they were development projects. The policy also requires that the resettlement plans form an integral part of the basic project design.
3. The Policy assures compensation for the loss of all assets by calculating an amount equivalent to 'replacement cost'. It further states that the oustees should be assisted in the process of transition, and granted solatium for the period of transition at the relocation site. The displaced should be given opportunities to get a share in project benefits.
4. The Policy requires that the project authorities minimize the distance between departure and relocation sites so as to facilitate the resettlers' adaptation to the new socio-cultural and natural environment. It also suggests that during the preparation of the resettlement plans, the resettlers and the host populations shall participate in the process of conflict resolution.
5. The Policy envisages that the process of rehabilitation should be treated as an opportunity of development for the new settlers by giving them infrastructural and service facilities and empowering them with training and aptitude.
6. Finally, the Policy is also concerned about maintaining the ethnic value and social relationship of indigenous communities. It proposes to treat the informal customary rights, a natural right to the land or other resources acquired for the project, and hence to be compensated adequately. In substance, it accepts that the absence of a legal title to land shall not be the basis for denying compensation and rehabilitation.

Some of the current guidelines of the World Bank about rehabilitation and resettlement are:

1. The current guidelines for involuntary resettlement in Bank-supported projects provide for: (a) adequate compensation of lost assets; (b) assistance with relocation and support during the

transition period; and (c) assistance in re-establishing former living standards. Prior to 1980, when the first Bank guidelines were published, responsibility for resettlement lay solely with the borrower. Bank's loan documentation tended to be concerned mainly with land acquisition, timely evacuation of people out of the project area and payment of compensation, with less consideration given as to where they were to be resettled and how their livelihoods were to be re-established.

2. The Bank was the first international organization to adopt guidelines on involuntary resettlement. Concerns for the displaced persons gave rise to the following basic policy directives:
   - project design should avoid or minimize the need for involuntary resettlement;
   - projects should ensure that those who have to move receive benefits from the project that displaces them; and
   - projects should provide the displaced people with the means to improve their former living standards, or at the least, ensure that they are not worse off than before relocation.
3. The Bank specified procedures and institutional arrangements for dealing with resettlement issues in the several phases of the project cycle and for supporting borrowers in their adherence to the Bank's resettlement policy. These procedures deal comprehensively with resettlement planning and implementation, with resettlement planning as an integral part of project design, and community relocation as a development programme.
4. With the Bank's recognition that technical support might assist in the satisfactory outcome of resettlement, there came detailed technical guidelines, '3' issued in 1988, for preparing and appraising involuntary resettlement components, including how to include resettlement in financial and economic analysis, and what performa cost tables were required; the same period also saw the publication of relevant technical papers.
5. Treatment of the legal issues associated with involuntary resettlement was also taken up. The paper recommended: (i) A detailed review of the domestic legal framework, including statutes governing the power of eminent domain, the right of the government to expropriate private land for the public good. (ii) The notion of just compensation, i.e., replacement value.

(iii) Review of rights of people displaced who do not have legal title to the land, even though they may have occupied it for generations and (iv) An opinion on whether the judicial provisions for redress are adequate.

6. Bank guidelines made provision for the protection of indigenous populations. Initially, it was expected that these people would be left undisturbed as far as possible, given the special importance of land for these communities. As a general policy, the World Bank will not assist development projects which knowingly involve encroachment on traditional territories being used or occupied by tribal people, unless adequate safeguards are provided.
7. Subsequently, there came a progressive broadening in the range of the Bank's policy considerations for involuntary resettlement, including that special consideration should be given to protect those who may not have established or legal rights—minorities, the landless, women indigenous and ethnic groups. Meanwhile, the approach to indigenous people also changed in 1991. It requires consultation with the indigenous people to determine whether they wish to participate in the development process or whether they prefer to remain apart to protect for their cultural traditions.

Paranjpye and Kewalramani (1997) criticize the Bank policy, since it does not clearly identify the minimum level of basic human rights which must not be isolated or diluted by using the argument of economic exigencies or trade-offs. The policy should have indicated the threshold level or the cut-off point for rejecting a project at the inception stage. Besides, the policy also does not describe a clear mechanism by which a share of the benefits can be determined. In practice, this never happens. The Bank guidelines are not properly implemented. For example, the baseline surveys, which is one of the first tasks, are done casually. Further, there are inherent problems in re-establishing standards of living, which is difficult, expensive and more time-consuming than visualized by the policy. Hence, it remains an idealistic policy with high standards without the will or the seriousness to demand compliance, resulting in utter failures at the implementation level.

Implication of World Bank Policy

The single most important message of the Bankwide Resettlement Review (World Bank 1994) is that good resettlement can prevent impoverishment, and even reduce poverty by rebuilding sustainable livelihood.

The Bank made significant progress during 1986 to 1993 in three major fields:

1. *Influencing policies:* Resettlement works when governments want it to work. The 1986–93 period was marked, according to the Review, by some notable policy successes. Stimulated by a Bank sector project in 1990, Brazil's Electrobras developed satisfactory resettlement guidelines for the country's power sector. Colombia adopted similar sectoral guidelines in 1992. China, with Bank involvement, improved its policy guidelines in the water resources sector. In 1993, India's National Thermal Power Corporation (NTPC) adopted a sectoral rehabilitation policy for all its operations. Major multilateral and bilateral donors also have recently issued resettlement guidelines similar to the Bank's, for instance, the Inter-American Development Bank in 1990;
2. *Avoiding or reducing displacement:* The Review states that the Bank has become more effective in assisting countries in avoiding resettlement, or reducing its size wherever technically and economically feasible. The redesigning of the Saguling high dam in Indonesia, for instance, lowered dam height by five metres, thus avoiding the displacement of 35,000 people. In the Cote d'lvoire forestry project, the Bank proposed revisions and set substantially higher standards for those to be relocated. In Ecuador's Gyayas, flood control project, the redesign of the canal layouts completely eliminate the need to displace anyone; and
3. *Restoring income:* The ultimate test of consistency between resettlement operations and policy is income restoration and improvement. Bank-financed projects that resettle people productively on land and in jobs tend to restore income far more effectively than projects that deliver compensation without institutional assistance. Incomes were found to be successfully restored particularly when resettlers were enabled to share in the immediate benefits created by the every project that displaced them. Examples include helping resettlers develop aquaculture

and fisheries in the new reservoirs (Indonesia), moving them into the newly irrigated command areas (China, and some projects in India), or favouring them to cash in on the commercial opportunities created around the newly-constructed infrastructure (Argentina. China, Turkey).

It must be noted here that there are enormous variabilities of experience between projects and countries. Performance in income restoration is of particular concern in some countries, such as India and Indonesia, which have numerous projects entailing displacement, but do not have a countrywide policy or legal framework for resettlement with income restoration. Thus, some of the factors which account for the uneven performance of resettlement operations are: (i) compensation provisions and property acquisition practices do not provide enough resources to allow resettlers to purchase replacement lands and other assets; (ii) the overall financial resources earmarked for the resettlement often fall short, often by large amounts; (iii) the institutions charged with managing resettlement often lack the legal framework, mandate and skill needed to help resettlers and their hosts; and (iv) the affected and host communities are not adequately participating in the resettlement process. Local knowledge is rarely used in designing resettlement programmes or finding viable solutions. Effective legal mechanisms are often lacking. Top-down planning and weak institutional field presence exacerbate the problem.

Implication of World Bank's Policies in South Asia

In South Asia, the absence of national resettlement policies in countries like Pakistan and Nepal has been a key factor in preventing a systematic practical approach to planning resettlement. In India, where many resettlement operations in both non-bank and bank-assisted projects have failed to restore the living standards of many displaced people, (Ganguly Thukral and Singh, 1994). There is neither special federal legislation nor explicit policy statement to define the country's general resettlement norms. Most states in India still lack state level resettlement policies; they use expropriation laws which provide for compensation only but do not provide for socio-economic rehabilitation.

Of the 14 states in which bank-financed projects were under implementation during that year, only three states have statewide

R&R policies and five states have government orders regarding resettlement. There are both growing bottom up demand and increasing official recognition in India, that a shift towards a full-fledged socio-economic approach to resettlement issues, rather than an eminent domain expropriation approach, is necessary and must be formally instituted as part of the country's formal policies and legal frameworks. (Joshi, 1991; Dhagamwar, 1989; Mathur, 1994; Ganguly Thukral and Singh, 1995). According to Joshi (1991), when following needs are realized, resettlement operations will be much better.

1. There is a strong need for developing a R&R policy and a well-endowed machinery to implement the policies.
2. However, a policy alone cannot determine the R&R outcome. A review of a number of irrigation projects shows that, though the R&R programme related to the displacement caused by the irrigation project was governed by the same policy framework, the outcomes were significantly different (Parasuraman, 1994). The action of the implementing agencies are required to be welfare-oriented.
3. Experience from the Sardar Sarovar and other industrial, irrigation and power projects show that large-scale displacement, specific to the nature of project, cannot be sustained. The very fact that the three state governments involved in Sardar Sarovar project have three different policies with differing entitlements to the displaced, though people are displaced by one dam. Uniform policy is needed.

When the effects of development activities, determinates for the poor and the downtrodden, efforts should be made to bear the cost of their livelihoods and safeguard life-supporting modes of their economy. Since development projects are a necessity, the rehabilitation and resettlement policies are even more necessary and significant to achieve the common good of the displaced people.

Implications of World Bank Policy in India

Recognizing the adverse impact on human beings, the sufferings and hardships caused by involuntary settlement, the World Bank Policy states as its first requirement, that "whenever feasible, the involuntary resettlement must be avoided or minimized and alternative developmental solutions must be explored" (Cernea, 1988). Notwithstanding this policy, there have been cases, when projects have been designed and approved without examining such possible alternatives. Lack of provision of psycho-sociological consideration in the Land Acquisition Law 1894 and also Land Acquisition Amendment Act 1894, further weakens the implementation of the Bank Policy. Though rehabilitation has normally been envisaged as a planned change effort, evidences suggest that implementation of each project, called for an ad hoc policy of its own. The Bank Policy can be made effective only, if a well-defined National Policy is designed. Introducing of psycho-sociological perspective in the Land Acquisition Law will also greatly enhance the efficacy of Bank Policy. Therefore, the need for a well-defined national policy is a first pre-requisite for effective implementation of resettlement and rehabilitation projects (Sinha, 2006).

It is very well realized that loss of Common Property Resources (CPRs) results in economic, social and cultural dispossession and impoverishment for the oustees, especially the CPR dependants. For poor households in rural India, particularly the landless and other assetless communities, including women, the CPRs have always been a critical source of basic livelihood. Fruit and other edible forest produce, firewood and deadwood for use and sale, common grazing areas, use of public quarries, and medicinal herbs account for a significant share of a poor household's resources. Thus, the loss of the CPRs results in a major income loss or increase in expenditure.

Social disorganization takes place with the type of changes that are brought about by the displacement process. These forces lead to major changes in the social structure of the communities in general and especially of tribal societies. Their family life may be disrupted. The traditional social control mechanisms may be weakened and even lost. Consequently, social tensions may increase. Also social support networks tend to disintegrate and that has far-reaching consequences for the community. Social networks often help people cope with poverty through personalized strategies such as informal loans, exchange of food, clothing, durable goods, mutual help with farming, building houses and caring for children. Loss of such multifunctional, yet virtually invisible social networks through displacement acts as a hidden but serious cause of impoverishment through displacement. Such loss is higher in projects that relocate people in a dispersed manner rather than in social groups and units. In such cases, it is very difficult for the oustees to reconstitute similar social structures and networks.

R&R Policy in India

India in the early 1980s has witnessed a sensitization towards the ever growing and all pervasive problems of resettlement and rehabilitation. Opinions of the donor agencies as well as national and international organizations concerned with the social cause, shifted towards protection of human rights. As a result, there was hue and cry favouring the enactment of a sound national resettlement and rehabilitation policy in India, ingenious enough to solve the problems of the oustees. As such, efforts are constantly made towards the composition of such a national policy (Verma, 2004).

Despite large-scale displacement of people by various development projects since independence the country lacks a comprehensive resettlement and rehabilitation policy. It was in 1993 that the Ministry of Rural Development drafted a national rehabilitation policy. In the Indian federal structure, resettlement is a state issue, but only a few state governments have come out with a comprehensive R&R policy to resettle project affected people (Kothari, 1996). Draft of a national resettlement policy has been the subject of widespread consultation amongst state governments and within the NGO community in many parts of the country. This discussion has focused on dealing with displacement from forest and common property resources, as well as on general displacement. Discussions on a national policy have been taking place for several years. In 1989, a National Working Group on Displacement was formed through an NGO initiative. This also involves government officials and a draft national policy on developmental resettlement of project affected persons was prepared. Since then, four drafts have been prepared encompassing an ever-widening group of people—from 'oustees' of 'river valley projects,' to 'persons affected by reservoir projects,' and now to the 'rehabilitation of persons displaced as a consequence of acquisition of land'.

The Ministry of Rural Development prepared the draft of a national policy for rehabilitation of persons displaced as a consequence of land acquisition. Responsibility for the progress of government discussions now lies with the Ministry of Rural Areas and

Employment, which has been designated as the nodal ministry. This shift in responsibility is perhaps one indication that there is a recognition that the responsibility for successful R&R cannot really be given to one particular ministry only but is central to the agendas of many. The current draft has been circulated to 15 ministries, including finance, water resources, social welfare, environment and forests, power, coal, home and surface transport, as well as to the Planning Commission. This document has been the text used by the NGO community over the past years to put together a draft alternative after widespread regional discussion. This draft alternative has been submitted to the Ministry of Rural Areas and Employment for their consideration.

Some states and autonomous organizations have formulated their specific R&R policy under the pressure from donor agencies. But in the absence of a national policy, ad hoc and part time measures are being adopted, treating similar cases with different procedures, which are the breeding grounds for discrimination.

The draft emphasizes equity, fairness, justice and equality on the distribution of burdens and benefits. The draft recognizes the right to settle and reside in any part of the country, the special rights of tribals, the customary rights to common property resources of those dependent on the forests, and also those classified as 'encroachers'. It recognizes that the 'displaced' are actually 'uprooted from the soil'. It emphasizes the need to ensure rehabilitation in any displacement process and stresses the need to ensure that the displaced persons actively participate in their own rehabilitation. There is also recognition that the adverse impacts of involuntary displacement are much wider than those just associated with loss of land.

It is formulated on the expectation that future developments will increase rather than decrease the pace of displacement, as more and more land is required for infrastructure expansion. As per the revised Land Acquisition Act, it is indicative that R&R is likely to remain as an imperative activity, which has to be undertaken prior to developments.

An analysis portrays that the government is absolutely serious about the rights of the victims of various development projects and their duties towards the sufferers. But a closer look at the vicious problem brings out an entirely different picture of the situation. To date there is no national resettlement and rehabilitation policy in India. The process of formulation of a national policy was kicked off way back in 1989. Since then, the policy is under discussion in various offices. Complex bureaucratic procedure and the involvement of more than one agency responsible for the finalization of the policy have complicated the whole issue. Since several ministries share the load, no one seems to be serious about the agenda and the purpose behind such an important law favouring the rights of the displaced. It is still assumed that the efforts made towards rehabilitation are ad hoc, reactionary, charitable and do not address the rights of the victims. The whole issue of negligence and apathy towards the problem can well be exemplified by the fact that since last 15 years, nothing concrete has taken place and recommendations are still on paper only (Verma, 2004).

The rehabilitation policies that have been in preparation for two decades have gone through at least four drafts; each of them has been an improvement over the previous one. Fernandes (2004) has described the process in detail.

In February 2004, the Government of India promulgated the National Rehabilitation Policy for Project Displaced Persons. The policy stipulates that landowning project-affected families (PAF) will be given land for land, subject to a maximum of one hectare of irrigated or two hectares of unirrigated land, subject to availability of revenue or waste land in the district. Other provisions relate to house and other benefits. The landless who lose their house will be given a new site free and the families below the poverty line will be given Rs 25,000 for building a house also. There are also provisions for granting some minimum agricultural wages to the affected families and Rs 10,000 for building shop. In this respect, Fernandes (2004) observes, "The policy makes no distinction between the type of projects and their size. It offers a few shops to justify massive land acquisition. It finds a face saving exit by limiting its application to projects displacing more than 500 families".

The draft national policy has been revised and now implemented. However, for specific projects, packages and guidelines are accepted. It is stated that the PAPs should be free to negotiate, and quick payment of compensation has to be encouraged. Resettlement should be treated as part of the project itself, and the welfare and development of the PAPs should be a precondition. It should be the responsibility of the acquiring authority to establish that the proposed project is the best among available alternatives to achieve the given objectives, with minimum displacement. Further, the concept of comprehensive rehabilitation and reasonable settlement should be adopted while preparing and executing R&R plans.

The definition of project should cover every activity, public, semi-public or private, which results in acquisition of land or displacement or disturbs the habitat and way of people. All persons whose source of livelihood, place of residence or other property is affected notwithstanding the legal status enjoyed by them in relation to the concerned location, resource base for their livelihood and subsistence, shall be deemed to be project affected persons.

Judiciary on R&R

The judiciary in India has taken much initiative in ensuring a proper R&R policy for the project affected people. The provision in the law for representative petitions, which enables the grouping together of rights of persons similarly situated, and public interest litigation provide relatively easy access to courts, and acknowledge the existence of a community of interest. The provisions in the law for representative petitition, which enables the groupings together of rights of persons similarly situated and Public Interest Litigation (or Social Action Litigations is more appropriately termed) (Baxi, 1988). The reliefs that the courts have been petitioned to provide range from the scrapping of projects as they are based on a misconception of what is in the public good; to halting project work till the displaced are rehabilitated in a manner that does not treat them as a cost of the project; to hold the project authorities to the promises made in their endeavour to find acceptability during the planning process; to assert a right to spaces for participation in the process; to considerations of equity, and for infusing into the process of displacement a recognition that there are fundamental rights which are non-negotiable. Even where eminent domain and public purposes may be invoked; or for enhancement within the law of compensation which will make the compulsory exchange less inconsonant with justice (Ramanathan, 1996).

The reasoning of the court is influenced by the statute. The displaced, whose rights have been represented but marginally in the law, have had to resort to the assurances of policy; and policy has no more than persuasive effect. Also, courts are reluctant to adjudicate on the exigencies of policy implementation. Acquisition, on the other hand, is a well entrenched state power, reiteratively reinforced by the judiciary.

The NTPC policy for rehabilitation, for instance, was the basis of directions which went out from the court on how displacement was to be effected, and the displaced treated. [Banwasi Seva Ashram v State of Uttar Pradesh (1992)]. There is, however, no right to the promises of policy. The test firing range near Itarsi uprooted tribals. Rehabilitation of the displaced tribals apparently failed. By the government's own admission, 81 persons had lost their lives between 1972 and 1993. The unanswered questions about displacement and rehabilitation continued unaddressed. [Sudeep Mazumdar v State of Madhya Pradesh 1994 Supp 2 SCC 327].

State Level Policies

Till now, there are four states which have enacted statewise R&R policies namely Maharashtra, Madhya Pradesh, Punjab and Karnataka. Another state has developed a sector specific R&R policy, which is West Bengal Coal mining areas. Apart from that, four other states (Andhra Pradesh, Tamil Nadu, Orissa and Gujarat) have issued government orders/resolutions. The Government of Maharashtra has developed a progressive policy to deal with people not successfully rehabilitated under previous water projects.

Three state governments have so far passed laws to this effect so that project affected persons can be resettled or rehabilitated after displacement. Initially, no distinction was made between resettlement and rehabilitation. The two concepts were used interchangeably. This confusion can be seen when we go through the Law of Resettlement of Project Displaced Persons in Madhya Pradesh, 1985, The Maharashtra Rehabilitation of Project Affected Persons, 1986, and The Karnataka Rehabilitation Act, 1987. Except Orissa, the other states in India do not have any policy on R&R. The industrial and mining projects have their own policy on R&R.

Sector-Specific Policies

There are also companywise, and sector specific policies, such as those developed by the National Thermal Power Corporation and Coal India Ltd. which reflect upon policy issues. It has been observed that creating of alternative productive assets for PAPs on a sustainable basis remains the biggest challenge before the projects or NGOs. Many state governments and ongoing projects like mining or those of the NTPC have evolved their own R&R policies, which incorporate all possible components of a good R&R but rehabilitation remains as elusive as ever. Though some praiseworthy work is visible in the Singrauli NTPC project or training in carpet weaving by the Rihand NTPC project, these are not enough to rehabilitate the affected families. Likewise, several skill upgradation and training programmes for the young are initiated by some projects, and the trained PAPs again expect the project to provide them with regular jobs. The result is that the initial enthusiasm to train PAPs soon turns into a liability for the projects.

The need towards a policy received acknowledgement in the plan of various organizations. National Thermal Power Corporation and Coal India have prepared their own policies. Power Grid Corporation is in the process of doing the same. The Government of Orissa has prepared a policy to be issued in water resource developments in the state. Other projects, such as the Tamil Nadu Urban Development Project, and the Bombay Urban Transport Project have prepared their own project-specific policies. Those urban projects aim to address issues such as 'illegal encroachment', rights of tenants and of absentee landlords.

Orissa and Rajasthan have policies for water resource projects. The policy of Orissa was promulgated in 1994 and of Rajasthan in 1997. The state of Orissa has formulated a policy for the persons displaced by industry. Land for land is considered as the main method and it also includes provision for providing free of cost transport to the new site. R&R provisions for Rajasthan do not provide land for land but permit it as a welfare measure. There is a provision for allotment of a homestead plot.

Rehabilitation of PAPs

Thus, due to the lack of a detailed and comprehensive R&R policy, the process of resettlement and rehabilitation of uprooted people has been minimal and not very successful (Morse and Berger, 1992). Because of the dismal record of resettlement, government and project authorities do not view resettlement as their responsibility. Resettlement plans are not properly designed. The plans are not based on sociological studies which could indicate the social problem of the people to be resettled. The authorities do not make proper efforts for resettlement and rehabilitation. The opportunities provided to the affected people to register their grievances are merely theoretical. In practice, they have very little chance to question the awards.

Main objective of the rehabilitation should be to restore to good condition and to recognize the rights of the persons concerned.

In urban areas, the acquisition of land does not require displacement of all residents from all parts of the land acquired. The R&R should recognize that the displaced and affected people have the right to the benefits because they are sacrificing their way of life and have paid for the urban development. Providing facilities and opportunities to them means the right of their development as well as of the urban areas.

Basic Principles and Alternatives

Explaining the economic perspectives on resettlement and rehabilitation, Goyal (1996) highlights some of the principles for resettlement and rehabilitation.

Cash for Land

This is the principle of compensation on which the Land Acquisition Act 1894 is based. It identifies one particular dimension of deprivation (land dispossession) and proceeds to put a price on it, which is market-based. In a sense, it is the narrowest interpretation of loss, and completely eschews structure and process.

Parasurama (1994), identifies factors that have generally been important with respect to the proper use of more adequacy of compensation; help to the people in making prudent investments; and investment opportunities. As has been noted above, there is often undervaluation of land acquired and the sum paid cash for land principle is inadequate for people to rehabilitate themselves on their own. Empirical studies suggest that house repair and construction are major categories of expenditure. People use the money given in lieu of and on house construction over and above the money paid for homesteads because of inadequate compensation.

Land for Land

The land-for-land principle is particularly pertinent in the case of tribal areas, where rights to land may rest with the community rather than individuals. Land markets are generally weak or non-existent in such contexts and it is difficult to assign a value to land based on its market price. The absence of well-defined private property rights in land also makes it difficult to decide who has a rightful claim to compensation. The land-for-land principle, aside from its other advantages, obviates these difficulties.

Job Opportunity

Getting a 'regular job' in the project remains the single most important factor influencing the whole process of R&R. For PAPs, the main demand (and aspiration) is a regular job in the project. Most projects being hi-tech do not have many low-skilled jobs to rehabilitate the PAPs. Those few jobs like health worker, gardener, canteen boy, security staff (in the project township) and sweeper are also not offered by projects on a regular basis, due to the recent trend of awarding such jobs on 'contractual basis' for reducing the overhead costs. This creates bitterness among the PAPs who consider the projects as anti-PAPs. The projects also avoid extending a firm commitment to PAPs about the quota of regular jobs to be awarded to PAPs.

Standard of Living

Income restoration (or livelihood replacement), it is argued, tops the priority list of the displaced persons. The focus on income restoration is also seen as a rational response to the widely observed impoverishment of project-affected persons. Cernea (1998), while comparing the findings of several empirical studies, found that the ultimate common underlying broad spectrum of reported displacement consequences is the onset of impoverishment (Mathur, 1995).

Bargaining Approach

This approach involves giving the displaced persons a right to refuse displacement and leaving it to project authorities to put forward a rehabilitation package which the displaced persons find acceptable. This is the most obvious way of giving the displaced persons bargaining power that would make it possible for them to negotiate substantial share of project benefits.

Right of Livelihood

Right to livelihood is a constitutional right. Under Article 21 of the Constitution of India, the right to life includes the right to livelihood. This is a very important right conferred by the Constitution because no person can survive without means of livelihood. That, which alone makes it possible to live, must be deemed an integral component of the right to life. If the right to livelihood is not treated as a part of the constitutional right to life, the easiest way of depriving a person of his right to life would be to deprive him of his means of livelihood to the point of abrogation. Such deprivation would not only make life devoid of its effective content and full meaning, but it would also make life impossible.

Land Acquisition Act

Singh et al. (1992) say: "In the absence of a Central Act on Displacement and rehabilitation, the whole process of dealing with the issue of displacement remains ad hoc and piecemeal, even today." Again they nullified the utility of Land Acquisition Act of 1894 and its amended form of 1984 by saying that, "the process of acquisition remains meaningless to the illiterate masses since they are unaware of any notices that are issued until they receive their individual notice. By then it is too late to exercise their limited rights under the Amendment Act 1984."

Land Acquisition Act should be used to calculate social cost of all resources which will be destroyed or put to alternative use—land, air, water, forest, wasteland, even individual trees. The social cost/replacement value or even irreplaceable value should be given as compensation. This will be probably so high that it will deter mindless, wasteful acquisition and lead to more economic, almost miserly use of resources (Dhagamwar, 1989).

Role of NGOs

The policies and practices of the state came under scrutiny with the social movements and work of NGOs with DPs. The social movements and the NGOs primarily emphasized the perspectives of gender, equity and recognition of rights of women, children and old people. They examined the existing norms for the policies, practices and the role of the state and criticized them because they further marginalized or victimized displaced families. The attention of the NGO movement, particularly those concerned with tribal rights, as well as that of some donors, has been drawn to the issues surrounding displacement, because of increased interest in matters of sustainability and human rights. These focused during early 1990s around the Sardar Sarovar Project.

Consequences for Women and Downtrodden

In the past, when a family was displaced, compensation was paid mostly in cash or kind as against the immovable property. Compensation was generally paid to the adult male member of a family. There was no special consideration for women, children or old persons in the family. The category of women 'female headed household' was neglected and the woman had to suffer even greater hardships along with her children and other dependants. Consequently, there was significant deterioration in the quality of life of women, children and old people. Irrespective of the patrilineal or matrilineal system, the ownership of property largely remained with the male member of the family. Women were denied their right over family property, as they have not been seen as an equal owner of the property. Women lost control over land and Community Property Resources as well as Natural Resources along with other assets, and consequently, they were further marginalized within the family.

With very little information available about the impact of displacement on the quality of life of women, children and old people, more emphasis was given to understand their needs and concerns. Based on the understanding of their needs, one of the remedies suggested and accepted is the participation of these members in R&R plans at all levels.

According to Kothari (1996), PAPs are not a uniform category. Prior to displacement, they were divided on social, economic and gender basis. Accordingly, post-displacement experiences also vary and are influenced by their pre-displacement statuses. Those with sizeable lands or educational/occupational skills and are younger are at a distinct advantage compared with the marginal farmers or unskilled labourers (mostly the SCs/STs). Those who succeed in converting their compensation money into productive assets (like operating a shop, tractor/trolley for contract work or purchasing land for land), in fact, gain from the displacement. The same holds true for those few lucky ones who get regular jobs in the project. The gainers are, in fact, the most vocal against the project. The left out either wait indefinitely for a job and other benefits from the project, or become reconciled to their fate. Women, the aged and marginalized are the main sufferers and need priority in any rehabilitation programme.

Issues

Resettlement and rehabilitation issues need to be taken far more seriously than they have been in the past. So far, R&R has tended to be considered as some kind of 'externality' development projects, and investment in R&R has been minimized. This approach has led to widespread impoverishment of project-affected persons, and also to conflict between them and project authorities that have had extremely high financial and human costs. It is in this context that we have set out a case for a national policy on resettlement and rehabilitation.

Baviskar (2004) has put forward issues of tribals affected in the Narmada valley. There are various searching questions about the whole NBA struggle and whether they had made the correct choices, now that they saw themselves surrounded by water. While no one expects anyone to change their minds about the inherently problematical nature of resettlement, the set of options and limitations—the calculus in terms of which people evaluate situations, both strategically and morally—has shifted in some ways, opening up some new options, and closing down others. At present there is a debate going on about the development and resettlement. A common ground has to be explored in the policy where development goes on along with the welfare of the displaced. A new approach may force the government to put severe controls over what constitutes public purpose and certain type of acquisition could be prevented.

Urban Policy in Mumbai

There is no specific policy for the people affected by the land acquisition in urban areas. In such a situation, in urban areas the authorities may negotiate with villagers to share their problems. During the process of resettlement, they should take care of the common civic amenities including schools, health, transport for the affected families. When land is acquired for use as dumping ground for industrial waste, industries must be asked to find ways of minimizing industrial waste and then of disposing or recycling that small quantity.

In all our cities, housing colonies are constructed for betterment of the people. No eviction should be allowed for this purpose. Sometimes, builders share the land with original resident. Two examples can be given here. In Andheri, a suburb Mumbai, slum dwellers were given space equal to what they had, but built up with high plinth, which protected them from flooding. This came to not more than 300 sq ft. They were also given water and electricity connections. From the first floor upwards two bed room flats were constructed and sold at market prices. In Pune, half the space covered by a sprawling slum was used for building three storey tenements and rest of the space was used for constructing multistoried apartments. In both cases the builders made their profits. Needless to say, in such situations interaction between the families is inevitable and is a healthy bonus. Neither side remains a dark mystery, to be feared and hated. A policy of compensation, with a welfare approach in R&R should be adopted in urban areas.

Policy for Land Acquisition in Urban Areas

Land in urban areas is acquired under the provisions of Land Acquisition Act 1894. Mainly agricultural lands are acquired for urban development. A notification is issued in the newspapers and in state gazette. The awards for compensation are issued to the affected persons. Compensation is given in monetary form. Only in some cases, house plots are allotted at a reserved price. No resettlement and rehabilitation measures are taken. The affected persons have to make their own efforts for relocation and rehabilitation.

The process of land acquisition, resettlement and rehabilitation adopted for development of Navi Mumbai could be taken as a model for framing the polices for resettlement and rehabilitation in urban areas (see Box 7.1).

Because of R&R measures adopted by the CIDCO, the migration from old villages could be restricted. Allotment of 12.5 per cent developed land improved their economic status. Training and employment opportunities provided them better occupational avenues. The Gaothan Extension Scheme could retain a part of the old villages. Further, environmental concerns were also taken into consideration. Several people started building material shops to fulfil the demands of building industries. Being organized and locally influential, they took advantage of the situation.

Box 7.1

Resettlement and Rehabilitation in Navi Mumbai

For development of Navi Mumbai, 344 sq km of land was acquired under the Land Acquisition Act 1894. This included mainly agricultural land and salt pan lands. Main responsibility was undertaken by the city and Industrial Development Corporation (CIDCO) of Maharashtra.

Special Land Acquisition Officers were appointed by the Maharashtra Government. The compensation was determined as per government rate, which was according to market prices prevailing at the time of land acquisition. They were also given 12.5 per cent of their developed land. Agreement for rehabilitation measures was made between the CIDCO and Zamin Bachao Samiti. It paved a way for further land acquisition.

Rehabilitation measures included occupational training of the inhabitions of the project area with payment of stipend. Provision was made for financial assistance of college education and technical training for the needy children of PAPs and necessary assistance in free education, books and scholarship. Efforts were made to increase their income from non-agricultural sources. Some provisions were made to meet out the needs of affected villages and their development

CIDCO developed the existing villages in the form of improved Gaothans. Ten per cent of the village land was allotted for Gaothan Extension Scheme. About half of this land was used for development of roads, drainage, open space and social facilities. Basic services and alternative sources of income were generated for people affected by land acquisition. Several people were provided employment by the CIDCO.

The case Navi Mumbai shows R&R measures could be affectedly taken under the existing provisions. In this context, Deshmukh (2001) rightly observes, "If we consider the benefits given to PAPs under various welfare and rehabilitation measures, there is no need for a separate rehabilitation policy. On the contrary no other project in Maharashtra or even in India would have offered so many benefits to PAPs under the rehabilitation measures. No other project would have taken care from all angles as has been done in the case of PAPs under Navi Mumbai project." Where there is a will, there is a way.

The Rehabilitation and Resettlement Bill, 2007

Bill 98 of 2007 aims to provide for the rehabilitation and resettlement of persons affected by the acquisition of land for project of public purpose or involuntary displacement due to any other reason, and for matters connected therewith or incidental thereto. It has to be enacted by Parliament of the Republic of India and shall come into force after publication of the notification.

The provision of this Act shall apply to the rehabilitation and resettlement of persons affected by acquisition of land under the Land Acquisition Act, 1894 or any other Act of the Union or a State for the time being in force; or involuntary displacement of people due to any other reason.

Objects and reasons described for the Act are as follows:

1. Provision of public facilities or infrastructure often requires the exercise of powers by the State for acquisition of private property leading to displacement of people, depriving them of their land, livelihood and shelter, restricting their access to traditional resource base and uprooting them from their socio-cultural environment. These have traumatic, psychological and socio-cultural consequences on the affected population which call for protecting their rights, in particular of the weaker sections of the society including members of the Scheduled Castes, the Scheduled Tribes, marginal farmers and their families.
2. There is an imperative need to recognize rehabilitation and resettlement issues as intrinsic to the development process formulated with the active participation of affected persons and families. Additional benefits beyond monetary compensation have to be provided to families affected adversely by involuntary displacement. The plight of those who do not have rights over the land on which they are critically dependent for their subsistence is even worse. This calls for a broader concerted effort on the part of the planners to include in the displacement, rehabilitation and resettlement process framework, not only those who directly lose land and other assets but also all those who are affected by such acquisition of assets. The displacement process often poses problems that make it difficult for the affected persons to continue their old livelihood activities after resettlement. This

requires a careful assessment of the economic disadvantages and the social impact of displacement. There must also be a holistic effort aimed at improving the all-round living standards of the affected people and families.

3. A National Policy on Resettlement and Rehabilitation for Project Affected Families was formulated in 2004, which came into force with effect from February, 2004. Experience gained in implementation of this policy indicates that there are many issues addressed by the policy which need to be reviewed. There should be a clear perception, through a careful quantification of the costs and benefits that will accrue to society at large, of the desirability and justifiability of each project. The adverse impact on affected families—economic, environmental, social and cultural—must be assessed in participatory and transparent manner. A national rehabilitation and resettlement framework thus needs to apply to all projects where involuntary displacement takes place.
4. The aim is to minimize large-scale displacement, as far as possible. However, where large numbers of families are affected, it must be mandatory to do social impact assessments and provide all required infrastructural facilities and amenities in the resettlement area. More particularly, where the Scheduled Tribes people are being displaced in sizeable numbers, a well thought out Tribal Development Plan must be put in place. Furthermore, such a policy must specify clear timeframes within which the implementation of the rehabilitation package as well as utilization of the land shall be accomplished. Also it should lay down an effective monitoring and grievance redressal mechanism.
5. The National Rehabilitation and Resettlement Policy, 2007 has been formulated on these lines to replace the National Policy on Resettlement and Rehabilitation for Project Affected Families, 2003. The new policy has been notified in the Official Gazette and has become operative with effect from the 31st October, 2007. Since the inception of Land Acquisition Act, 1894 for the first time a legislation namely, the Rehabilitation and Resettlement Bill, 2007 has been developed on the lines of the provisions of the new policy, so as to give a statutory backing to them and provide for Social Impact Assessment, making of scheme and plans well defined rehabilitation and resettlement benefits for the affected families.

6. Many state governments have their own rehabilitation and resettlement policies. Many public sector undertakings or agencies also have their own policies in this regard. The Rehabilitation and Resettlement Bill, 2007 provides for the basic minimum requirements that all projects leading to involuntary displacement must address. The Bill contains a saving clause to enable the state governments, public sector undertakings or agencies, or other requiring bodies to continue to provide or put in place greater benefit levels than those prescribed under the Bill.
7. The Rehabilitation and Resettlement Bill, 2007 will be primarily applicable to the rehabilitation and resettlement of persons adversely affected by the acquisition of lands for projects. However, involuntary displacement of people may be caused by other factors also, and the provisions of the Bill may apply to the rehabilitation and resettlement of persons involuntarily displaced permanently due to any reasons.
8. In brief, the Rehabilitation and Resettlement Bill, 2007 will provide for the basic minimum that all projects leading to involuntary displacement must address the grievances of the affected persons. A social impact assessment of proposals leading to displacement of large populations through a participatory, informed and transparent process involving all stake-holders, including the affected persons will be necessary before these are acted upon. The rehabilitation process would augment income levels and enrich quality of life of the displaced persons, covering rebuilding sociocultural relationships, capacity building and provision of public health and community services. Adequate safeguards have been proposed for protecting rights of vulnerable sections of the displaced persons.

The Land Acquisition (Amendment) Bill, 2007

A Bill further to amend the Land Acquisition Act, 1894 is to be enacted by Parliament of the Republic of India.

The provisions of the Rehabilitation and Resettlement Act, 2007 shall apply in respect of acquisition of land by the appropriate Government under this Act.

In this Act, the expression "person interested" includes:

1. all persons claiming an interest in compensation to be made on account of the acquisition of land under this Act;

2. tribals and other traditional forest dwellers, who have lost any traditional rights recognised under the Scheduled Tribes and Other Traditional Forest Dwellers (Recognition of Forest Rights) Act, 2006;
3. a person interested in an easement affecting the land; and
4. persons having tenancy rights under the relevant State laws.

The expression "cost of acquisition" includes:

1. compensation awarded including the solatium and other amount and interest payable thereupon:
2. demurrage to be paid for damages caused to the land and standing crops in the process of acquisition;
3. cost of acquisition of out-project land for settlement of displaced or adversely affected families;
4. cost of development of infrastructure and amenities at resettlement sites;
5. additional cost of resettlement as may be required after admissible adjustment of rehabilitation and resettlement cost against compensation awarded to affected persons or families;
6. administrative cost of acquisition of land including both in-project and out-project areas lands; and
7. administrative cost involved in planning and implementation of resettlement and rehabilitation packages for providing physical rehabilitation and resettlement to the entitled and interested families, displaced or adversely affected on account of in-project acquisition of land.

Eight

Sociological Perspective on Urban Dynamics and Displacement

In the years following independence, urban areas are considered as potent avenues of expansion and regeneration of modern India. The process of urbanization has led to transformation in the social, economic and cultural lives of people. Although, the country is predominately rural, the increasing rate of urbanization is a dominant indicator of development. Generally, urbanization is explained through population changes and movement of people from rural to urban areas. Now, spatial and functional aspects have been included in the dichotomies of urbanization. It is realized that it involves basic changes in the behaviour and social values of the people.

There are some issues related to industrial development, population increase and service growth in the context of urbanization. Expansion of industries in urban areas sometime becomes a major cause of population concentration and subsequently, the factories are to be shifted to distant areas. The population concentration also results in creation of slums and unauthorized construction. The service sector and infrastructure facilities are lacking in cities. These are the results of unplanned growth of cities. There has been increasing population pressure on urban areas, which are ill-equipped to sustain it.

Classification of the cities depends on their prominent features. Cities grow initially according to agglomeration of economy and multi-centred urban structures. Gradually, the smaller towns grow into large and intermediate towns. The postulates of urbanization (Geyer and Kontuly, 1993) are in the forms of primate city, intermediate city and small city. Other forms are large cities, mega cities or Million cities. Million cities have relatively high population growth and some of them are fast growing in recent years. Due to congestion and crowding, the urban sprawl moves into the adjoining area.

Rural and urban areas depend on each other. Urban areas provide services for marketing of agricultural products, educational and health services. The recent trends of privatization and liberalization have benefited the cities more compared with towns; and the towns compared with villages.

The process of urbanization explains the nature of city growth, spatial pattern and mobility. Urbanism is now seen as a way of life and phenomena of city residence. Theories of postmodernism have provided a fresh approach to urban phenomena. It is based on radical break with the past. It could be possible only when we resolve the problems of congestion and delivery of service in urban areas. The emerging problems are centred on the safety and security of urbanizers. The traditional habitat, ways of transportation and communication require a total revamping of urban structure. This poses the question, whether the growth of urban centres should be restricted or limited on the basis of emerging structures.

The problem of urban population varies according to their scale and intensity of population growth and density. The prime cause of the population boom in the city is migration. Due to this pressure, the water supply, sewerage drainage system fails to cope up with the requirements. The city roads become unfit for supporting the large traffic flows. Rapid development led to population redistribution and changes the shape of cities. The city requires expansion. Consequently, agricultural land has to be transformed into residential and industrial land. There are several cases of unauthorized construction and encroachment. Public land is wrongly acquired for private purposes. Further, there are problems of slums. The problems are likely to degenerate the community networks and transform them into an alienated form of urban development.

Land acquired for urban development displaces agriculturists, poor and tribal people residing at the fringe areas of the city. There is always a need to acquire more and more land for residential colonies, industries, educational institutions, offices, tourist resorts, roads and infrastructural facilities. Large areas of land are acquired but the problems of evacuees' resettlement and rehabilitation are neglected.

How the way of life of the displaced households differs from that of city people and rural folk? Whether the change in residence and occupation has transformed their behavioural patterns? There are many more questions which need to be answered in the context of displacement.

Displacement of People

Oommen (2006) views displacement as development pathology. According to him, "As for displacement, it is explicitly recognized as a development pathology. Yet displacement is widely perceived as inevitable in the course of development. Thus, the rural is to be displaced by the urban and agriculture by industry, the simple or traditional technology by the high, complex or modern technology. However, a moment's reflection would unfold that what goes on is not only displacement but also accretion. The pathological obsession with a particular direction of 'development' and displacement it entails is playing havoc with people and hence the present spotlights on it".

It is now very well recognized that displacement unravels the patterns of social organization and production system. The acquired land had been a collective source of livelihood as agricultural labourers and service providers indirectly depended upon it. The displaced people undergo a process of disempowerment, as the status which was linked to ownership of land, is delated. They have to explore new occupational avenues in open market situation and search for a hearth in new social environment.

The problem of urbanization-induced displacement is different from the displacement caused by dam site industrial and infrastructure projects. In specific projects, the resettlement and rehabilitation costs could be part of project cost, whereas in case of the land acquired for urban development such costs are not covered. The government policies are restricted to the Acts of land acquisition, which provide for only monetary compensation.

Displacement in urban areas causes movement of people in surrounding areas, occupational change, and marginalization. The loss of access to common property, increased morbidity and mortality result into their downward mobility. Majority of the people affected by land acquisition were backward classes, Scheduled Castes and Scheduled Tribes. Their living conditions are deteriorated and it often produces social conflicts and tensions. The displaced live under the condition of deprivation and hardship.

The living condition of people affected by land acquisition in urban areas reveals that about one half of them are squatters; majority of them are without proper legal document about the land on which they reside. Majority of them were facing impoverishment although they were marginalized for the cause of development. The variations in living conditions are greater because of the zone (area) of land acquisition, their caste and class. Tribals had their traditional ways of living. These were disturbed because of shifting and scattering.

Methodology

The problem of displacement and resettlement is of critical nature and requires flexible approach. The people affected by land acquisition are on the move either for search of a new place for resettlement or for alternative occupational avenues. They have to adapt themselves with new forces. When they are planning to shift, they are in a transient situation. The remaining have readjusted themselves with smaller pieces of land in their possession.

In studies on displacement, the ethno surveys and multi-method data collecting techniques are considered appropriate. Since community linkages are to be explored, cluster network methodology is also relevant for the resettlement and rehabilitation study. Keeping in view the expansion of city from time to time, multi-stage cluster sampling method has been used. In six zones, 30 clusters were identified. While interviewing 10 respondents from each cluster, a total sample of 300 persons affected by land acquisition were included in the sample.

A semi-structured interview schedule was used in the study. For assessing the behavioural and situational change, a Likert type scale was administered. The use of local media reports and study of land acquisition notifications and office records was very helpful. The situation analysis of area of study and field observations provided insight into the major issues of displacement and the case studies provided qualitative information. An attempt was made to gather the views of leaders and officials.

Both qualitative and quantitative techniques have been used for the analysis of the data. These include content analysis of newspaper reports, case studies, focused interviews and scrutiny of documents. The descriptive survey data has been analyzed using frequencies, chi-square, mean and factor analysis.

Land Acquisition and Compensation

A major drawback in resettlement and rehabilitation is the inadequacy of institutional framework. The Land Acquisition Act provides for payment of only cash compensation and only to those who have a direct interest in the title to such land. The Act provides acquisition of land under a vaguely defined concept of public purpose. By limiting the entitlement to monetary compensation, the multiple dimensions of the loss of depression is not taken into account. It is well understood now by most of the agencies that the scope of the Act is very limited and its provisions are grossly inadequate.

From the absolutist point of view, the displaced cannot be adequately compensated for what they lose. There are social and cultural considerations when the whole 'way of life' is disturbed. However, it required that at least the standard of living of the displaced remain as high after the resettlement as it was before. This should include the aspects of social and cultural status along with the economic indicators.

Plurality of interacting entities is involved in effective resettlement and rehabilitation of the people affected by acquisition of land in urban areas. There are a number of organizations, departments and interest groups. These crucially impinge upon the requirements of the displaced—residentially or occupationally. This needs converting of segmental into comprehensive approach. There is an inherent tendency of R&R to limit to a narrow sequential and 'rules-linked' approach. This approach is generally observed in government departments or among the concerned functionaries. Often, there are accusations by one political party that its own failing has been due to the default of another party. Shifting of responsibilities often leads to accumulations of tensions.

The land acquiring agencies care more for their administrative convenience instead of paying attention on oustee's adjustment. The administrative procedures delay the process of land acquisition and payment of compensation. It creates more problems for the affected people when there is a long gap between the issue of urbanization for land acquisition and actual takeover of the land. Sometimes, the city level agencies find it difficult to implement the schemes because of the delays at the state level. The situation is also true in the reserve direction when state government grants approval and city authorities have no funds to pay compensation. In the absence of proper planning, the R&R programmes, stay as ad hoc arrangements, disjointed and uneven across different levels of the decision-making. Senior administrators take more time in imbibing the spirit and philosophy of R&R programme. It is imperative that all relevant, desired and naturally helpful communications flow among administrators, affected people and NGOs.

Utilization of Compensation

The prevalent way for compensating the people for acquisition of their land is cash for land. Although, the transactions are made through banks, yet it is a form of cash available to affected people. It could be utilized by them according to their needs, comforts and luxuries. It is possible for the educated people to utilize the compensated amount properly. On the other side, the poor uneducated agriculturists are likely to misutilize the amount. But the situation of displacement is critical. They have to struggle for resettlement, which forces them to take rational decisions.

The top priority of the people affected by land acquisition is purchase and construction of house. This is followed by purchase of land. A major portion of amount is kept as savings. This is a period when there are conflicts within the family and thus the some portion of the amount is divided among the family members. All this is followed by social needs including marriage and feasts. Children demand vehicles and means of entertainment. A little amount is also spent on alcoholism and addiction. In the process of resettlement, there was unplanned spending on several items.

The utilization of compensation is greatly affected by the area of land acquisition. The priorities of utilization change according to the period of displacement. Economic status and education are other factors influencing the patterns of utilization. Castewise variations are also seen in spending the amount of compensation. Classwise difference is significant in purchase of land and expenditure on construction or purchase of house. Some of the compensated persons have become entrepreneurs in the process of resettlement.

Nature of Social Conflicts

The conflict begins with the notifications of land acquisition and ends years after resettlement. Displacement is not limited to dislocation from the land; it is also displacement in social and occupational activities. Thus, there are tensions within the family also in the social sphere. The aggravated form of tension results in explicit agitations, struggles and movements supported by non-governmental organizations, political parties and leaders of caste, tribe and community. The government official threats, forcible evictions, shifting, search for new hearth, change in occupations, construction of house, purchase of land are the major problems. These combined together at one period of time dislodge the people affected by acquisition of land in urban areas.

The attitude of government authorities is apathetic. It lacks human perspective, lacks in planning and land acquisition. Involuntary resettlement leads to increased stress and health hazards. Local movement in urban area, migration and relocation result into psychological and social stress. When caste or tribe-based settlements are disturbed, these become a means of breakdown in community network. When people are displaced, their production systems are likely to be dismantled and links with customers are often severed.

Many of the displaced people had bitter experience with their hosts at the place of relocation. Interests of the state, land mafia and upper class of the society, and their attitude towards the problem of resettlement, are also the factors influencing the nature of social conflict. Sociological interventions could pave a way for conflict resolution.

Social tensions among the people affected by land acquisition vary according to the area of displacement and the agency dealing with payment of compensation. Tribal people are affected more than the other groups and their resistance is comparatively more aggressive. Although 'sangarsh samitis' are generally formed but these are not effective in urban areas. The affected people continue their agitations for better compensation deal. Awareness about the rights of the oustees has been increasing and now NGOs are coming forward to support their cause.

Social conflicts vary according to the nature of displacement and resettlement. The first category of relocated includes people who move to a new location after the acquisition of their land. The second category, termed as transient, includes those who are squatters and likely to move in future. The third category includes such people whose land has been acquired partially. They are stationary and continue to stay at the same place. There is a series of stages beginning from the issue of notification to the residential and occupational resettlement. Major conflicts and agitations were observed at the time of evacuation of the acquired land.

The squatters, tribal and persons devoid of proper land documents agitate vigorously than that of the others. Zonewise difference in formation of struggle committees was significant. The size of land acquired, caste and class do not affect the formation of the struggle committees, as majority of the people do not participate actively. Political leaders and NGOs gear up movements. The affected people plan to continue their agitation. With the result, government agencies use threats and force to get the area evacuated. During the process of resettlement, many people construct houses on unauthorized or agriculture land for which they fear to get ousted in future.

Urbanization and Social Change

Because of the haphazard growth of cities, their undesirable outcomes are increasing. Infrastructure facilities are lacking. The pressure of population has created problems of resources and organization. Urbanization is a boon for some of the rich who flourish. It is catastrophic for squatters and poor who are impoverished. Yet the cities are seen as a centre of employment, entertainment and amusement. The city life provides challenges, facilities for education and occupation and a source of fortune change. It attracts rural people who adopt urban way of life and subsequently find it difficult to readjust in rural areas. Because of the inflow of population and increasing density there is always a need to acquire land for urban development. This leads to displacement of several people. There is a tendency among the poor section of population to resettle on unauthorized or agricultural land. They hope that these will be regularized in future. It gives rise to unplanned growth and creation of slum areas. The social structure of the urban centres is continuously changing.

Social and Occupational Change

The consequences of land acquisition in urban areas are seen in the form of impoverishment and marginalization. The problems were more critical for those who were agriculturists, illiterate, aged and without the authorized document (patta) of their lands. Certain changes occur in their social and cultural life. Displacement not only affects change in habitat but also in livelihood resources and occupational activities. The agricultural mode of production was associated with traditional occupations economy and joint family. Adoption of the urban way of life and change to modern occupation and mobility gave rise to nuclear families. When land was acquired for development of roads, the affected persons took advantage of the situation, some of them started roadside commercial activities.

Change in the economy caused deterioration in their living conditions. Women were disturbed more; many of them had to work outside home. Tribal women were exposed to extramarital relations or prostitution. The transfer of rural areas in the urban administration set-up deprived them of participation in Panchayati Raj system. Change was also observed in indicators of the class, e.g., possession of land, monthly income, monthly expenditure, occasional expenditure, main occupation and their self-assessment of economic status. The economic status of the Scheduled Castes and Scheduled Tribes was lower than the general and other backward classes; land acquisition showed deterioration in their social status.

The people affected by land acquisition had to spend considerable amount on construction of house or purchase of land. Changes in their expenditure on family and social needs were also witnessed. More people were indulged in the labour market. There was an increase in the number of people starting their own business. The change revealed that the poor and displaced have become poorer. The change in movable assets was observed. The number of animals possessed by them decreased. The affected people not only suffered a deprivation from of natural and community resources, their income from subsidiary occupations was also reduced. In spite of it, they wanted to possess motorcycle, television and other sources of entertainment.

Behavioural and Situational Change

Some behavioural and situational changes were observed among the people affected by the acquisition of land in urban areas. Because of this phenomenon, there were trends of disintegration and quarrels in the families. Education of children suffered. There were considerable problems in marital affairs. The marriages and effective marriages (*Gauna*) were delayed. There were changes in nature of food, consumption of alcohol and other addictions. There was an increase in the expenditure on medicines.

There was avoidance in performance of social and religious rituals. Factor analysis revealed five dimensions of the behavioural change after the acquisition of land. These are: marriage and migration, living conditions, status symbols, morbidity, and addiction. For analysis of the problems of the displacement and resettlement, it is necessary to pay attention on these aspects.

Policy Implications

Resettlement and rehabilitation are understood as humane concerns in the context of social justice to the displaced people. United Nations guidelines provide a scope for identification of their rights and protection of their standard of living. World Bank, while implementing its projects, emphasizes minimization of displacement, participation of stakeholders, recognizing the rights of the victims of displacement and protection of the interests of the host populace. The World Bank also focuses on psychological, social and cultural factors including the problems of powerlessness and alienation. The policy gives importance to the welfare and development of the indigenous groups, ethnic minorities, pastoralists and other marginalized groups, such as women. It assures compensation for the loss of assets equivalent to the replacement cost. Further assistance with relocation and support during the transition period is also covered. Further, it specifies institutional arrangement for dealing with resettlement issues. The Bank Policies are seen as major guidelines in influencing polices of the various nations, reducing displacement and restoring income. Several nations in South Asia have focused their attention on the problems of the displaced because of international concern for resettlement and rehabilitation.

In India, the land is acquired under the provisions of Land Acquisition Act 1894. It deals mainly with the issues of monitory compensation. Although the Act has been amended, no significant change is witnessed in the direction of resettlement and rehabilitation. A national policy for rehabilitation of persons displaced, as a consequence of land acquisition, has been drafted but has not yet been implemented. The draft emphasizes equality, fairness, and justice in the distribution of burdens and benefits. In February 2004,

Government of India promulgated the National Policy for Project Displaced, which has provision of allotment of piece of the land to the affected persons. The policy provides some relief to the PAPs by granting them some other benefits. By and large the welfare approach in R&R is still missing.

There are some state laws and sectoral policies for the affected persons. In such cases, the PAPs get some more benefits. The state polices vary from state to state. The problems are observed in inter-state projects, where compensation packages vary from state to state. The judiciary in India has taken initiatives in ensuring proper compensation. It has also resolved conflicts between the state and the NGOs. The courts have provided relief in several cases.

Because of the dismal record of resettlement, the government and project authorities do not view resettlement as their responsibility. There are limited opportunities for the affected people to register their objections. The consequences of the present policies are adverse for the people affected by the acquisition of land.

The displacement in urban areas is increasing at an alarming rate. More and more villages are being included in the urban belt. The acquisition of land transforms their life. Many are subjected to impoverishment. Yet there are no specific guidelines for rehabilitating the affected people in urban areas. The model of resettlement and rehabilitation adapted by CIDCO in development of the township of Navi Mumbai is worth following. It has demonstrated that proper rehabilitation measures could be undertaken even under the present provisions of Land Acquisition Act.

Results Achieved

1. Mostly agriculture land is acquired for development of urban areas. It includes land for housing projects, public offices and institutions, industrial units and roads.
2. The affected population is mainly from agriculture sector and lower economic strata. The average land acquired per person is about six Bighas. Most of the land losers are illiterate or little educated. Very rarely, they had alternative sources of income. However, some have benefited by selling land to property dealers.
3. The notification for acquisition of land is issued by the Urban Development Department of the Government of Rajasthan,

Jaipur. Subsequently, the land is acquired by the Urban Improvement Trust. In some cases, the land is acquired by other government agencies for development of roads, industrial areas and civil facilities. The compensation paid for land was much lower than the prevailing market rate. In few cases, alternative residential land was allotted to the displaced households. Additional benefits given to outsees varied according the agency acquiring land.

4. Public authorities identify and issue notification for acquisition of large tracts of land on the periphery of the city for urban use on the basis of a Master Plan. The determination of compensation rate is done according to market price of the agriculture land. Now 30 per cent solatium is also granted. Even then, poor farmers are the losers in the absence of a resettlement and rehabilitation package. Because of agitation, political interference, legal complications and financial constraints, public authorities acquire lands several years after the notification. The private property dealers take advantage of this situation by developing colonies and getting the land converted into residential land. The intervention of dealers either delays the acquisition of land or benefit land mafia.
5. The private property dealers form housing societies and get the map of new colonies approved by the Urban Improvement Trust. The UIT instead of allotting land to the colonies, allot land to each landowner directly. Cooperative housing is not encouraged. The property dealers generally pay cash to the agriculturists and take their signatures on stamp papers. They sometimes cheat and take more land into their possession. In some cases, the payment is executed in gold also.
6. Many of the people affected by land acquisition spent large sum of money on house and land. The agriculturists who are well educated and business-oriented utilize the compensation amount properly and flourish. Yet, in several cases, their children purchase motorcycles and household goods. Some money is also spent on death feasts and marriages. There was slight increase in expenditure on liquor and drugs.
7. Behavioural and situational changes occur in change among the displaced households. Emotive and status aspects of family and marriages are changing along with the status of women. Their

health status is also deteriorated. Old age problems and mortality rate show some increase. Cultural changes are seen through participation in religious activities and death feasts. In the changed situation, the displaced tend to become addicted to alcoholism and gambling. During the process of resettlement, there appears a small family size and breakdown in joint family system. There is greater movement from place of residence to place of work along with migratory trends. More efforts were required for maintenance of standard of living. The agriculturists and illiterate suffered more than the educated and business class.

8. There are changes in the status of women. Their family and work roles are changed. Women work outside home for others. In cases of acquisition of agriculture land, they work as labourers. Young girls tend to discontinue education for supporting family. Few cases of indulgence in prostitution were also reported.
9. The government policies differ in resettlement and rehabilitation of the displaced persons. Only monitory compensation is paid for the land acquired. In some cases, alternative land or residential accommodation has been allotted on reserved prices. A large majority of the affected people suffer in various ways.
10. Nature of land acquisition and resettlement varies in large and mega cities. Several evacuees whose lands have been acquired are not spatially displaced. They continue to stay in the same vicinity. When the land was acquired for Navi Mumbai, the CIDCO took adequate resettlement and rehabilitation measures. They were allotted 12.5 per cent developed land. Once resettled, they have started commercial activities, e.g., sale of building material and household industries. They operate influentially in these areas.

The Testing of Hypothesis

Seven hypotheses were formulated at the beginning of this study. These were tested through field observations, focus interviews, case studies and descriptive sample survey. The results obtained in the context of these hypotheses are presented here.

1. *Social-physical situation of the people whose lands are acquired, is disrupted because of the shifting from the native place. The caste network supports them in resettlement at the new site.*

It has been observed that the social-physical situation of the people whose land is acquired is disrupted. But in urban areas, all of them are not required to shift from their native place. About 50 per cent were stationary, they stayed at the same place where they were located before the acquisition of land. About 15 per cent were in *transient* situation and were planning to shift in future. Nearly 35 per cent were *relocated.* Non-possession of proper document of the land (patta) was one of the major problems for several people. Many stayed in unauthorized houses or on non-converted land. The caste network was not supportive in resettlement. Occupational linkages were more relevant in this context.

2. *Major portion of the compensation amount is spent on fulfillment of social needs, e.g., death feasts and social ceremonies. There is also a tendency to purchase household equipment, vehicles and entertainment items.*

It is not true that major amount of compensation is spent on fulfillment of social needs. The people affected by acquisition of land give priority to their household needs. They spend more on construction of a house and purchase of land. Although some amount is spent on social needs but these do not have priority over the household needs. Because of the pressure from younger generation, they spend some amount on purchase of vehicles and entertainment items. Although the affected people do not maintain proper record of expenditure out of the compensation amount, but they are rational in their approach. However, property dealers and their relatives sometimes cheat illiterate and poor people, which leads to misutilization of compensation amount.

3. *Households receiving adequate compensation for the acquired property and occupational guidance invest major share for improving their occupational status either by modernizing working conditions or by occupational entrepreneurship.*

This hypothesis is relevant but lacks evidence from the existential conditions. Neither the compensation was considered adequate not there existed any formal system of occupational guidance. Informal channels of guidance did matter but their effect could not be measured. The activities followed after the receipt of compensation amount do reveal some examples of occupational modernization and entrepreneurship. But majority of the affected agriculturists are diverted to labour market.

4. *Those oustees, who have been engaged in agricultural activities and are illiterate, find it difficult to change their traditional occupation. The agricultural castes suffer more than the other groups because they neither find it easy to purchase alternative land nor are they capable of taking up other occupation.*

   Field observation and results of the descriptive sample do prove this hypothesis as true. A large majority of the agriculturists are finding it difficult to purchase alternative land because of the rise of the prices of land in urban areas. Their search for agriculture land in fringe areas generally becomes a futile exercise. Their problems are aggravated when they are cheated by property dealers in land purchase. When the search results in a failure, they do try for alternative occupations, but most of them are forced to work as labourers. Among the agriculturists, the tribal groups have suffered more than the others. Many of the tribals, who were engaged in share-cropping and depended on the landowners, also suffered because of the acquisition of land.

5. *During the process of displacement and resettlement the number of domestic animals decreased but dependence on subsidiary occupations increased.*

   The results show that the hypothesis was partly true. The number of animals possessed by the affected families showed a considerable decline. The natural resources and the community land which was earlier available for grazing of the animals has now been utilized for urban development. As the number of animals has declined, the number of families engaged in subsidiary occupations has also decreased. Due to the meagre income from these occupations, the displaced could not depend entirely on it. Their dependence on other occupations was more than on the subsidiary occupations.

6. *Women play a significant role in supporting the family during the process of resettlement and rehabilitation. They shift themselves from the family role to income generation role and start working for others.*

   The hypothesis was proved true. The women played a supportive role during process of resettlement and rehabilitation after the acquisition of land. This was truer for women of lower class. Many women of this category had started working as labourers. Several women had also started working as household servants in nearby colonies. Women also provided emotional support to their husbands. However, some women suffered more because of the consumption of liquor and drug addictions by the male members. Few women were also exposed to prostitution.

7. *Marriages are delayed and joint families are broken because of displacement and rehabilitation.*

   The hypothesis was proved to be true to a great extent. It was observed that effective marriage (*Gauna*) and arranged marriage were delayed during the process of resettlement. The affected people had to pay more attention to construction or house purchase of land and alternative occupation. Because of the decline in social status, which was related to possession of land, the search for a desirable match also posed problems. The organizations of marriage had become more expensive. The rising property disputes in the families resulted in disintegration of joint families. Agriculture, as a mode of production, was related to joint families. Acquisition of land resulted in division of property, which further affected the institution of joint family.

Urban, Suburban and Rural Population Flows

The trend of urbanization in India reveals movement of people from rural areas to cities and from smaller towns to larger ones. The process has been geared up after the independence of the country. In the present form, it is infinite and likely to continue in future also. The percentage of persons living in urban areas is found to be increasing. It is due to the development and modernization of urban areas. Business, education, hospitals and employment opportunities are concentrated in cities. The lack of such facilities pushes the population from rural to urban. On the contrary, development avenues and glamour of cities pull the people to it. The rural areas have been confined to primary source of production and urban areas have taken up the secondary and tertiary activities.

Suburbanization in India is an extension of central cities and development of satellite towns around it. Though these are intended to release the burden of population from the cities, during the course of time these become part of the city. The process continues as more and more suburban areas are developed and merged into the city. Development of suburban localities is a strategy for extension of cities. This extension requires land acquisition resulting in displacement. Such a displacement could be total or partial. It could be residential or occupational.

Movement of population from 'urban to rural' is not generally observed. Rural area could attract urban people temporarily or occasionally. The people who are used to urban way of living find it difficult to adjust in rural areas. The kind of comfort and luxuries, which are available in urban areas, do not exist in rural India. Moreover, social status is also associated with urban living. People of Mumbai may view people of Udaipur city as somewhat backward and villagers still more backward. On the other side, the people of rural areas consider the people of urban areas as more advanced and developed. This is also because of the differentiated activities performed by the urban and rural people. Rural people are bewildered in large cities when they visit them occasionally. The kind of density of population and fast commuting of people surprises them. In a way, there is a marked contrast between the living of mega cities and small remote villages. When the rural youth is exposed to urban areas for education or occupation they prefer to be urban rather than rural.

Failure of rural areas to pull people for permanent residence is one of the reasons for concentration of people in urban areas. Moreover, there are limited opportunities for employment and professional growth in rural areas. If rural areas do not have the kind of facilities available in urban areas, the flow of population from urban to rural cannot be achieved.

Labelling Village as Urban

It is an established fact that development attracts people. Synonymously, 'urban' attracts 'rural'. It is interesting to note, that when we cannot change the trend, we can at least label 'rural' as 'urban'. As soon as some developmental indicators are noticed in a village, e.g., industrial, commercial, educational or religious activities, there is a demand to raise the status. Consequently, a municipality is established. With the result even small areas, having a population of less than 5,000, are notified as 'urban'. This way, the rural becomes urban as soon as some developmental facilities are available in a rural area. This is one of the ways of showing an increase in urban population in India. What will happen when few such urban indicators are noticed in most of the villages? Keeping a futuristic perspective, we need to pay attention on the existing definitions of 'urban' and 'rural'.

Whether small places with a population of less than 5,000 should be considered as urban? Whether the definition of cities having a population of one lakh should be accepted for 'urban'? Whether the criterion of classification of cities according to the population categorization should continue in future also? The definitions have implications for future development, extent of land acquisition and displacement.

Checking Growth of Cities

There is a possibility that haphazard growth of cities may pose enormous irresolvable problems in future. There is a need to determine the optimum level of cities on the basis of population, area, density, industry, social and environmental concerns. Considering the optimum level, the expansion has to be delimited. This is essential because it could restrict acquisition of rural land surrounding the cities and minimize the displacements. It could also reduce the sufferings of rural people at the cost of urban people. We need to find out ways of development of rural areas in such a way that they benefit from the process of development.

In many developed countries, rich people live in villages and poor in cities. The nature of villages of the developed and developing countries varies significantly. In developed countries, the facilities enjoyed by urban people are available in the villages. Moreover, there is more space available at their disposal along with well-planned greenery and a better environment. There are express highways and planned roads connecting rural and urban areas. This results in the flow of population from urban to rural. In India also, the concept of farmhouses is emerging. But because of lack of facilities in rural areas, most of the people maintain such houses as their occasional habitat. For changing the flow of population, President of India, APJ Abdul Kalam (2002), has made reference to a project, Provide Urban Facilities in Rural Areas (PURA). The project was discussed with him by Panchayat heads belonging to various political parties converged at Kanchi to discuss development. He was struck by the fact that spiritual leaders were helping to focus programmes for development. We should gear up the process of development of villages. The expansion of educational, medical and health, industrial and commercial should be diverted from urban to rural. All this could be feasible by proper planning in this direction of linking cities with rural areas with roads, transport and communication linkages. In this context, we could take the base of network society.

Network Society

Mannual Castells (1996) emphasizes on the flows he sees as characteristics of what he calls 'network society'. It is viewed in the context of the global city, the process of networking and flows is more pertinent here. "A process by which centres of production and consumption of advanced services, and ancillary local societies are connected in a global network, while simultaneously downplaying the linkages with their hinterlands on the basis of information flows. Inside each country, the networking architecture reproduces itself into regional and local centres, so that the whole system becomes interconnected at the global level."

For changing flows from 'rural to urban' to 'urban to rural' a broad sweep would be required. In this respect, the conception of people about the superiority of urban people over the rural and of large cities over the small has to be changed through the global networking at all levels. Tony Lane's views on sense of superiority are revealing. According to him, "The swagger derived from an inherited collage of beliefs celebrating the significance of a complete seaport economy at the heart of global empire of the modern epoch" (Lane, 1997). It leads us to assessment according to theoretical approaches of postmodern urbanism.

Postmodern Urbanism

Postmodern urbanism operates with a conception of a radical break with the past. The new globalized postmodern city is seen as a homogenous intervention that somehow flattens history and culture. The local/social is seen to dissolve under the influence of global/economic (Munk and Melville, 2004). These authors further discuss the process of 'globalization', a process supposedly describing the new global local intermingling or interpenetrating. The term is denoted to a new hybrid blend or fusion. Amin (1997) explains it as hybrid generated by 'in here-out there' mingling. Most of the Indian cities are in the process of globalization as they retain local identities and adopt global inter-linkages. The main issue remains unanswered. Whether the globalization of cities would restrict their boundaries and restrict the flow of rural population towards the urban. If globalization leads to further inmigration in cities, the cities will continue to displace the people of rural areas encompassed in urban belt.

Postmodern Ruralism

In Indian context, we wish to propose a new concept of *ruralism*. This is viewed as an effort to radically break the flow of rural population to urban areas. It could be based on ideally developed villages having widespread linkages. Such villages would not only restrict migration of people from rural to urban areas but attract people from urban to rural areas. We could then plausibly reverse the trend. This type of approach may engineer thinking globally but acting locally. The approach will regenerate villages, if the problems of poverty and unemployment are resolved at the village level. It would require radical change in infrastructural facilities of rural areas. The process of rural regeneration could be achieved through an integrated radical approach of changing rural life by inducing modern facilities of housing, road, education, health and communication and other linkages. At the same time, care has to be taken for the development of rural-local. Further, the physical transformation should not down-grade the social and cultural status of the locals.

Transforming National Perspective

There are opposite views of hyperglobers and skeptics, optimists and pessimists, and homogenizers and hetrogenizers. A balancing perspective has been adopted by Held et al. (1999) in the form of 'transformationalists'. According to him, globalization not only reinforces old patterns of inequalities but also forms new social hierarchies which penetrate all regions of the world, thus recasting the traditional patterns of inclusion and exclusion. However, significant opportunities for empowerment of individuals, communities and social groups also exist (Martinelli, 2001). Taking this view in consideration, there could be increased hybridization of cultural traits. The old and the new could co-exit simultaneously; the gap between the rural and urban, and local and global could be reduced. The society could be transformed, so could be rural areas adopting urban facilities. The indigenous rural identities could be reduced. The society could be transformed, so could be the rural areas adopting urban facilities. The indigenous rural identities could be retained along with the physical changes. All this is considered for the sake of limiting the expansion of cities to an optimum level and providing more developmental facilities in rural areas. This could also minimize displacement.

Applying Theories of the Transformation

Twentieth century social theory, especially in its more critical and Marxist-oriented forms, has been precisely been concerned with the move from liberal capitalism to organized capitalism. (Crook et al., 1992). The direction of modernization involves identifying of the processes of differentiation, commodification and rationalization. The most themes for the process of displacement and rehabilitation of the people affected by acquisition of land in urban areas could be analyzed by variations of the notion of differentiation. Displaced persons remain more or less differentiated to the extent the approaches of resettlement and rehabilitation are relative to the policies and packages that are relative to operation and function. The differentiated system exists in various types of displacements. The variations exist in rehabilitation of project-affected people, in dam site displacements and urban area displacements and also in other types, e.g., natural and man-made disasters.

Because of differentiation in approaches and policies of various states, there arise social tensions and conflicts. The conflicts increase when supported by political parties and NGOs. The conflicts are observed between the state and the NGO; between bureaucrats and the displaced, between evacuee-resettlers and host population. All this occurs because policies are person-oriented rather than the community-oriented. They focus on village evacuation instead of village preservation. They change the occupational activities from primary to secondary. In this process of transformation, the families are disintegrated, the women are burdened, the social conflicts increase and several people are alienated. The struggles are temporal and do not last for long periods. Ultimately, the people affected suffer for years to come.

Social Consequences for the Displaced

In the absence of any formal system of resettlement and rehabilitation, various social consequences are observed for the affected families and the individuals whose lands have been acquired. These consequences have been observed in five dimensions: (1) Land loss and resettlement, (2) Social and occupational change, (3) Household management, (4) Behavioural and situational change, (5) Social relations and status. The consequences in each dimension have been shown in Table 8.1.

Table 8.1
Social Consequences of Land Acquisition

Acquisition of Land	*Social Consequences*
Land loss and resettlement	Impoverishment and marginalization, difficulties in purchase of land, difficulties in house construction, arranging necessary facilities, loss of comforts, adjustment with host population, isolation and alienation.
Social and occupational change	Difficulties in getting finance, lack of skill, occupational training, lack of education, lack of motivation, lack of social support.
Household management	Women work outside house, complete or partial unemployment, misutilization of compensation.
Behavioural and situational change	Marriage and migration, living conditions, status symbols, morbidity, addiction.
Social relations and status	Disturbed community ties, loss of social status, socialization of children, helplessness and powerlessness.

Displacement indicates a process of expropriation of land and resources. It causes traumatic psychological and socio-cultural consequences. Loss of land affects production system, family and marital relations, kinship groups, community network, income and expenditure patterns, and management of household affairs. The priorities of life are changed and there is a trend of impoverishment. According to Singh (1996), "In spite of the intentions of the government to provide comfortable rehabilitation to the affected population, no attention has been paid to psycho-sociological consequences associated with the process. Though rehabilitation projects are often viewed as a 'planned change effort' with developmental objectives, they are rarely implemented in a manner to achieve those objectives. People have been made to experience psychological shocks, undergo trauma, more often resulting in mental illness." Accordingly, the various stages depict: antecedent condition for displacement, perception of the situation, effects on individual, manifest behavioural patterns, rehabilitation programmes and further problems and demands.

Scudder-Colson Relocation Theory

The social consequences of relocation could be assessed by the theory of Scudder and Colson (1982). The theory has greatly influenced relocation literature and resettlement planning in recent years. Briefly stated, they argue that relocation, whether voluntary or compulsory, is a stressful experience. Members of communities undergoing relocation react in predictable and broadly similar ways "partly because the stress of relocation limits the range of coping responses of those involved" (Scudder, 1985). The problem and stresses accompanying forced relocation also characterize other types of relocation although to a lesser degree. During the most stressful period, i.e., the period leading up to relocation, the move itself, and the first few years of adjustment thereafter, people tend to behave in conservative, risk-avoiding ways, clinging to familiar practices and groupings. As, and if, communities re-establish themselves economically and socially, they leave this period of stress and insecurity. They now begin to behave in more innovative and risk-taking ways; and their attitudes become increasingly flexible, individualistic and open-ended. It is evident in the case of communities that have resettled. This is because of the simplified cultural repertoire, and the break down of pattern of community organization and the movements that occur during resettlement. It makes for less restraint on diversity and individual initiative as the relocated communities re-establish itself.

de Wet (2005) has criticized this model, because it is formulated to explain similarities, rather than differences in people's reactions to involuntary relocation. It can do so only by operating at a fairly high level of generality. It has, therefore, been recognized that what is also required is an approach to the analysis of relocation which is able to account, in greater detail, for the nature of people's reactions to involuntary relocation, both in its more stressful stages, and in the longer term. In as much as relocation involves the movement of people from one place to another, it brings about a change in spatial setting or context in which people find themselves, and to which they have to adapt. It has been suggested, therefore, (de Wet, 2005) that a focus on this element of spatial change will provide us with a means of accounting for similarities and differences in greater detail.

The Scudder-Colson relocation theory has greatly influenced resettlement theory and resettlement policies in many countries. Micheal M. Cernea's (1990) risk model explains how resettlement projects can cause impoverishment. Scholars are working in various countries, and researching on both empirical and theoretical issues.

Alternative R&R Approaches

Displacement disrupts a whole way of life. The displaced can never be adequately compensated for what they have lost. This perspective applies more to people of traditional culture and society as contrasted with the modern market economy and culture. There could be ethical problems in measuring traditional and cultural traits in terms of economic values. Indigenous people give more importance to their places of religious worship and ancestral habitats. The dissatisfaction among the affected people has been mainly because of the non-cooperative attitude of the officials dealing with compensation matters. The problems of the displaced could be assessed properly through personal contact and participatory approach. The avoidance behaviour and delay in payment of compensation further aggravates the prevailing critical situation of the people affected by the land acquisition.

The problems of displacement and resettlement are directly and integrally connected with loss and purchase of land in urban areas. Hence, there is a need for a policy and law, which could integrate social and occupational issues related to land. The Land Acquisition Act (1894), even after the amendment of 1984, does not recognize the rights of land losers about their rehabilitation. It disposes them by paying monetary compensation only. Major changes are required in the Act and in the policies dealing with land acquisition so as to make them welfare-oriented. Since, right to life is a fundamental right, rehabilitation should provide dignified and secure life to the displaced groups and persons. Ideally, no person should be displaced from the land, occupation or economic resources without proper resettlement. It is necessary to consider livelihood as the basis of compensation rather than the land and property. This requires resettlement and rehabilitation of the people according to their livelihoods and ways of life.

A national rehabilitation policy is only a first step. It is necessary to promulgate a comprehensive law of land acquisition, displacement and rehabilitation. The resettlement and rehabilitation are essential aspects of the issue of displacement. These are to be associated with all developmental projects in various sectors. A policy for urban development, considering all issues of displacement, could minimize the level and its effects. Along with this, the development of rural areas, communication and transport network could release the burden of urban areas. Alternatively, rural pockets could be developed in growing cities. These are also conceptualized as urban villages.

At present, the lands of agriculturists are acquired at a very low price for development of industries, residential colonies and commercial centres in urban areas. Development and use of such lands earn huge profits. When profits are earned, how these could be covered under the definition of public purpose? In case the land is acquired for profit making, the affected persons should be made shareholders of these profits. When government fails to adopt this approach, private dealers and land mafia takes advantage of the situation by intervening in the process of land acquisition. They motivate people who have been served notices for acquisition. They purchase land from them and get it converted from agriculture use to residential or commercial purpose. This affects the government schemes, which are suspended from time to time. The private colonizers, by development of various schemes, take advantage of these situations and earn profits. It is not only government and development projects that cause displacement but private agencies also dislodge people. In urban areas, the land mafia displace a large number of peasants. The property dealers create conditions that compel or motivate them to sell their land. It is an established fact that some people pay the price for development of others. The notion of sacrifice is contradictory when profit motive becomes a basis of development. It creates conflicts between land acquirers and land losers. If social costs of the land losers are covered, the displaced persons could be benefited. They could be made partners or shareholders in the process of development.

The rehabilitation must lead to a comprehensive development of the people affected by land acquisition. It could be a part of developmental strategy. The standard of living of the affected persons should substantially improved by rehabilitation. The development should not only benefit the organizations and agencies, which acquire land and property, but should facilitate the people who are deprived of their resources. With this approach, the oustees could be provided opportunities to develop themselves. The R&R should consider social and cultural factors while providing sustainable means of livelihood.

Bibliography

Advani, Mohan, 1990. Socio-economic Aspects of Resettlement and Rehabilitation: A Study of Rampura-Agucha Mines. Udaipur: Samajshastra Hindi Karya Samiti.

—, 1992. Resettlement and Rehabilitation Aspects of Rural Evacuees Affected by Gosunda Dam: A Sociological Study and Social Work Programme (Phase-1), Udaipur: Samajshastra Hindi Karya Samiti.

—, 1993. Resettlement and Rehabilitation Aspects of Rural Evacuees Affected by Gosunda Dam: A Sociological Study and Social Work Programme (Phase-2), Udaipur: Samajshastra Hindi Karya Samiti.

—, 1995. "Displacement Caused by the Projects of the Hindustan Zinc Ltd.: Using Socio-cultural Research Inputs to Facilitate Resettlements". In Hari Mohan Mathur (ed.), *The Resttlement of Project Affected People*. Jaipur: The HCM Rajasthan State Institute of Public Administration, 120–129.

Advani, Mohan and Sharma, C.L. 1993. Social and Occupational Aspect in Rehabilitation Evacuees Affected by Agucha Mines: A Sociological Study and Social Work Programme. Udaipur: Samajshastra Hindi Karya Samiti.

Agarwal, Anil, 1995. "Ecological Destruction and the Emerging Patterns of People's Protests in Rural India". *Social Action*, 35(l): 54–80.

Alam, Manzoor S. and Reddy, Geeta Ram, 1987. "Process of Urbanization and Urban System of India", In: Manzoor S. Alam and Fatima Ali Khan, (eds.), *Perspectives of Urbanization and Migration: India and USSR*, New Delhi: Allied Publishers.

Amin, A., 1997. *Placing Globalization, Theory Culture and Society*, 14(2).

Anderson, Nels, 1960. *Urban Community*. London: Routledge and Kegan Paul.

Atal, Yogesh and Mishra, Rajesh (eds.), 2004. *Understanding the Social Sphere: The Village and Beyond*. Jaipur: Rawat Publications.

Baboo, Balgovind, 1991. "Big Dams and Tribals: The Case Study of the Hirakund Dam Oustees in Orissa". *Social Action*, 41(3), pp. 288–303.

Banarjee, Paula, Chaudhary, B.R., Sabyasachi, Das and Samir, K., 2005. *Internal Displacement in South Asia the Relevance of the UN's Guiding Principles*. New Delhi. Sage Publications.

Bansal, B.L. and Aiyer, R., 2004. *Law of Acquisition of Land in India*. Delhi: Capital House.

Baxi, Upendra, 1988. "Norton Constitutional and Legal Aspect of Rehabilitation Displacement" in Walter Fernandis and F.G. Thukral (eds.), *Development, Displacement and Rehabilitation*. New Delhi: Indian Social Institution.

Baxi, Upendra, 2003. "Foreword", Vasudha Dhagamwar, Subrata De and Nikhil Verma. *Industrial Development and Displacement*, New Delhi: Sage.

Bayly, C.A., 1975. *The Local Roots of Indian Politics - Allahabad* 1880–1920. New Delhi: Oxford University Press.

Berry, B.J.L., 1962. "Some Relations of Urbanization and Basic Pattern of Economic Development", in F.R. Pitts, (ed.). *Urban System of Economic Development*. University of Oregon.

Bhagat, R.B., 1993. "Components of Urban Growth in India with Reference to Haryana: Findings from Recent Census". *Nagarlok*, 24(3), July-September, pp. 10–14.

—, 2002. "Challenges of Rural-urban Classification for Decentralized Governance". *Economic and Political Weekly*, 37(25): pp. 2413–2416.

—, 2004. "Dynamics of Urban Population Growth by Size Class of Towns and Cities in India". *Demographic India*, 33(1), pp. 47–60.

Bhuskute, R.V., 1997. "The Maharashtra Rehabilitation Act 1999", in Walter Fernandes and Vijay Paranjpye (eds.). *Rehabilitation Policy and Law in India: A Right to Livelihood*. New Delhi: Indian Social Institute, pp. 169–191.

Breese, G., 1969. *Urbanization in Newly Developing Countries*, New Delhi: Prentice Hall.

Census of India, 2001. *Final Population Totals*, Series 21. Jharkhand: Director of Census Operation, Jharkhand.

—, 1991: India, Series I, Paper-2 of 1991. *Provisional Population Totals: Rural-urban Distribution*.

Cernea, Michael M. and Scott Guggenheim (eds.), 1993. *Anthropological Approaches to Resettlement: Policy, Practice and Theory*. Boulder, CO: Westview Press.

Cernea, Michael M. and Moigne, G. Le, 1989, *The World Bank Approach to Involuntary Resettlement, Water, Power and Dam Construction Handbook*. England: Reed Business Publishing Ltd.

Cernea, Michael M., (ed.) 1999. *The Economics of Involuntary Resettlement: Questions and Challenges.* Washington D.C.: The World Bank.

Cernea, Michael M., 1988. Involuntary Resettlement in Development Projects: Policy Guidelines in Bank-financed Projects (Technical Paper No. 80). Washington D.C.: The World Bank.

—, 1990. "Involuntary Resettlement and Development Projects". In Hari Mohan Mathur (ed.). *The Human Dimension of Development: Perspectives from Anthropology.* New Delhi: Concept Publishing.

—, 1991. "Involuntary Resettlement: Social Research, Policy and Planning". In Michael M. Cernea (ed.) 1991. *Putting People First: Sociological Variables in Rural Development.* (2nd ed.), New York and London: Oxford University Press.

—, 1995. "Social Integration and Population Displacement: The Contribution of Social Science", *International Social Science Journal,* Vol. 67(1), pp. 91–112.

—, 1996. "Public Policy Response to Development Induced Population Displacement", *Economic and Political Weekly,* 31(24), pp. 1515–23.

Childe, V.G., 1950. *The Urban Revolution, Transaction of Planning Review.* Vol. 21(3).

CIDCO, 1991. New Bombay: Development Plan as Modified up to March 1991. New Bombay: CIDCO Bhavan.

Crook, Stephen, Pakulski, Jan and Walter, Maleolm, 1992. *Post-modernization: Change in Advanced Society.* London: Sage Publications.

D'Souza, 1958. *Social Structure of a Planned City: Chandigarh.* Delhi: Orient Longman Limited.

D'Souza, Alfred (ed.), 1978. *The Indian City: Poverty, Ecology and Urban Development.* New Delhi: Manohar.

D'Souza, Victor S., 2003. "Urbanization as a Perspective for Social and Historical Analysis" In R.S. Sandhu, (ed.) *Urbanization in India-Sociological Contribution.* New Delhi: Sage.

Dale, Reidar, 2004. *Evaluating Development Programmes and Projects.* New Delhi: Sage Publications.

Dasgupta, Manas, 1990, "New Problems: Dam Sardar Sarovar Project", *The Times of India,* Baroda. July, 26.

Davis, Kingsley, 1962. "Urbanization in India: Past and Future". In Roy Turner (ed.), *India's Urban Future,* University of California Press, pp. 3–26.

de Wet, Chris, 2005. *Development-Induced Displacement: Problems, Policies and People,* Oxford: Berghahn Books.

Desai, A.R., 2003. "Urbanization and Social Stratification" in R.S. Sandhu, (ed.), *Urbanization in India: Sociological Contribution*. New Delhi: Sage.

Desai, Anjana P., 1985, *Spatial Aspects of Settlement Patterns: A Study of the Narmada Command Area of Mahesana District, Gujarat.* New Delhi: Concept Publication.

Deshmukh, S.B., 2001. "The Project Affected Villages and their Rehabilitation". In R.N. Sharma and K. Sita (eds.) *Issues in Urban Development: A Case of Navi Mumbai*. Jaipur: Rawat Publications.

Dhadave, M.S., 1989. *Sociology of Slum*. New Delhi: Archives Book.

Dhagamwar, Vasudha, 1989. *Rehabilitation Policy and Institutional Changes Required*. In Walter Fernandes and Enakshi Ganguly Thukral (eds.), pp. 171–184.

—–, 1990, "Long Long Way from Home: The Search for a Rehabilitation Policy". New Delhi: *Mainstream*.

Dhagamwar, Vasudha; De, Subrata and Verma, Nikhil, 2003. *Industrial Development and Displacement: The People of Korba.* New Delhi: Sage Publication.n

Dubey, R.M., 1972. Impact of Urbanization on Population: With Special Reference to KAVAL Towns of Uttar Pradesh, Agra: University Thesis.

Dutta, S., 2000. "Partnerships in Urban Development: A Review of Ahmedabad's Experience". *Environment and Urbanization*, Vol. 12, April, pp. 13–26.

Excerpts from MARG, 1990. *The Land Acquisition Act and You*. Pauls Press and Jain Book Agency. *The Land Acquisition Act, 1894 with Short Notes.* Universal Law Publishing Company.

Fernandes, Aloysius, P. (ed.), 1990. *Workshop on Rehabilitation of Persons Displaced by Development Projects*. Bangalore: Institute for Social and Economic Change and MYRADA.

Fernandes, Walter and Asif, Mohammed, 1997. *Development-induced Displacement and Rehabilitation in Orissa, 1951–1995: A Database on Its Extent and Nature*. New Delhi: Indian Social Institute.

Fernandes, Walter and Ganguly Thukral, Enakshi (eds.), 1989. *Development, Displacement and Rehabilitation: Issues for a National Debate*. New Delhi: Indian Social Institute.

Fernandes, Walter and Menon, Geeta, 1987. *Tribal Women and Forest Economy: Deforestation, Exploitation and Status Change*. New Delhi: Indian Social Institute.

Fernandes, Walter and Naik, (1999). *Development-Induced Displacement in Goa 1965–95: A Study on Its Extent and Nature*. New Delhi: Indian Social Institute and Goa: Indian National Social Action Forum.

Fernandes, Walter and Paranjpye, Vijay, 1997. "Hundred Years of Displacement in India: Is the Rehabilitation Policy an Adequate Response?" In Walter Fernandes and Vijay Paranjpye (eds.). *Rehabilitation Policy and Law in India: A Right to Livelihood.* Pune: Econet and New Delhi: Indian Social Institute.

Fernandes, Walter and Raj, Anthony S., 1992. *Development, Displacement and Rehabilitation in Tribal Areas of Orissa.* New Delhi: Indian Social Institute.

Fernandes, Walter, 1991. "Power and Powerlessness: Development Projects and Displacement of Tribals". *Social Action*, 41(III): pp. 243–70.

—–, 1996. "Development, Displacement and Rehabilitation: Principles of the NGO Alternative". Paper Represented in the Workshop Organized by The World Bank, NDO. March, pp. 12–14.

—–, 1996. Resettlement Studies and Specific Issues: Sharing in the Benefits of Development. Keynote Address, Refugee Studies Programme, University of Oxford, September, pp. 9–13.

—–, 1998a. "Development-induced Displacement in Eastern India". In S.C. Dube (ed.), *Antiquity and Modernity in Tribal India: Continuity and Change Among the Tribals.* (Vol. I) New Delhi: Inter India Publisher, 217–301.

—–, 1999. *The Land Acquisition (Amendment) Bill 1998: for Liberalisation or for the Poor.* New Delhi: Indian Social Institute.

Fernandes, Walter, Menon, Geeta and Viegas Philip, 1988. *Forests, Environment and Tribal Economy: Deforestation, Impoverishment and Marginalization in Orissa.* New Delhi: Indian Social Institute.

Fernandes, Walter; Viegas, Philip; Menon, Geeta and Chandy, K.T., 1985. *Forests, Environment and Forests Dweller Economy in Chattisgarh.* New Delhi: Indian Social Institute.

Gadgil, Madhab and Guha, Ramchandra, 1992. *This Fissured Land: An Ecological History of India.* New Delhi: Oxford University Press.

Ganguli, P.G., 1965. "Need for a National Policy on Urbanization", *Economic and Political Weekly,* July 29, 13: p. 1215.

Ganguly Thukral, Enakshi and Singh, Mridula, 1995. "Dams and Displaced in India, in H.M. Mathur and M. Cernea (eds.) *Development and Resettlement: Focus on Asian Experience.* New Delhi: Vikas.

Ganguly Thukral, Enakshi, (ed.). 1992. *Big Dams, Displaced People: Rivers of Sorrow, Rivers of Change.* New Delhi: Sage Publications.

Ganguly Thukral, Enakshi, 1989. "Dams: For Whose Development?" In Walter Fernandes and Enakshi Ganguly Thukral (eds.). *Development, Displacement and Rehabilitation.* New Delhi: Indian Social Institute.

——, 1995. "Development, Displacement and Rehabilitation: Is there a Need for a Gender Perspective". *Mainstream*, November 11, pp. 24–26.

——, 1996. "Development, Displacement and Rehabilitation Locating Gender", *Economic and Political Weekly*, 31(24), pp. 1500–1503.

Ghurye, G.S., 1964. "Bombay Suburbanites: Some Aspects of their Working Life". *Sociological Bulletin*. 13(2), 14(2), 27–35.

Giri, Anand Kumar (ed.), 2004. *Creative Social Research Rethinking Theories and Methods*. New Delhi: Vistar Publications.

Gopal, Y.S., 1976. A Study of the Migrant Component in Indian Urbanization. Thesis. Trivandrum: University of Kerala.

Government of India, 1985. Report of the Committee on Rehabilitation of Displaced Tribals Due to Development Projects. New Delhi: Ministry of Home Affairs.

——, 1988. Report of NCU. New Delhi: Government of India Press.

Goyal, Sangeeta, 1996. "Economic Perspectives on Resettlement and Rehabilitation", *Economic and Political Weekly*, 31(24), pp. 1461–67.

Graham, S., 1999. "Cities of Connection and Disconnection" in J. Allen, D. Massy and M. Pryke (eds.) *Unsettling Cities*. London: Routedge.

Guggenheim, Scott, 1990. Development and Dynamics of Displacement, in Aloysius P. Fernandes. (ed.) *Workshop on Rehabilitation of Persons Displaced by Development Projects*. Bangalore: Institute for Social Economic Change and MYRADA.

——, 1993. "Peasant Planners and Participation: Resettlement in Mexico" In Michael Cernea and Scott Guggenheim, *Anthropological Approaches to Resettlement: Policy, Practice and Theory*. Boulder, CO: West View Press.

Gupta, Dipankar, 2000. *Mistaken Modernity: Indian Between Worlds*. New Delhi: Harper Collins.

Gupta, K.R. (ed.), 2004. *Urban Development Debates in the New Millennium*. New Delhi: Atlantic Publication. (Vol. 1).

——, 2005. *Urban Development Debates in the New Millennium*. New Delhi. Atlantic Publication. Vol. 3.

——, 2005. *Urban Development Debates in the New Millennium*, New Delhi: Atlantic Publication. (Vol. 4).

Hakim, Roxanne, 1996. "Vsava Identity in Transition: Some Theoretical Issues". *Economic and Political Weekly*, 1492-1499.

Hauser, Philip M. and Duncan, O.D. (eds.). *The Study of Population: An Inventory and Approval.* Chicago. University of Chicago Press.

Held, D.A. Mcgrew; D. Goldbaltt and Perraton J., 1999. *Global Transformation.* Cambridge: Polity Press.

Hesselberg, Jan. (ed.), 2002. *Issues in Urbanization*. Jaipur and New Delhi: Rawat Publications.

Hoselitz, Bert. F., 1962. "Role of Urbanization in Economic Development: Some International Comparisons" in Turner, Roy (eds.), *India's Urban Future*.

Human Development Report: Rajasthan 2002 and 1999 and Rajasthan Health TTMVFP UNDP Definitions. Human Development Report: Rajasthan 1999.

Indian Institute & Health Management Research, 2001. *Health Infrastructure*, Jaipur: IIHMR.

——, 2001. *Rajasthan Health Scenario: Family Welfare, Reproductive and Child Health*, Jaipur: IIHMR.

Jacobson, L. and Prakash, V. (eds.), 1971. *Urbanization and National Development*, California: Sage Publications, Beverly Hills.

Jain, M.K., Gosh, M. and Kim, W.B., 1992. Emerging Trends of Urbanization in India. Occasional Paper No. 1 of 1993. New Delhi: Office of the Registrar General and Census Commissioner.

Jairam, N. (ed.), 2004. *The Indian Diaspora: Dynamics of Migration*. New Delhi: Sage Publications.

Joshi V., 1991. *Rehabilitation: A Promise to Keep, A Case of SSI*. Ahmedabad: The Tax Publication.

Kantesbovskaya, L.V., 1976. "Some Definitions of Urbanization in Geographic Literature and the Relevant Ideas", in S. Manzoor Alam and V.V. Pokshishevsky (eds.), *Urbanization in Developing Countries*. Hyderabad: Osmania University Press.

Kenneth, Gillion, 1968. *A Study in Indian Urban History*. Berkeley: University of California Press.

Kidwai, A.H., 1979. *Urban Growth: A Historical Perspective, Problem De Croissanee Urbadine Dans Le Monde Tropical, Trends et Document De Geographic Tropical*. CEGET, No. 45.

Kothari, Smitu, 1995. "Development Displacement: Whose Nation is it? PCD. People-centred Development Form". New Delhi: *Lokayan* Bulletin. March-April.

——, 1996. "Whose Nation? The Displaced as Victims of Development". *Economic and Political Weekly*. 31(24): pp. 1476–85.

Kumar, Sarvottam, 2005. *Rural Male Out Migration*. New Delhi: Vista International Publishing House.

Kundu, Amitabh (ed.), 2000. *Inequality, Mobility and Urbanization: China and India*. New Delhi: ICSSR and Manak Publications.

Lampard, E.E., 1955. "The History of Cities in Economically Advanced Areas". *Economic Development and Cultural Change*. Vol. III, pp. 61–92.

Lane, T., 1997. *Liverpool, City of the Sea*. Liverpool: Liverpool University Press.

Lynch, Owen M., 1969. *The Policies of Untouchability: Social Mobility and Social Change in a City of India*. New York: Columbia University Press.

Mahapatra, L.K., 1986. "Evolving a Plan for Social Inputs in Rural Blocks with People's Participation". *Manav*. II (1).

—, 1996. Good Intentions or the Policy are not Enough: Reducing Impoverishment Risks for the Tribal Oustees. Paper Presented in the Workshop Organized by The World Bank NDO: March, pp. 12–14.

Majumdar, D.N., 1986 Urbanization in Northeast India. (Research Project), Sponsored by ICSSR, New Delhi.

Majumdar, Paramita, 2004. *Dynamics of Urban Development*. Delhi: Abhijeet Publication.

Majumdar, Veena, 2003. *Peasant Women Organize for Empowerment: The Bankura Experiment*. New Delhi: Sage Publications.

MARG (Multiple Action Research Group), 1998. *Shahpur Jat: A Village Displaced*. New Delhi, MARG.

Martinelli, Alberto, 2001. "Global Governance, Power Accountability and the European Union", *Sociological Bulletin*, 50 (1).

Massey, S. Dougls, 1993. "The Methodology of an Ethnosurveys" in Donald J. Bouge et al. (eds.) *Readings in Population Research Methodology*. Illinois: United Nations Population Fund.

Mathur, Hari Mohan (ed.), 1995, *Development, Displacement and Resettlement: Focus on Asian Experiences: Focus on Asian Experience*. Jaipur: The HCM Rajasthan State Institute of Public Administration.

—, 1995. *The Resettlement of Project-Affected People*. Jaipur: The H.C.M. Rajasthan State Institute of Public Administration.

Mathur, Hari Mohan and Marson David (eds.), 1998. *Development Projects and Impoverishment Risks: Resettling Project Affected People in India*. New Delhi: Oxford University Press.

Mathur, Hari Mohan in Collaboration with Michael M. Cernea (eds.), 1995. *Development, Displacement and Resettlement: Focus on Asian Experiences*. New Delhi: Vikas Publishing House.

Mathur, Hari Mohan, 1996. Impoverishing Risks in Involuntary Resettlement: Coping with the Advance Effects of Development Projects. Paper presented in the Workshop Organized by the World Bank, NDO, pp. 12–14.

——, 2004. "The Impoverishing Potential of Development Project". In Yogesh Atal and Rajesh Mishra (eds), *Understating the Social Sphere: The Village and Beyond.* Jaipur and New Delhi: Rawat Publications.

Menezes, 1991. "Compensation for Project and Displacement: A New Approach". *Economic and Political Weekly*, 26(3), p. 2465.

Mills, Edwin S. and Becker, Charles M., 1986. *Studies in India Urban Development,* New York: Oxford University Press.

Ministry of Information and Broadcasting, 2006. *India: A Reference Annual.* New Delhi: Government of India.

Mishra, Sunil (ed.), 2000. *Voluntary Action in Health and Population: The Dynamics of Social Transaction.* New Delhi: Sage Publications.

Mohan, Rakesh and Pant, Chandrashekhar, 1982. "The Morphology of Urbanization in India: Some Results from the 1981 Census". *Economic and Political Weekly,* 17(38), pp. 1534–1540.

Mohan, Rakesh, 1985. "Urbanization in India's Future", *Population and Development Review,* 11 (4), pp. 619–645.

Morse, Bradford and Berger, Thomas, 1992. *Sardar Sarovar: Report of Independent Review*, Ottawa: Resource Futures International.

Mukerji, Debashish, 1997. "Victims of Progress". *The Week*, February, pp. 23-28.

Munk, Ronaldo and Melville, Ruth, 2004. "The City, Globalisation and Social Transformation: A View from Liverpool". In K.R. Gupta (ed.) *Urban Development Debates in the New Millennium.* Vol. I. New Delhi: Atlantic.

Murickan, Jose, George, M.K., Emmanuel, K.A., Boban, Jose and R. Prakash Pillai, 2003. *Development-Induced Displacement.* Jaipur and New Delhi: Rawat Publications.

Narasaiah, M.L., 2005. *Urbanization and Child Labour.* New Delhi: Discovery Publishing House.

National Policy, 1993. *NTPC. Resettlement and Rehabilitation Policy.* New Delhi.

O'Leary, Zina, 2004. *The Essential Guides to Doing Research.* New Delhi: Vistar Publications.

Panday, Ganesh and Panday, Aruna, 2004. *Nagriya Samajshastra* (In Hindi) New Delhi: Radha Publication.

Papola, T.S., 2002. *Rural Industrialization and Agricultural Growth: A Case Study of India*. New Delhi.

Paranjpaye, V. and Kewalramani L., 1997. "Swamped by NTPC Fly Ash: A Review of Rehabilitation Policy". In Fernandes, W. and Paranjpaye, V.

(ed.), *Rehabilitation Policy and Law in India: A Right to Livelihood.* New Delhi. Indian Institute.

Parasuraman, S., (1994). *Displacement and Resettlement: Experience from Development Project in India.* Surat: Centre for Social Studies.

Pathak, N.R., 2004. *Dictionary of Sociology.* New Delhi: Vishva Bharti Publication.

Philips, WSK, 1990. *Social Stratification and Mobility in Urban India.* Jaipur and New Delhi: Rawat Publications.

Prakasha Rao, V.L.S., 1983. *Urbanization in India: Spatial Dimensions.* New Delhi: Concept Publishing Company, xxi–327.

Prasad, B.K., 2003 *Urban Development: A New Perspective.* New Delhi: Sarup & Sons.

Pulin, K. George and Parikh, Indira J., 1995. *Crossroads of Culture: A Study in the Culture of Transience.* New Delhi: Sage Publications.

Rajasthan. *District Action Plan.* Udaipur: CMHO (FW).

Ramaiah, Savitri, 1996 *Impacts of Involuntary Resettlement and Level of Living of the Project-affected Persons*: Paper Presented in the Workshop Organized by The World Bank: NDO. March.

Ramanathan, Usha, (1996). "Displacement and the Law". New Delhi: *Economic and Political Weekly.*

—–, (1999). "Public Purpose: Points for Discussion", in Walter Fernandes (ed.). *The Land Acquisition (Amendment) Bill 1998*", New Delhi: Indian Social Institute, pp. 19–24.

Rao, M.S.A., 1974. *A Reader in Urban Sociology.* New Delhi: Orient Longman.

Rao, M.S.A., Bhat, Chandrashekar and Kadekar, Laxmi Narayan, 1991. *A Reader in Urban Sociology.* New Delhi: Orient Longman.

Rao, T.V., 1996 *Human Resources Development: Experiences, Interventions, Strategies.* New Delhi: Sage Publications.

Redfield, Robert and Singer, 1972. "The Cultural Role of Cities". *Economic Development and Cultural Change,* 3: pp. 53–73.

Redfield, Robert, 1941. *The Folk Culture of Yucatan.* Chicago: University of Chicago Press.

Reissman, L., 1964. *The Urban Process.* New York.

Rostow, W.W., 1937. *The Stages of Economic Growth.* Cambridge.

Samaddar, Ranabir (ed.), 2003. *Refugees and the State: Practices of Asylum and Care in India, 1947–2000.* New Delhi: Sage Publications.

Sandhu, R.S., 1989. *The City and Its Slums: A Sociological Study.* Amritsar: Guru Nanak Dev University Press.

Sandhu, R.S., Singh, Sarup and Sandhu, Jasmeet, 2001. *Sustainable Human Settlements: The Asian Experience*. Jaipur and New Delhi: Rawat Publications.

Sandhu, Ravindra Singh (ed.), 2003. *Urbanization in India: Sociological Contributions.* New Delhi: Sage Publications.

Scudder, Thayer and Colson, Elizabeth, 1982. "From Welfare to Development: A Conceptual Framework for Analysis of Dislocated People". In A Hansen and Oliver Smith (eds.). *Involuntary Migration and Resettlement: The Problems and Responses of Dislocated People.* Boulder, CO: West View Press.

Shah, A.M., Baviskara, B.S. and Ramaswamy, E.A. (ed.), 1997. *Social Structure and Change: Development and Ethnicity.* New Delhi: Sage Publications, Vol 4.

Shahpur, Jai, 1998. *A Village Displaced: A Study in Self-Rehabilitation*. New Delhi: *MARG*, p. 125.

Sharma, B.D., 1978. *Tribal Development: The Concept and the Frame*. New Delhi: Ruchi Prakashan.

Sharma, R.H., 2003, "Involuntary Displacement: A Few Encounters", *Economic and Political Weekly,* Special Article, March 1st.

Sharma, R.K. and Jain, S.P. (ed.), 2006. *Udaipur Guide and City Map.* Udaipur: Chirag Publications.

Sharma, R.N. and Sita, K. (ed.), 2001. *Issues in Urban Development: A Case of Navi Mumbai.* Jaipur and New Delhi: Rawat Publications.

Sharma, R.N. *Economic and Political Weekly*. March 2003

Sharma, Rajendra K., 2004. *Indian Society: Institution and Change*. Delhi: Atlantic Publication.

——, 2004. *Urban Sociology*. Delhi: Atlantic Publications.

Shriniwas, K., 1998. *Basic Demographic Techniques and Applications.* New Delhi: Sage Publications.

Singh Mridula, 1992. *Displacement by Sardar Sarovar and Tehri, A Comparative Study of Two Dams.* New Delhi: Multiple Action Research Group.

Singh, Inderjit, 2001. Provisional Population Totals: Rural-urban Distribution of Population, Paper–2. New Delhi: Controller of Publications.

Singh, Rajesh, 1996. "Managing Rehabilitation Under Development Projects: A Psycho-sociological Perspective". *MDI Management Journal,* 9(2).

Singha, Roy, Debal, K. (ed.), 2001. *Social Development and the Empowerment of Marginalised Group Perspective and Strategies.* New Delhi: Sage Publications.

Sinha, B.K., 1996. "Draft National Policy for Rehabilitation: Objectives and Principles". *Economic and Political Weekly,* 31(24), pp. 1453–60.

Sinha, C. Prabhas (ed.), 2006. *Disaster Relief Rehabilitation and Emergency Humanitarian Assistance.* New Delhi: SBS Publishers and Distributors.

Sinha, Pradip, 1978. *Calcutta in Urban History.* Calcutta Firma KLM Private Ltd.

Sridhar, K.S., 2004. "Approach to Urbanization in India: Theory, Policy and Challenges" in K.R. Gupta, (ed.). *Urban Development Debates in the New Millennium. Studies in Revisited Theories and Redefined Praxes.* New Delhi: Atlantic Publishers.

Srinivasan, Bina (ed.), 1996. *Restless Boundaries: A Study on the Urban Displacement of Woman in Baroda.* Mumbai: Vikas Adhayan Kendra.

Tati, Gabriel, 2005. "African Migrant Entrepreneurship, Social Networks and Informal Urban Economy: The Case of the City of Pointe-Noire (Congo-Brazzaville) P.No. 191". In R.K. Gupta, *Urban Development Debates in the New Millennium: Studies in Revisited Theories and Redefined Praxes.* New Delhi: Atlantic Publishers, Vol 3, pp. 191–259.

Taylor, I., Evans, K. and Fraser, P., 1996. *A Tale of Two Cities, Global Change, Local Feeling and Everyday Life in the North of England. A Study in Manchester and Sheffield.* London: Routledge.

The World Bank, 1980. Social Issues Associated with Involuntary Resettlement in Bank Financed Projects. Operational Manual Statement No. 2.33. Washington D.C. The World Bank.

——, 1990. "Operational Directive 4.30, Involuntary Resettlement". *The World Bank.* Washington D.C. The World Bank.

——, 1991. "Operational Directive 4.20, Indigenous People". *The World Bank.* Washington D.C. The World Bank.

——, 1993. Introduction to Environment and Social Assessment Requirements and Procedures for World Bank Financed Projects, Environment Department.

——, 1994. Resettlement and Development: The World Bank Review of Projects Involving Involuntary Resettlement. The World Bank/Environment Department. Written by Michael M. Cernea, and Scott Guggenheim. Washington D.C. The World Bank.

——, 2006. *Equity and Development, World Development Report.* The World Bank and Oxford University Press Publications.

Thompson, W.S., 1935. *Urbanization. Encyclopedia of Social Science*, Vol. XV. Macmillan.

Tilly, C., 1964. *The Vendee.* Cambridge: Mass, pp. 16–17.

Vaswani, Kalpana, 1992. "Rehabilitation Laws and Policies: A Critical Look". In Enakshi Ganguly Thukral (ed.). *Big Dams, Displaced People: Rivers of Sorrow, Rivers of Change.* New Delhi: Sage Publication, pp. 155–169.

Verma, Manish K., 2004. *Development, Displacement and Resettlement.* Jaipur: Rawat Publication, p. 264.

Vyas, H.N., 1993. Displacement, Compensation and Rehabilitation: A Study of Submergence Area Evacuees. (Ph.D. Thesis in Sociology) Udaipur: Mohanlal Sukadia University.

Vyas, N.N., 1995. "The Social Consequences of Resettlement of Tribals of Southern Rajasthan: A Case Study of Kadana Project". In H.M. Mathur, (ed.) *The Resettlement of Project Affected People.* Jaipur: The HCM Rajasthan State Institute of Public Administration.

Wirth, Louis, 1938. "Urbanization as a Way of Life". *American Journal of Sociology.* 44 (July), pp. 3–24.

Yadav, B.S. and Sharma, Sudha, 2004. *Urbanization and Rural Development.* New Delhi: Shree Publications and Distributors.

Zwingmann, N., 1989. "The Nostalgic Phenomena and its Exploitation" in N. Zwingmann et al., (eds.), *Uprooting and After.* New York: Springer Verlag.

Index